No God, Some Instructions...
Would Have Been Nice!

To mom & dad's tax Lady and friend!

[signature]
"Their Daughter"

The Story of My Life...Slightly Fictitious Memoirs

Outskirts Press, Inc.
Denver, Colorado

Outskirts Press, Inc.
http://www.outskirtspress.com

ISBN: 978-1-4327-1277-8

Outskirts Press and the "OP" logo are trademarks belonging to Outskirts Press, Inc.

PRINTED IN THE UNITED STATES OF AMERICA

Chapters

Preface

Introduction

Preface

I think this is the part of the book where I'm supposed to make you want to read the rest. Just remember that curiosity killed the cat. In light of that warning I will proceed anyway.

This is my story. It's fifty years in the life of a plain old American raised before the Ten Commandments were illegal and fence-hopping immigrants weren't. I don't have a fancy name—it doesn't even end in an "i." I've never been on television. I've accomplished next to nothing. My family and friends seem to think my life was rather funny and should be put into print. Of course it's always funny when it happens to the other guy.

It's not like I didn't notice all of the bad juju in my life, I guess I was just too busy trying to get through it. When I sat down and started to outline my life I could have actually been the poster child for Murphy's Law. Being extremely opinionated and a writer doesn't help one's odds on things going right either.

As Paul Harvey once said, "It is the writer who makes a fool of himself and reveals how shallow he is by putting his every thought he has on paper, where everyone can see it, read it, and put it away to read again tomorrow." I love Paul Harvey. We think alike. Anyone should know better than to write his or her mental glitches down. Problem is, it always seems like a good idea at the time.

I'd also like to say that the names have been changed to protect the innocent, or me, from being sued. Whichever comes first, but you people know who you are.

This is my journey through this thing we call life. I am a product of the Fifties—before cell phones, computers, identity theft, and fifty-foot aisles of different kinds of cereal. I don't mind anyone laughing at my misfortune. Sometimes I have to laugh myself. And, well, I hope no one sues me because then I will have to get even via my own judicial system.

Oh, and you may notice that I change from first, to second, to third person throughout the book. That's because all three of us have something to say. And grammar: forget it, *ain't* is a word I found in the Webster's unabridged dictionary. Fragments. If there were one word to describe my life that would be it. So don't get your panties in a wad if a sentence is missing a subject. I've often missed the subject. My editor advised me to warn you that I make up words. I also like my participles to dangle now and then. Put that in your tight little bun, Mrs. Dinger.

I'm not going to thank anyone yet. Let's wait and see how they act.

Introduction
I Believe

Everyone has beliefs. My sister believes that Heaven looks like Famous-Barr and has one-hundred percent off coupons every day. My brother believes you should never head out at 4 A.M. to fish with four kids unless you have a minimum of two cases of beer to wash down your bagel. My mother believes my father is the man of the house. My father doesn't.

I believe that everything that happens to us makes us who we are. Each event, person we meet, and kind or unkind word is stored in our memory, or on our hard drive—as the geeks like to say. Only a good blow to the noggin or a hit of carefully directed volts from the men in the white coats can really erase anything we have been subjected to. I believe lighting may have the same effect. If you don't have medical insurance, it may be an option if you want to halt some of those annoying and detrimental reruns.

I believe that most people never bother to update their programs and continue to fumble around in the land of DOS. Some don't because they can't conceive the theory and some because it's too much work. I'm running on a Tandy 67K most of the time. I believe that is enough for me, though I could use a little more RAM.

I believe, because I have been told many times, that I am not politically correct. I'm not socially acceptable at times either. I hate mincing words and I hate the direction my country is headed in with all of this liberal dribble. Someone is not vertically challenged, they're short; nor is Wilt Chamberlain vertically enhanced, he's a fricking giant! Illegal is illegal no matter how you phrase it. Two words won't make it right. Politically correct is iniquitous; it has the word *politic* in it. I rest my case.

I believe in freedom of speech for all, not just those who want to silence others. I don't believe that slinging cow dung all over the Virgin Mary is art or an expression of freedom of speech. I believe if it is disrespectful or hurtful to others you have no *right* to do it, and need a good therapist if you think you do.

I believe in God. I will also refer to God on many occasions: my God, the right God. I'm not asking you to believe in Him (though it beats burning in Hell). There has to be something greater to it than you and me just happening. I'm going to say the word God a lot. It's my right via that freedom of speech thing that has been greatly distorted over time. I might say some other things that the ACLU and other fame-seekers don't agree with. Who cares? I once accidentally told a joke about a guy with a wooden leg to a guy with a wooden leg and I lived through that.

I believe that our government is a bigger mess than my checkbook. Most politicians are crooked as a dog's hind leg and damn arrogant about it. Neither will ever be rectified without starting over from scratch. I hate politics, politicians, and store clerks that stay on the phone while they check you out. I believe they should hang up and give me their undivided attention. It would be nice if, after they are elected, politicians paid a little attention too.

I believe I am an activist, though many call me a fanatic

and a crusader. I believe you have to fight for what you believe in. You can't change the world with your remote from the sofa. However, I do not consider suing a means of changing the world. I've never sued anyone and I've been wronged a lot. Not that I didn't get even. I believe everyone should take responsibility for their own actions, especially if they act stupid.

I always fight for the underdog. The little guy needs a lot of help nowadays. But I don't believe that a free ride is helping anyone. Welfare is making us a fat and lazy nation.

I believe we are destroying our planet and going to be in deep doo-doo someday. I am an environmentalist though I've probably wasted a lot more paper writing than I've ever planted in trees. I believe that everyone should hug a tree once in his or her life. There is just something about wrapping your arms around a big old oak that towers fifty feet into the sky. Trees are life. Trees have witnessed hundreds of years of history, shading both the pilgrim and the yuppie. Though they'd probably laugh their butts off if they could read our history books. Well, if trees had butts.

I believe in equality for everyone until they break the rules. I believe rules were not made to be broken. A bad person made that saying up. I believe the Ten Commandments are the only real rules we need. And of course, we need the rules of the road because most people drive like idiots. The only reason we have ten million laws now is because nothing is right or wrong anymore. Everything is subject to someone else's interpretation. Somebody out there is trying to color the entire world gray and that won't work, unless you are a dog.

I believe it's okay to be an American. I'm not a German/French/English/American, just an American. I hate all of these prefixes to being an American. What the heck is wrong with being an American anyway? This is the greatest country in the world. From the four corners of the earth people are tying to get here; they risk life and limb to live in America, then they demand to be called by the messed up country they ran away from. If you don't want segregation don't segregate yourself. I'm not going to say go back there if it was so great, but I want you to know I'm thinking it.

I believe that America has a history and history shouldn't be changed to suit newcomers. When history is changed it isn't history anymore—it's lies.

I believe the term Redneck is being greatly overused. Redneck is a not-so-nice way of saying someone who's real, who has an American history, and is proud of it. I may be a Redneck, but I've never been one for putting labels on things. Excluding food and medicines, as they are very helpful there.

I believe if it works, don't try to fix it, and if it's broke let someone else do it, especially if you don't know what the hell you are doing.

I believe we should all question life. Not the theory of relatives or that time-space issue, but important things. Like why store coupons are suddenly expired when you check out—they were good when you left the house.

I believe home parties are for people who don't know how to throw a real party. Why don't you just sell the stuff around your own house and cut out the middleman?

I truly believe life is a very perplexing journey. It's a journey dragging a big overstuffed bag of insecurities millions of miles missing one of those convenient little wheels on the bottom. It's a journey to death and the grave with a whole lot of crap happening on the way. The second I found out I couldn't take any of my stuff with me, stuff that I worked my butt off to get, I said, "screw this, I'm lightening my load!" I quickly detached from material possessions, though my husband will deny that. Stuff is a fluffer of life, and life can get way too fluffy if you let it.

I believe that life can be good but it is also full of disappointments. That is life. My life seems to get really tangled up on a regular basis, worse than icicle Christmas lights. I have to admit that I've spent time in the nut ward trying to untangle life; it's not a major vacation destination spot but hey, if it's covered by your medical insurance? It's an all-inclusive arrangement: drinks, meals, activities, and drugs—you won't get a deal like that from Apple Vacations.

When it comes down to the bottom line I believe we are here for a reason. We start out as a little blob of nerve endings at the mercy of other unskilled human beings looking for answers, direction, and meaning. We grow into a big blob of nerve endings, still searching for the same stuff. If you hate your parents, think twice, they were kids too once. If you hate your kids, they will be parents some day. If you hate those little paper things they put on the end of lamb chops, don't order them.

Life is a journey and if you get tired, that's normal. If you get discouraged that's normal too. If you like to laugh at other people's misfortune, that's normal. It's fun to watch someone besides yourself make total fools out of themselves. It's fun to look at some poor sap that has it worse than you. It gives you the strength to buck up and go on. I've given out a lot of incentive over time.

I believe that life is short only if you die young. I've been here fifty years; it feels like five hundred and fifty. Most of those were child-rearing years. Those people who say "life's too short, eat dessert first" at least got half of it right. Always eat dessert.

Life only seems short when you get near the end, but on Monday morning it's long. Life is the longest thing you will ever do and there are no *do-overs* unless you're into that reincarnation thing. Either way you're not going to get to fix your mistakes, especially if you come back as an otter.

I believe that the power of chocolate is extremely underestimated. If I consume enough of it, I can see into the future. I can see Heaven.

Now that you know what I believe in, I will begin the journey of my life over again. I will take you from my birth to this moment in time as I type…on the surface you may see me as a crazy woman covered in a rich chocolate coating. As you read further you may envision a circus clown dog paddling in a riptide. Preferably a clown covered in chocolate. However you see me is fine as long as there is chocolate involved, because it makes the journey a lot more enjoyable.

This is my story.

Chapter 1

I Am Born

I am born. After that it's pretty much a blur. I'd love to sound insightful and say that I remember resting peacefully in my mother's arms or floating in the womb, but who am I kidding? Heck, I can't even remember why I go down the basement ninety percent of the time. People who say they remember stuff from a past life are scary and not just because they have such a keen memory. If I had done this before, I sure wouldn't be bragging about having to come back and try again to get it right.

I can't say that everything in this story is accurate, because my mind isn't what it used to be. Not that I was ever an Einstein. There are two things I know for certain about my arrival into this world for the first and only time. Two things I was told by my father. One, they had to break my collarbone to birth me. Which I think should have told them I never wanted out. Two, I came into the world *ass backwards* and have been going that way ever since.

My earliest memories are maybe at the age of four or five. I remember napping with my sister on the floor, in our panties, under an open window on a hot summer day. I loved napping then and I love it still but you can't do it in just your panties now because certain people won't let you sleep. I remember playing—unstructured free play—running amuck if you will. I remember running all over our neighborhood with no fear of being abducted. Though our parents may have thought about it on a bad day, it certainly wasn't a concern.

It's odd the things we remember most, things that stick in our mind and resurface on a regular basis. Whenever my life feels like it is spinning out of control I remember a contraption we had in our backyard called a Twirl-A-Way. My sister and I spent many a day twirling away. It was two seats on a cross bar and the faster our little legs could push the faster the blood would rush to our little blockheads. This might explain some of my dizziness in life. I don't know what happened to the Twirl-A-Way but I do know that enough alcohol will mimic the same effect.

I believe my childhood was pretty normal for growing up in the Fifties. I remember getting yelled at, slapped, reminded, and glared at on a regular basis. Most of the time that was by neighbors for running though flowerbeds or throwing rocks. When we got home we got yelled at again. Parents in the Fifties never threatened to sue anyone for correcting their little darlings. We had no rights; I did document most of it just in case.

My younger brother and I had a raging civil war from the moment I saw he posed a threat to my share of the food supply. We fought from sun-up to sun-down and spent the rest of the time planning each other's demise. He would tie bricks around my Barbie's neck and toss her in the wading pool to die. I would put hot sauce in his iced tea. He would carve open my baby doll and stitch her up with black wire. I would stomp on his favorite plastic tractor with a steel axle. While incapacitated with a hole clear through my foot I would wrack verbal damage on him by repeating his speech impediments. I would constantly remind him that he was the only blond in the family, a milkman delivery. It was one endless fight and excellent training for what lay ahead.

I don't feel bad about forgetting a lot of my life. Most people don't remember their childhood by their late forties. Maybe we don't want to remember or maybe we just plain can't. I'm pretty sure I had ADD, ADHD, and ADANYTHINGELSE. But, when I was a kid there were no fancy medical terms for it, you were just *acting stupid.* I was raised before all of this politically correct crap, when you could call someone an idiot because they were in fact a total idiot. Those were the good old days—a lot of people you called an idiot took a good long hard look at themselves and tried to change. Today's idiots are waltzing around in rose-colored glasses messing the world up for all of us because no one is allowed to tell them they are an idiot.

I never knew I had a problem. People didn't ponder over kids like they do now. When we were kids we were supposed to be looking for lighting bugs and cookies, not abnormalities in our gene pool or marketable gifts of talent. It amazes me, the potential parents see in their kids today. In the Fifties success was getting them through high school and out of the house shortly thereafter. Very few kids in the Fifties were told they could be famous or a star. Most kids were told they'd see stars if they didn't shut up and sit down. When we were kids we were annoying little mess-makers. I'm sure that was a lot more fun than working on a television set twelve hours a day.

Now that I look back at my childhood years with eyes enlightened by modern medicine, I see that a niece or nephew from each family has since been treated for ADD. They had to get it from somewhere; it must have passed through us. At first I felt bad about that, but after twenty years of raising my boys, I'm good with it. I'm eagerly awaiting the joy of watching them raise my grandchildren with the same abnormalities.

I remember falling down a lot as a kid, crashing my bike, tripping, and running into invisible objects. My knees were four inch scabs for the first ten years of my life. I didn't have some mysterious disorder. Back then there was no beating around the bush to save feelings—you were just a klutz. As I look back I'm not sure but I think feelings were something that was invented in the Seventies. Either way I forged onward through life's many childhood disasters. Which is the best part of being a kid: you are oblivious to the outcome. No matter how stupid you acted one day, you'd go to bed, sleep like a baby, and do it all over again the next day and shamelessly top your stupidity.

I like to watch little kids nowadays. They remind me of pinballs in a pinball machine, ricocheting off everything in their path. Most of them will never have a clue that they have problems because parents today are too scared to tell them so. They blame everyone else and pump the kids full of Ritalin instead of just coming out and telling them they are broke. Too many parents today fear it may stifle their creativity. Give me a break—it may save society millions in incarceration fees.

I think my parents knew I was broke. "Well, Bob, I guess two out of three isn't bad."

My dad once asked me to take empty soda bottles in one of those handy cardboard carriers to the basement and bring up some other ones. I did. Forty-something years later I still hear that story and hold to my original plea. He should have said "full ones" if he wanted soda, because all the bottles were different. I earnestly changed every single one of them. Oh, but my parents didn't rush me off to a psychiatrist or pump me full of pills, they just shook their heads. They shook their heads a lot. I thought I was quite entertaining. I still think I'm entertaining and they are still shaking their heads.

My mother was a housewife; it was okay to be a housewife back then. She was a great mom, a lot like Beaver Cleaver's mom, very busy minus the pearls. She wore pantsuits. I was amazed at her knowledge of everything, and her exceptional cooking skills. Our house was squeaky clean, and we always had clean pressed clothes. She rearranged the furniture a lot—thanks god the toilet was anchored to the floor.

Shirley Mae once made herself up like a huge mouse and went to a neighbor's house chewing on a very large chunk of cheese. It was not Halloween. She did lots of funny things, and dad always managed to get her home safely. I think I got my sense of humor from her; I like to dress up too.

I've realized in these last few years, though, I never actually knew the woman. Of course as a kid back in the Fifties and Sixties you weren't supposed to know your parents. You were just supposed to do what they said. I remember my father reminding us on a regular basis that children were to be seen and not heard. I always wanted to ask him why God gave me a voice box, but then I would have been heard.

Many kids today call their parents by their first name; I thought my parent's first names were Mom and Dad. No, I didn't find it odd that everyone else's parents had the same names. We actually had four girls in my third-grade class named Sharon. With an "n."

My father was and still is a bigger mystery to me. He was a hard worker, a good provider, and made a really scary puffy face when we were bad. He watched wrestling, fixed stuff, and loved spinach. I hate spinach. He did whatever Mom asked him to do, and I don't think I ever heard them argue. Well, except the one time they tried to hang this really weird ivy wallpaper. But hanging wallpaper can drive anyone into a frenzy. Look at Hitler.

My dad and I never really got along very well. He had his heart set on a boy after my sister. What do you do with three bookends, if you know what I mean? We are also a lot alike: we're both outspoken and very feisty scrappers. Sometimes it's hard to look at yourself in the mirror, especially in the morning without make-up. Not that my dad wears make-up.

Most of the time our relationship was like fingernails on a blackboard and many a comment was made over our years together. Being a parent isn't as easy as it seems, especially when you are the parent. I about chewed my lips off my face with my firstborn. Unfortunately a few of my father's comments stuck with me longer than my uterus did. I'm sure a few of the men in my life have suffered due to our rocky relationship. Yet I have no feelings of remorse. Each new male that enters my life makes me wonder why I let the last one live.

My sister Judy was the normal one of us kids, kind of the buffer in the family. Though I think it has taken its toll on her over the years. She kept my brother and me from demising each other. She did things right and always appeared to know what she was doing, unlike me. Judy always had a plan and a direction, even if she made a few U-turns.

Judy was also my life preserver, even though I've always wanted to let go she kept me hanging on. By letting go, yes, I mean the desire to die, to leave this world, to throw in the towel, cash in the chips, clock out. Why death scares so many people I have no idea. It is a bigger part of life than life itself. The actual *act* may be no picnic but the end results are promising. No more work, pain, bills, traffic, restricted diets, belly blubber, disappointments, failures, politicians, restricted diets, (oh I already said that but you get the general idea, all of the bad things are *out of here!*).

I need to stress this issue because it too has had a huge bearing on my lifestyle. When you go through life without a real fear of death you take a lot more chances, you don't worry about mistakes, and you eat a lot of butter. I'll never worry about what I didn't get to do, I'll feel relieved that I didn't have time to do it. Like skydiving. Why does the notice of impending death make people want to jump out of a plane? What, three weeks is too long now?

People like me also take great pride in planning our own funeral; this is our big event. Some people look forward to retirement, I look forward to an extended dirt nap. I've ordered up the *Toast & Toss*. It's a third of the cost of a regular funeral and no one will be saying, "she looks so natural," cause you're just a mound of ash. What was I, the walking dead, while I was here? No one should tell someone his or her deceased loved one looks nice or natural lying in a coffin, even if it is an improvement.

I read once of a woman who said she would never buy life insurance: she said, "When I die I want it to be a sad day for everyone." I have life insurance but I'm leaving it to my cats so they can buy all the catnip they ever dreamed of.

Let's face it—funerals suck. I don't want a bunch of people standing over me bawling, "she was such a great person." Bullshit. If you liked me so much why didn't you return my calls or buy me lunch while I was here? Oh, and I hate all that squeaky organ music playing. I'm ordering some good old country tunes; they're just as depressing but at least you can sing along if you take a notion. I've also heard a million times there will be no more butterflies and beautiful sunsets to enjoy, blah, blah, blah ... for every beautiful sunset I've seen, I've had over a hundred horrible, bowel-wrenching mornings. I guess if there is one thing that proves I've been going backwards all of my life it's my desire to get out of life instead of getting into it.

The Bible says we are all here for a reason and we all have our crosses to bear in life. I like the Bible, some versions better than others; it's nice to have a choice. Some of it sounds like today, only two thousand years later with better weapons and SUVs instead of chariots. The one thing I can't agree with is its concept of women. But then, it was written and rewritten hundreds of times by men. Everyone knows you can't trust men. I'm pretty sure that a disgruntled husband in one of the translation rooms slipped in the word "obey."

Either way, my cross seems to be the big D—as in depression—and I'm pretty sure I got it from my mother. She once said, while watching a movie of people lost on a desert, "Oh I'd just lay down and die." At the time we all thought it was funny, we're a sick bunch. She recently acquired colon cancer, her desire to live was greatly lacking. She sweetly stated, "Well, I've had a good life," smiled and proceeded to *lie down and die.* Of course my sister the life preserver whipped her into survival mode and she is still with us today. For fifty years, whenever the lead breaks on my pencil, I just want to lie down and die.

Unfortunately you can't just give up and go home. When God wants you he will come and get you. I'm pretty sure there is a reason I'm here. I've tried to do the *It's a*

8

Wonderful Life list for myself, but my small insurance policy always outweighs the good things I've done. Instead of saving my brother I tried to eliminate him and I don't think that any town I've ever lived in even knows I lived there. I don't think many would miss me. No one calls me now. I know my husband would just keep on working until another woman saw the potential in him and hog tied him into marriage. Then he'd go back to work. And my kids, well, my kids would have sucked another adult dry and forgotten to call them, too.

I think while we are here we have to muddle through life the best we can with what God gave us. Crummy part is some got a whole lot more than others. Life isn't fair, that is for sure, especially for women. My shrink once said, "*Fair* is where farm animals win blue ribbons." I think he needs help.

I'm not so sure on that whole Adam and Eve story. I think women took the brunt of the punishment and had she not been fixing lunch for Adam things might have been different. How about I give him back his rib and see if he cooks or just grabs an apple too.

I don't think that God really anticipated how we would react when he said to *go out be fruitful and multiply*. Heredity is an interesting yet frightening thing. It's like taking a bunch of rusty and relabeled cans in the garage, stirring them all together, and pouring it on the yucca plant to see what happens. Does anyone really know his or her ancestors? I mean the stuff's been running down the hill for thousands of years now. Great-Uncle Fernando may appear to have been quite the brave adventurer stowing away in a cargo ship to find a new life in America. He also may have been wanted in ten counties for a variety of odd or unlawful hobbies.

How I became *me* will always be somewhat of a

mystery despite modern science. When I hear all this hoo-hah about cloning I always have to wonder who the hell thinks they are so darn perfect as to do it again. I don't think there is anyone that wouldn't change something about themselves, even if it were that bent little monkey toe you can't get a ring on snugged next to your pinky toe.

You will find that in this book I tend to get sidetracked. One minute I'm talking about being born, the next I'm debating deformed appendages. But guess what: that, my friend is life. Nobody stays online 24-7! In the middle of church you're wondering if the stain stick you put on the butter spots a week ago will still work. In the middle of sex you're wondering why the hell he can't clip the hair out of his ear like you ask. In the middle of a board meeting you're wondering who got their BA from a matchbook school and why society allows them to run around unattended. If you're wondering if you're crazy most of the time, you're not. I read in a magazine once that if you can still question your sanity then you're not nuts. Though that doesn't mean you're completely *okay* either.

Anyway, back to the crosses we must bear and learn to deal with. Whenever I get depressed I have the desire to write things down. Some people take pills, some exercise, I write things down. I started writing as soon as my little hand could wield a pencil. Even at the age of eight I knew I was different and knew that someday my name would be in print. I was different—so part of that was very insightful for an eight-year-old. I remember making up little surveys in school and passing them to friends. Do you like boys? Do you think the Easter Bunny is real? Is the sun electric? What is the answer to numbers seven, twelve, fifteen, and twenty-two?

I figured even if no one wanted to hear what I had to say, I'd write it down for later use. I have stacks of writing that, when I look back on it, well, most of it makes no sense. But I'm saving it because I have been through many phases and someday something may just click. I've been waiting fifty years for something to click. Sometimes a bone will pop real loud and I get all excited—then nothing happens.

I have to say that being a kid was probably the easiest and best part of my life even if I can't remember most of it. It's definitely a lot better than being an adult. Yeah, you're in charge and can drink, but man, it was a lot easier when someone else made the decisions and took the fall if they were wrong. I can't wait for my second childhood—because I'll be old enough to do all of the stuff I wasn't allowed to do back then and no one can spank me. Unless, of course, it's appropriate for the activity at hand.

I don't remember a lot about my early school years either, maybe because of that ADD thing. I do remember hating to sit still and wondering what all the other kids found so darn interesting about story problems. It wasn't my problem, so why did I have to solve it? Who cares how long it takes for the train to get there as long as they are serving dinner and something chocolate. My favorite classes were recess and lunch, in those I excelled. Too bad they weren't graded. It definitely has carried over though because I don't work now and still love to eat.

I used to have to wear a dress every day to school. If it was cold we could put long pants under it for recess. That annoyed me because the boys didn't have to wear a dress over their pants on hot days. Even as a grade schooler I noticed a need for liberation in certain areas, so I went on strike and didn't wear *any* pants under my dress. I do remember always being a rebel, though authority figures described it differently.

I went to a private Lutheran school for the first eight

years of my education. They taught me about God and morals. When I entered the public school system, they taught me about reality and immorality. I liked the public school system better. They didn't care what you did or what you had as long as your butt was in a seat when the bell rang and it produced state aid. I remember walking up to my mother as innocent as a newborn babe my second day of public junior high, I asked her what the F-word meant. I'd heard it at least a thousand times and it seemed to work well with every form of speech, so as a writer I didn't want to miss out on such an amazing adjective. She gasped like a trout out of water on a hot river bank, clasped her hand over my face, and demanded I never utter that word again. I didn't listen.

My teenage years were restless and painful. Puberty is restless and painful. What a great time to cram your head full of important facts—when you are at the most unstable stage of your life. All you can do is concentrate on untimely zits and everyone else's body developing before yours. Who cares if Clayton Columbus crossed the Strait of Panama and discovered herbs? Who cares what the square root of twenty is—aren't roots supposed to be in the ground? And who the hell ever decided to add alphabets and numbers together? We need to get our education when we are interested in it, after our faces have cleared up and we've gotten laid. Then we can concentrate.

Everything is a catastrophe during puberty. I had appendicitis for thirteen years, and finally after endless frustration, stomachaches, diets, and missed school, the mystery was solved. As I lay doubled up in pain barfing, Dr. Ben declared, "I'm opening that kid up, I have to know what is wrong!" Kind of like when something is stopping up the toilet one day and running through the next. Sooner or later you've just got to yank it and bust it open. This would be the beginning of life-long medical problems, either real or imagined.

You have to understand something about me. I'm not normal. My symptoms never seem to be in the right place or to follow the textbook. All of my appendix pain was very high in my rib cage, probably why they tried to cure it with diet. Now when my toe hurts my doctor knows to do a brain scan. They never find *anything.* Anyway, I was rushed to the emergency room, where my appendix broke on the operating table. Everyone was amazed! They said another ten minutes and I would have been dead. Shortly thereafter I started my period and wished I was.

My monthly blessing of cramps lasted for twenty-eight days and felt like someone had vise grips clamped on my ovaries. This may help explain my kids—cracked eggs. Worse than the pain was the desire to eliminate every living organism in my path. My father never understood the female mysteries, so three times a month he and Bobby left town. I've always loved the saying, "If something can bleed for seven days and not die, don't mess with it." Words to live by, men! I also identify greatly with the movie *Sybil,* because we both have way too many people inside us on any given day. Yeah, sometimes it's crowded, but you're never lonely either.

What it came down to was, my dad was right about one thing: I should have been Bobby. He never had cramps and for that I wanted to nail his foot to the floor and watch him run around in circles with his head on fire.

Somewhere in the puberty phase my father and I really started butting heads, probably because I figured after I started my period I was never going to grow that penis he wanted. As a teenager you live to annoy adults anyway, so I did my best to uphold the unwritten code. I now had two battling partners at home. I added PMS to my ADD and

ADHD, which is a quite impressive string of letters after your name even though none of them ever raised my pay scale. The medical diagnosis of PMS was yet to be discovered. No fancy explanations, you were just being a bitch. There was no sympathy for anyone who was just being a bitch, so every month I would sit in my dark room questioning my existence, asking God to come and get me, and planning the demise of my brother. Some things never change.

I didn't have much going for me as a young lady. I went from fat to rail-thin and a tad shy of six-foot one night while I slept. I wore glasses—four eyes and frog face (that one came from my brother, but I don't know what it had to do with glasses). When I was little my mom used to put a bowl on my head and cut around it, and then trim my bangs up to my scalp line. When I got older she would give me Toni home perms, torquing perm rods on my head so tight my eyes looked like dime slots on a gumball machine. I think my mom really wanted to be a beautician. She wouldn't let me shave my legs either, she said it would come in darker. I already looked like an orangutan—so what? I'd look like a gorilla? I was often mistaken for a boy between my hairdo, excess hair, and lack of boobs. Some things never change.

Back in the Fifties kids didn't get a lot of *life* information. I remember eagerly awaiting health class only to find out they were actually talking about health. I got better information off of the bathroom stall walls. The opposite sex was a mystery to me. The first boy I had a very distant crush on in high school got killed. The rest of them I dreamt of killing. My best friend and I used to write boys' names on our notebooks, wear fake rings, and claim our boyfriends were older and went to another school. What was the point of that? Is it a wonder no one ever asked us out? The two mercy dates I did have were painfully long with a constant fear of invasion by a male. Not so much because my mother told me *it* was very valuable, but more because I didn't want anyone to know how little my boobs really were after the Kleenexes were removed from my bra.

I never went to any high school dances or parties, or any things, probably because my imaginary boyfriend was always working. It didn't really bother me though, because whenever I tried to talk to boys my vocabulary instantly shrunk to three words: I, I, I, and my glasses felt like those giant sunglasses you get from a carnival supply. I tried to take my glasses off whenever a cute boy was around, but after a few trips to distant neighborhoods I decided it was more important to see the bus numbers.

So, like most homely pubescent girls I hid in my room and dreamt of my knight in shining armor, awaiting my rescue. Where was Toby Keith's song, *There Ain't No Knights in Shining Armor,* then? This is information I could have used. I refuse to tell little girls fairy tales. Cinderella should have packed up her rodents, hit the road, and let those ugly sisters clean their own rooms. She could have gotten a grant, a degree, and invented the pumpkin carriage, holding the patent to the first SUV. Who needs to be rescued when you're famous and filthy rich?

I used to dream about being filthy rich. The first thing I did in my dream was to sell off my brother to a caravan of traveling gypsies. Of course my parents didn't mind because I was fifthly rich, and their favorite. The second thing I did was purchase contact lenses. That was way before they invented silicone implants, or I'da bought them too. Now I'd buy a new liver and bladder so I could start drinking again.

I've never had a lot of friends in my life at any given

time. Maybe because people just don't understand me or didn't enjoy sitting in the closet putting pins in my brother's voodoo doll. Too many friends are a lot of work and costly around the holidays. I prefer one really good friend, one you can trust. When they start counting and I go off to hide, I want to know that they will actually come and look for me. Staying in the clothes hamper too long will make your family wonder about you.

Growing up is tough no matter what era you are in. Every generation has peer pressure, it just comes in different forms. When we were little kids friends used to dare us to ride our little red wagon down the *big* hill blindfolded. Let me tell you, an old oak tree at fifty mph can mess you up worse than a few puffs of pot. People think it was easier in the old days, but I disagree. Daring someone to walk a highway overpass rail or put a whole brick of firecrackers in an Easy Bake Oven never goes out of style. Busted bones or a finger blown off hurts no matter what era you're in!

No one ever tried to get me to try pot. I guess they thought I was already high. The only thing I've ever been pressured into was my swimsuits.

I think the biggest danger to kids today is TV. The only threat TV ever posed us was going blind from sitting too close. And of course radiation from the color TVs. Our parents never had to worry about us watching something unsuitable; there were only four channels and a thing called censorship (can't explain it now, it's way too complicated). The only thing I want to say on it is this. I think it is our responsibility as adults to screen and protect our children from all of the sick and demented crap in the world for as long as we can. We learn what we live, and if kids sit in front of a TV all day watching violence sooner or later they are going to act it out on something. I'm glad my parents didn't let us watch some stuff—my mind went downhill fast enough on its own. Heck, I thought about shredding my brother long before Freddy Krueger ever came into play.

Growing up is a lot easier to do than to look back on and analyze. Some things you just shouldn't stop and think about, like dancing on a table when you take a notion. All this New Age theory and thought has only made our kids as neurotic as their parents.

It's like Barbie dolls: they were mine and my sister's best friends. Of course we only had one Barbie and she had to do various jobs, mostly housekeeping. Now Barbies must carry a warning label: *Caution: Parts on this doll may appear to be larger or smaller than achievable in actual life.* Litigation wants to make her boobs smaller, her waist bigger, and further diversify her employability for fear of the emotional effect on young girls. They even have a Barbie in a wheelchair. That's just want a cripple wants, a crippled doll. Who thought that one up? The last Barbie my great-niece showed me had feet on it like walrus flippers.

Barbie was a great invention, but they don't need to keep reinventing her. What about us Barbie beginners? Mattel is going to have to make all of her body parts droop for me to assimilate now. It's a toy, just play with it.

Can you imagine parents of the Fifties suing Mattel because their kid was stupid enough to eat a tiny pair of high heels because there was no warning to say otherwise? We would have gotten a half a loaf of bread shoved down our throats and a slap upside the head if we ate our toys.

There are a lot of things I think I remember from my childhood, but I'm not so sure if they are real or just a side effect of aging now. Sometimes my sister remembers the same event very differently, she's never the one that initiated the plans that caused the punishment. However I distinctly recall her saying, "Hey, let's do this…" and then sending me off down the road to a disaster.

I hate remembering bits and pieces, especially when a cop stops me. I could write a lot more bits and pieces of my childhood, but hell, they don't even make sense to me. One thing I do remember clearly was having fun. We had fun as kids and we played hard, though none of it was structured teams or lessons. We played streetlight tag in the dark, built forts (with curtains of course), and then fought neighborhood wars over them. We dug holes in the yard for my dad to step in while mowing. We ran five thousand miles beating our legs with sticks to make the horses go faster. I had to play Horses or my sister wouldn't play with me. We rode our bicycles until our tires wore out. We played under the sprinkler in the summer and in the snow in the winter. Kids today think they have to have tons of friends or events going on all the time. Not in the old days. We used our imagination and played with ourselves.

As I look back on my childhood I see that it laid the groundwork for the life I have lived. All of a sudden my mother's warnings of *someday you're going to be sorry* have shed great light on an otherwise empty statement. It seems like I was a child for a very short time. Once I turned sixteen and got behind the wheel of a car things got very complicated. I was expected to be responsible. *Expected* is the key word there.

If I could do it all over again, I wouldn't. Especially the wagon thing.

18

Chapter 2

I Marry the First Guy that Comes Along

I can remember it like it was yesterday, the day I met Richard. Well, let's just call him Dick. Dick is the father of my two sons, Pete and Repete. (Remember the names are changed.) Dick was pink, with spots. He wore a tan sport coat and gray pants. The tie didn't match either, but gosh, was he funny. Diana from high school worked with Dick and felt compelled to ruin my life. To this day she often asks if I can ever forgive her. No. Actually I can, but just to be safe, she gets a "no." In case she has another single friend.

Dick had just been awarded an Oscar Mayer wiener ring from a gumball machine and after our introductions he took to his knee and asked for my hand in marriage. I refused the wiener ring and told him to come back when he had a big diamond. He did, but the wiener came with it anyway, though it somehow morphed to six-foot-one.

The best part of Dick was he was fun and freedom from the typical teenager oppression at home and the much-dreaded boredom of youth. When you're young and you're sitting around with nothing to do you call it boredom; when you're old and sitting around with nothing to do you call it a rest. Either way you have nothing to do. Why doesn't it bother you when you're old?

Dick was real, not just a name on a notebook, so just the sheer joy of producing a living, breathing male to all those stuck-up pom-pomers was intoxicating. And Dick was older, just like my imaginary boyfriend, but he could actually purchase beer. My dad never worried about us drinking even when my sister bounced down the basement steps on her butt. He'd just shake his head and say, "go to bed." He assumed we would figure it out on our own. We didn't. After the soda bottles he shouldn't have assumed anything.

Back in the Seventies drinking was cool. Anything that altered your mind was cool and far out, man. Drinking and driving wasn't even considered a problem, it was actually kind of amusing. Nothing was more fun than exchanging stories of your worst attempt to make it home alive after a good party.

No matter how many laws they pass about drinking and driving, people will still do it. Your judgment is impaired under the influence. When you're sober you responsibly state, "I know better than to drive when I've been drinking; here's my keys." But after a few too many drinks you're belligerently yelling at everyone, "Gimme dem damn keys, I'm not dunk!" They just want to get rid of your obnoxious ass. Hence, drinking and driving.

* Note: I do not advocate drinking and driving, before the letters start to pour in. I'm telling a story here so fire down and keep reading for amusement's sake. That is one

20

of the problems with people today, everyone gets their nose out of joint for every infraction and heads straight to court. We don't need to found an organization and make a law for everything that happens. Everyone can't sue someone every time someone dies. We all have to die somehow. Shouldn't we be taking up the *method* used with God instead of the courts?

When your life is changing a million miles a minute it's hard to keep a grasp on things. Jumping into the world of adulthood is like a nosedive into a drained pool, and sometimes you just have to escape from reality and think things out. It's not going to make sense sober or drunk so you might as well enjoy a good buzz, and chill.

I recall right before my wedding being totally wasted at a county park. I used to like to get drunk and go stare up at trees while bonding with nature. As I sat under a mighty oak crying because of some life-shattering trauma (I think Dick didn't like the china pattern I picked out), a cop stopped to see what the problem was. Boy was he sorry. He gave me a Kleenex or his sock and asked me some questions. I'm not sure what I answered or what he asked, but I distinctly remember him assisting me to my car. Though I don't recall my feet ever touching the ground. He put me into the driver's seat (no need to buckle up back then, because Dick had cut all the seatbelts out). He then instructed me to *drive* straight home and not drink any more. Home?

For the most part Dick and I had nothing in common but beer and laughter, which works well for a lot of relationships. I have always loved to laugh. I can find humor anywhere in anything. I laugh at stuff that's not even funny. Ask anyone. Dick had great jokes—little did I know that thirty years later he would still be telling the same jokes. He took me on float trips, bought me a car, and didn't care how big my boobs were. He was the absolute funniest when he was drunk, but aren't we all? If only to ourselves.

When you're eighteen years old you're not exactly analyzing for long-term mental disorders that appear to be fun. At forty if someone tells you they hid a Thermos in their school locker filled with grape juice and vodka you want to get them help, at eighteen you just want to get to the locker! If someone tells you he blew holes through twelve U-Haul trailers with a homemade cannon using only a trash can lid for a shield, now that's funny! Dick was a great storyteller, I thought they were made up.

I'm going to admit, I didn't weigh out my options, I didn't think things out, I didn't even consider the fact that all those spots were never going to go away. I just said yes. I wanted freedom, a wedding like my sister's, a big fluffy white dress, and that really cool ring. Little did I know that my freedom was about to come with more responsibility than I'd ever imagined. When you're eighteen you think you know it all. When you're staring at fifty you realize you haven't learned squat in fifty years.

I think this short era of my life was the best, next to being a kid. You've finally gained independence and your parents start to take you seriously and are glad you can no longer blame them. You can now go anywhere you want and not cry when you get lost. Well, sometimes. You are now allowed to be *seen and heard,* and the right to vote proves that. Big people no longer ask, "do your parents know where you are?" And best of all, you get a bank account and money of your own. Sure, later on when the service fees start piling up it won't be as great as it seemed, but it feels really good to write that first check out, and have it clear.

The best part of getting married is that everyone is

paying attention to you. That might seem self-centered and very "me," but once you reproduce, that brief shining moment in your life will become your happy place. It will never be all about you again.

Parties of any kind are good but wedding showers are the best. You get all sorts of gifts that make you feel grown-up, even if you don't know what to do with them. Who would have thought a waffle iron couldn't crimp hair too? And why does a soufflé dish look so much like a dog bowl? I didn't even know my aunt knew we had a dog. And, you never really think about towels until you have your own house. Amazingly enough, my mother was right: they do not wash themselves, nor can they get from the floor to the towel rack without assistance. Nothing makes you feel emancipated like your very own toaster.

The actual wedding was a whirlwind. Most are. All I really wanted to do was dance around in my six-hundred-dollar Cinderella dress. Dick wanted to drink. My poor mother drove herself crazy with all the details, and my dad with all of the bills. When I planned and paid for my second wedding I finally appreciated my parent's efforts. Well, at least for the wedding. Each phase of my life, especially having children, would be a new revelation of admiration for my parents.

The wedding ceremony took about thirteen seconds, or so it seemed. Before I knew it I was walking back down the aisle with a ring on my finger and a growth by my side. By the end of our wedding dance they had to cut Dick's size-thirteen shoe out of my once white floor-length veil. He said it didn't matter, I "was only wearing it once anyway." That's when I understood why my father asked before I walked down the aisle, "If you don't want to do this, you don't have to. The party is all paid for. We are having it either way." Why didn't I ever listen to my father?

Ah, but there just isn't enough time planning a wedding to think about stuff like the groom. Each phase is more exciting, more fascinating, building and building into the finished production that you've waited your entire life for. After playing *Barbie Gets Married* five hundred thousand times you're finally in Barbie's shoes. Well, not in reality because her shoes are, like, really tiny.

Weddings to women are like sex to men. Women can't get enough of them. Anyone's wedding. It's life fluffed to the billionth power. It's flowers and fantasy, it's silk and satin, bows and spending obscene amounts of money. And best of all, it's the joy of knowing another happy male is giving up his freedom to serve the woman he loves for eternity.

When it's your wedding it's even more overwhelming. I was so totally swept up in the moment of it all that before I knew what hit me, my years of lifelong dreams were over and I was married. Kind of like when you break down and buy one of the big thirty dollar fireworks, ssst... that's it? What can you do but curse the Chinese and move on.

You smash what's left of your glorious gown into the backseat of a hatchback Pinto dragging three-quarter barrels. Three of his buddies with ice-bucket hats and cumberbund bras stuff a passed-out lump in next to you while wishing you well. Suddenly it hits you as you climb over the seat to drive. "Man, what the hell was I thinking?"

I'm not even going to discuss my first honeymoon. It was a miserable time. I felt very awkward and uninformed at night and pissed off during the days. There weren't any sex therapists on TV back then and my parents were still spelling the word *sex* out after I had their first grandson. My mother's few words of pre-wedding-night wisdom were, "it's your wifely duty," which started to look a lot like ironing. Dick wasn't much help; I knew his suggestions weren't going to help me, so I just kept my mouth shut tight and kept ironing. I could have used a little spray starch.

I kept looking at Dick wondering who the heck he was as he ran around the amusement park trying to goose six-foot mice with his cotton candy. I wondered if my mother ever regained consciousness after Dick started to moon everyone on our way out, or if she missed that and it had something to do with the bill the caterer handed her. It seemed like my mind was bombarded with worries and concerns of things, strange things, things my mom should have been taking care of. Somehow, though, I felt responsible, it was quite an eerie feeling. Even as Dick twirled us into oblivion in the teacups, I wondered how mad my dad would be if I called him up and asked if it was too late to change my mind, and kick Bobby out of my room.

We took three hundred dollars from our wedding money, which was a lot of money back in the Seventies. I was making one dollar and eighty cents an hour, to give you a *range of value*. Dick ate it all in four days; he's a big guy. After our last night's stay in a small box made out of hot pink concrete blocks (it was only ten dollars a night) we headed home three days early to start our new life together, for however long that might be.

It was a horribly long drive home. The eight-track finally chewed up the Beatles *Abbey Road* cassette just outside of somewhere and we hadn't eaten anything but a bag of Fritos since we left. Words were few from me. I think I was in that Post Traumatic Shock Syndrome. Dick drove on, happily beating out the drum solos on the dashboard to his favorite Seventies tunes for the last five hundred miles. I have to say that he was always a happy guy even as Hell closed in around him.

Dick had bought a house before we were even married, thinking if he did I'd have no financial interest in it if anything should happen down the road. I wonder how he knew it wasn't going to work. Anyway, it was a nice little cozy three-bedroom one-bath bungalow in Fergaston, with strangled plumbing. It was on a pretty little street lined with vicious probing tree roots and a steady stream of annoying park traffic. We bought the house from a very old man named Mr. Blornaker; he took a step every thirty minutes.

The inside was a nightmare of drab Forties colors. Wherever they ran out of paint they picked up with the next shade of scary. I never imagined that people would paint around their furniture and wall hangings, but sure enough after they moved out a lot of their stuff; it looked like they were still there. We cheered it up with mod Seventies wallpaper and furnished it with Early Attic and Late Relative. I hated that house. I still have nightmares of waking up in it next to my "ex."

Dick moved in his new recliner. There he would stay for the duration of our marriage.

Most of the carpeting was what they used to call sculptured shag. Which means wherever their dogs hadn't chewed a hole there was a slight bump to the thinness. Our uneventful bedroom was adorned with green shag carpeting and a closet the size of a matchbox. To this day I can't stand shag carpet or believe that someone is actually trying to bring it back. It's a lot like a bad lawn; it is always in a state of dying. Yeah, a little water will perk it up but as soon as you walk on it, it's dead again. I actually raked our rug with the garden rake. It didn't help. It's hard to live in a house where you hate the flooring. That has been almost every house of my life. It's even harder to rectify that problem when you have no money. Anyone that says money can't buy happiness hasn't been poor with shag carpeting.

All of our windows were painted shut, and for a very good reason. After hours of hard work to free one, it fell out onto the driveway. But what could you expect for $14,500—what does that buy you now, a closet? Our house payment was $159.53 a month. You can't even stay in a nice hotel for one night for that. Later I would sell the house and triple my payment, because I am a financial wizard.

The perpetually wet basement was filled with mountains of Mr. Blornaker's junk. How do you tell someone who gives you an interest-free loan for your down payment to pack up and get out? And how silly of us to assume he would. For two years we welcomed him into our home to remove a lamp, or maybe an important paper—not the whole box. Some nights he would stop by and forget what he came for so we'd visit for a while. We'd try to spark his memory; he'd leave with nothing. It was apparent this could have gone on forever or as long has he had life left in him. We were surprised he was still breathing after two years. Then late one night I caught him digging in our back yard. He felt compelled to reclaim his deceased wife's rose bushes that I had planted a few days before.

We had offered to pack and transport the rest to him on many occasions, but he said, "Nah, that's too much work for you kids. I'll get it." One night after a half-barrel of beer Dick decided to just pitch the rest of his stuff out on the curb for trash pick-up. Besides, the creek in the park had backed the sewer into our basement again and most of it was aromatic brown mush. We agreed that when he showed up to uproot, sort, or just think, we'd both tell him that he had gotten the last of it. I mean, after two years he was still calling me Martha. How would he know?

He showed up unannounced one Halloween night looking for his pumpkin (pre electric, ceramic, or crazy foam pumpkins). Dick spun his lie, he was very good at it. I sat silent like a nervous beagle next to a puddle. Mr. Blornaker scratched his head and mumbled as he stared around the empty basement. After a while he asked if it would be all right if he came by just to visit. We both said no. From that moment on I truly feared aging and stepped up my request for God to come get me.

I learned a lot in my first six months of marriage. The first thing I learned about freedom is that it isn't free. I now go around and turn the lights off at my parents' house. Nothing is more liberating than your first electric bill. The second thing I learned is that you never really know someone until you live with them. I wish my mother had told me the latter first, it had a lot bigger effect on me than the electric bill.

Of course Dick and I went to a few marriage classes at our church to prepare us for marriage, but I have to say that was comparable to P.E. class being training for war. I think you need to know your marriage partner just like your enemy of war. One can't go into battle without a strategy. All our pastor talked about was loving each other, communicating, loyalty, and compassion. He never said anything about annoying traits, skid britches in the hall, boundless beer, or bill collectors.

I guess we both did the best we could with the information we had. I tried to play house like I had with Barbie. The only problem was I didn't know what to do with Ken now. With dolls after Barbie made him breakfast and sent him to work, we tossed Ken under the sofa. Now Ken was sitting in the recliner watching TV, making messes, and wanting service, and was way too big to stuff under the sofa. I tried.

I liked being a housewife. I was born to be a domestic goddess. Unfortunately I had to work full time because most of the time Dick was between jobs, sitting in his recliner, or hanging out with his buddies. A husband who sees work as a hobby can put a real damper on your plans and dreams.

My first real job was working in a clothing factory; I was a picker. I suggested we have big noses with our names on them to mark our clothes racks but the boss didn't find that amusing. Everyone said it was because he was Jewish. He was a great boss and I wished him Merry Christmas every year, probably because I wasn't politically correct back then either. I was the only person who ever wished him anything, right or wrong. He thanked me for including him in the holiday. Now I feel stupid.

Picking was a great job. On our lunch breaks we had rack races and took naps in the sweater boxes. I worked there happily until my sister came to work with me for a few weeks. She informed me that the heat, environment, and pay all sucked. It did. However, I wish she had not pointed that out, because for a brief moment in my life I thought I was doing rather well.

I've found out that the only difference between a job and a career is that one of them you're not ashamed of. When someone asks where you work, you either give yourself an impressive title or mumble a location. Like, I'm a neonatal nurse, or a technical engineer. Or if you just have a job like most working stiffs you simply state Twelfth and Washington. The rest of my life would be described in directions.

I think I worked very hard at getting nowhere.

This was not the best time in my life. As a matter of fact the only time I felt more disillusioned was when I woke up in the nut ward five days after I'm-not-sure-when. Most people in a nut ward (not the loony bin; there is a big difference) are only there because they had enough sense to question the bizarre behavior of others. If you can get past the med-induced narcolepsy you will find sane people driven crazy by their spouses. Outside of the alarmed doors are the real crazies, that was a unanimous vote.

My group counselor was great; I think we were taking the same medication. Every now and then she would tell us a story about her ex but make us all swear not to repeat it. Of course none of us ever did because after our next dose of meds we couldn't even remember who we were.

Our group also concluded that the best way to select a spouse would be to go to a family reunion before you say *I do*. One should talk to the uncles wearing the T-shirts that say, *"Rehab is for Quitters"* and definitely spend a little time with the auntie wearing striped toe socks with thongs in the middle of August. You should watch their eating habits: do they cook their meat first? Check out their vehicles too, are there oversized dog crates in back, but only children present? It's called a gene pool and it shouldn't be overlooked when joining a clan.

The nut ward was very enlightening. I still have the little papier-mâché happy ball I made there. Whenever I feel like my situation is hopeless and I have no control over the actions of others I dig it out and repeat the saying written around the middle. *The world isn't a perfect place; drink heavily.* I had to take that class a few times before I won my freedom. I threw away the happy ball that allowed me to pass.

I think the journey of life would be a lot easier if we didn't keep allowing people to ride on top of the big bag of insecurities we are dragging along. It's a shame that we have to reach eighty to figure out a Chihuahua is a lot less trouble than a spouse and kids. I can't blame Dick for everything, I know some of our problems were from my inability to make intelligent choices. Everything seems like a good idea at the time.

And another thing. I don't know why it would have been so hard for God to send people with instructions and some simple directions. It would be a lot easier on parents and children and He wouldn't have to listen to our whining 24-7. You wouldn't get a box with a bicycle in it and try to make it into an end table. No, because it says "bicycle" right on the package. Think of the agony we could be saved if we were labeled with a suggestion on arrival. School teacher: add eighteen to twenty-two years of education. Doctor: add twenty-two to twenty-six years of education. Psychotic: add drugs. Drunk: add booze. Think of the time and aggravation it would have saved both of us. They say God knows our destiny. Let's face it, most people don't have a clue, some hints wouldn't have messed up free-will that bad.

Along with those directions, He could have sent a few warnings, you know, like "don't use a hair dryer in the bathtub." Don't get married to be free. I mean, He *is* God; he had to see this stuff coming. But then it probably wouldn't have been as much fun for Him to watch us bumble through life trying to figure it out.

I think God has a great sense of humor. He made me. I also think He wasted eight arms on an octopus when a mother could have put them to good use. God and I have got a lot of things to talk about when I get there... might be why He doesn't come and get me?

Chapter 3

I Reproduce

I don't know what it is about our species that makes us want to reproduce. Every time I heard someone whining "we want to have a child," I offered to give them one of ours. What makes people think that their kids will be any different?

My lawyer once took my two boys and me to get an ice cream cone. I warned against it. Naturally the boys were leaking from every direction all over his nice car. Bluntly he asked me, after he unstuck his hands from the steering wheel, "why would anyone in their right mind want to have kids?" I had nothing. My mind was as blank as the expression on a cop's face when you try to tell him you couldn't stop at the red light because a huge wasp was in the car, buzzing at your eyes! It's really hard to sell a kids' cuteness when they are covered in ice cream, chocolate, and legal papers made into snowflakes.

About ten years later, he and his family came out to my

house for dinner. His four-year-old son stood on my new suede chair cushion wildly spewing buttered corn on the cob all over my dining room. He and his wife casually ate and talked of old times and new directions; they had either acquired what I like to call parental Alzheimer's or it was pay-back time. I gazed silently out into the back yard, trying not to notice the ritualistic corn-grinding dance. From the window I could see Pete and Repete shooting their corn and pork & beans out of soda straws into the pool filter. Hey... my lawyer had a pool?

Ah, but when you're a young women and your biological clock is ticking there's no sleeping through the desire to reproduce. Especially when everyone around you is having babies, cute, cuddly, sweet little babies. My immune system must have been down because I immediately contracted a raging case of baby fever from work. All I could think of was having a baby. Surely it would fulfill my meaningless life and make Dick a better husband. It is amazing how we rationalize the most bizarre possibilities out of hopeless situations. Reproduction has never fixed anything, not even artwork.

After months of badgering, Dick finally agreed, as long as it didn't involve his getting out of the recliner or giving up beer. It didn't. I got pregnant the day I threw my birth control pills away. Finally I had a purpose. I remember the first time I felt the baby move. It felt like a butterfly in my stomach. I was so excited. Eight months later it felt like a billy goat butt at the zoo when you take the little bottle away and try to feed another goat. I was terrified. I made a chocolate cake.

Pregnancy is a life-altering event. I think every cell in your body changes, as you are transformed into *a mother*. I think that is why parents and kids don't understand each other—a mother actually becomes something extraterrestrial.

Fathers aren't understood later because they are, men.

I change easily. I like change. I was so into "nesting" there wasn't time to worry, be scared, or think about the changes. Anyone notice a pattern there? Dick seemed real happy, too, sitting in the recliner, in between jobs, drinking a beer. I decorated the nursery alone, went to the doctor alone, swelled up alone, threw up alone, and got stretch marks alone. It was a magical time.

When you're poor you do cheap things. Back in the Seventies lots of people were poor, but you didn't notice it, probably because poor people hung together. That might have been before subsidized housing entered neighborhoods of 250K and up. Our meager little neighborhood had established a Wednesday night porch-dweller's club complete with hotdogs on a hibachi, beer, and TP for anyone who porch-pooped. Ricky and Lucy (changed) had gotten free tickets to a baseball game on porch night and needed to be chastised, as it was their night to buy the dogs. While we ran around decorating their trees with cheap one-ply tissue the lookout sounded the alarm, they were coming down the street. Everyone ran for our porch, I waddled frantically, slipped on the wet grass, and slid down the hill on my belly like a penguin down a snow mound. Everyone stared at me for a long time just waiting for the baby to drop out onto our thinly-seeded lawn. It didn't. That was the only lucky thing that ever happened to me.

Then one night very close to that nine-month mark, while I was soaking in the bathtub amazed at my huge belly, I realized the baby had to come out. The logistics just weren't there. All those things I thought made sense no longer seemed rational. Once again I wanted to call my parents and ask them if it was too late to change my mind. I've always said God made babies cute and little for two reasons: one, no one would keep a twelve-year-old and two, they come out a tad bit easier.

After sixteen hours of hard labor, an attack of Tourette's, and a few well-placed punches to Dick's head, Pete came out. I can't believe I didn't die. No words can express childbirth, but disemboweled comes pretty close. Dick bought a half-barrel of beer and six pizzas to celebrate with his buddies. He bought nothing for me or the baby; he didn't have enough money left. He did, however, leave the molded barrel floating in Pete's second-hand turtle pool, and the pizza boxes piled on the counter by the four day's worth of dirty dishes, laundry, and assorted auto parts. Somehow I knew that it wouldn't be a great homecoming and begged the doctors to please let me stay just a few more months.

Unfortunately, once again I was too busy to wonder, think, or even notice Dick. I was now the mom. I don't know exactly when my identity was miraculously changed, but it was. A lot like when Superman goes into the phone booth. Of course I was still the mild-mannered reporter, maid, cook, laundress, lawnmower, handyman, painter, money juggler, dog walker, and ironer but I really did acquire additional "powers." You know, the eyes in the back of your head and the ability to read minds. I was finally just like my mother. ☺

Now is when more directions from God would have come in really handy, because raising kids is definitely hit-and-miss, especially if they're fast.

The day we brought Pete home from the hospital my sister came with me. Dick was looking for a job. If it had needed to be saddled and a bit put in its mouth I had brought the right person with me. As Pete screamed bloody murder we both gazed at him in awe. Judi (now with an i) quickly pointed out that I was its mother and should know what to do. I didn't. Dick said raising a puppy first would prepare us for this. It didn't. This wild little thing couldn't be put into a box and definitely couldn't walk over to the newspaper.

I stuck the tape tab of the Pampers to his little thingy, and mind you the first paper diapers didn't retape. If you taped it you better hope it was on right because you needed a scissor to get them off! I squeezed the powder can up his butt causing his eyes to pop wide open and the room to look like a blasting zone. I fed him beets then rushed him to the hospital because he was bleeding from the rectum. He swallowed more change than a slot machine and never paid out. He fell down the basement steps, off the front porch twice, and rolled off the bed when Dick was on watch. He wandered out of the house at 2 A.M. to play in his sandbox—we slept right through it. I painted everything in his room with lead-based paint, who would have thought? He ate a half a box of crayons, but I didn't take him to the hospital for rainbow runs, so at least I was learning something. Oh, and I lost him in an amusement park but by then he was already talking so he caught up with me on my way out to the parking lot.

Pete never slept and he ate every two hours round the clock, an inherited trait from Dick. Dick felt it was my duty to care for the baby and do all of the night feedings, after all he was out looking for a job. I remember setting the alarm clock for his one o'clock feeding. Waking him at precisely one eliminated the bone-chilling screams echoing down the hallway that caused me to leap out of bed and slam into the wall every night. Little did I know I was setting a pattern for Pete's nightlife which would reappear in his teenage episode. I should have written this down.

Sometimes even a mom gets sick and one must do the impossible, ask for help. I had been stricken with the flu and Dick, in a moment of mental instability, agreed to take the one o'clock feeding. I set the alarm and had everything ready for him. Precisely at one Pete whelped out his demands. Dick snored on. After I extracted a handful of his armpit hair, Dick got out of bed and headed down the hallway. I snuggled deep into my covers and buried my head under my cheap, lump-ridden pillow. Pete cried on…

After about a half hour of begging God to come and get me *right now*, I decided to get up and see what the problem was. It could have been another tape-tab blunder. Pete was still in his bed buck-naked screaming bloody murder, so I knew it wasn't a diaper issue. Down the hallway drifted a strange aroma of toasted plastic and fried hops. Once in the kitchen I found Fred Flintstone melted to the bottle warmer, the icebox door hung open, and an empty beer can lay lifeless on the floor. I unplugged the bottle warmer with the broom since there were sparks present. A little trick I had learned from my dad. Dick was in the recliner, who'da thought? He lay snoring with Pete's teddy bear semi-diapered across his chest. I never asked him for help again.

A lot of my childrearing tactics I picked up from other people. If their kids were older than mine and didn't appear to be too screwed up I did what they did. Excluding my neighbor, her son Buddy was a real little devil. I always asked her what she thought she did wrong, trying to avoid it. But she would just shake her head and say, "I think he's just a bad seed." That really worried me. Considering I got my seeds from Dick.

Parents aren't always proud of some of their decisions and choices. I once hooked Pete's bib overalls back to the dog chain staked out in the middle of the yard, so I could paint the house. We couldn't afford a fence, and someone had to actually use the ten gallons of paint Dick bought. He seemed really content with a bowl of water and all the dog toys. Then years later at an amusement park we saw a woman with her kid on one of those child leashes. Everyone gasped with horror. "What kind of a mother puts her child on a leash?" my friend wailed.

"Shameful," I added.

As in all things, nothing can be all bad all of the time. Dick finally found a part-time job. It was actually full-time but he only went in part of the time. We finally had some money. Money is a very useful thing even if only for a short while. Those two weeks would be the last time I had extra money.

Dick's wild single friend Mooch (real name) had moved in. Let's just say he was passed out on the sofa almost every morning, or his fat head was stuck inside of my refrigerator eating anything without mold on it. They swore he didn't live there, but I saw the suitcase in his truck and didn't recognize a lot of the laundry.

One night they came home late and descended upon my very beautiful roasted chicken. They grunted, beat on their chest, and yelled out "Vikings!" Then they proceeded to rip the legs from it and gnaw on them while circling the table. Mooch dug into the mashed potatoes with two fingers. I ran from the house in tears, after all it was my first slow roasted chicken.

I was about to go crazy. It was as if Monday Night Football would never end. We usually had a hopped-up Chevelle parked in our front yard or the neighbor's, depending on how fast he took the turn onto Frostwood. Guns and Roses was drowning out *Mary Had A Little Lamb*, foreign skid britches covered the bathroom floor, and a beer tap now sprouted from the front of our hand-me-down Frigidaire. I was not happy. Now that Dick had a little friend sleeping over our communications had dwindled to throwing things at each other. The boys would often leave for a fun-filled evening of male bonding and beer. Naturally I would sit home alone and plan their demise. A lucky break for my brother.

In a moment of enlightenment I decided to pitch most of the guy's stuff out into the street. It was actually a Mr. Blonaker flashback. While they were gone I changed the locks on the doors and put up no trespassing signs. Dick got a key after one night of sleeping in the Pinto, whereupon he also swore in blood that no friends would ever move in again. We shook on it and agreed to start over as a family.

If at first you don't succeed, try, try again. That has to be the worst wise saying ever put to paper. Who are these people that make up this shit, I bet they've never been married.

After a wild New Year's Eve party in 1977, Repete was born. It was only an eight-month pregnancy—there just wasn't time for a full nine months. What was once a blur was now a total blackout. Every day was an unending routine of unfulfilling work, sterilizing bottles, washing diapers, and diverting creditors. Each morning started the same: with a swift blow to Dick's freckled sleeping head and a sweet apology. Every evening ended the same, with a blow to Dick's fricking freckled head and no apology.

I was slowly learning how to deal with married life and being a mom, but on-the-job training sucks when there is no instructor. At least I never chained Repete out in the yard. Didn't have to—I had his sixteen-month-old brother to help watch him while I painted!

The baby years fly by so fast because you're so busy with all of the maintenance stuff you don't have time to really enjoy them in their only cute stage. Colic, poop diapers, rank formula, strained spinach, diaper rash, suctioning out nose debris, unsticking heads from the crib, whining, more poop diapers, pediatric visits, spills, sleepless nights, poop diapers, banshee screeching for no apparent reason, poop diapers. It's a magical time and it just goes way too fast.

Again I found myself thinking of my parents. Every time something unnatural backed up the toilet I blessed my father's patience and plumbing skills. Every time I managed to save a table full of china and food from being dragged to the floor by a tangled airplane wing, I praised my mother for endowing me with her quick reflexes. Every time my brother taught my kids a new cuss word I anticipated his first reproduction, and planned his offspring's demise.

You know how some people say if you got one you might as well have two? Those people surely were not talking about kids; something was left out of that statement. What one doesn't do the other one will—there is no down time. While I was carefully extracting Cheerios from Repete's nose, Pete was over in our elderly neighbor's yard showing off a colorful box of Trojan balloons.

When Pete was finally committed to Kindergarten lock-up I thought I had a chance. Repete took over his absent brother's task of painting the dog with toothpaste and filling the tape player with Hot Wheels which are really hard to get out once the little wheels engage for rewind. I truly want to know what makes a kid put sticks and grass in a gas tank or their airplane in the toilet? This kind of stuff really makes a parent fear for their child's future. Probably like the empty soda bottles did to my parents.

The only real upside to having two kids close together is it gives the older one something to ride on that doesn't need a bunch of damn batteries.

One would think that when they were both incarcerated into the educational system that things would calm down. Wrong. Now you have teachers and principals calling to inform you that your darling reproduction has committed the unforgivable crime of refusing to return his lunch tray to the dish area. The only difference is you now have to drive back and forth constantly to repair the school's video property.

Every day is a test, a test of endurance. Can I, a grown adult, keep up with these strange little people? Can I stay one step ahead of them and ward off danger so they don't break themselves? How long can I live on four hours of sleep per night? Can children really live on Spaghetti-O's if it is all they will eat and not spit back? Every day is a questioning of your ability. My mother used to say, "Oh, Nancy, it's mostly common sense." I can't believe she even said that to me. Soda bottles, Mom, soda bottles.

The hardest part of being a parent is trying to be a good one. Anyone can be a bad one. I know lots of people that never did anything extra for their kids. They just let them grow, as if they had planted a kernel of corn on the earth. Not me. I was a room mother, a Cub Scout leader, a bake sale organizer, a carnival planner, a taxi, and a nurse. I worked, begged, and borrowed to make each holiday a memorable one. I threw balls until my arm fell off, I slept on a hardwood floor in a blanket tent, and ate Happy Meals until I was as hysterical about the free toy as the kids were. I lay awake at night contemplating their future as the president of the United States. And above all, I looked down with great shame on those parents who never did any of this for their kids. Someday they would be sorry. They were just cruising though life while a nanny or relative did all the legwork. I never gave up. I never said never. I kept on keeping on... I just knew in my heart that someday it would all pay off. I believe they call it, visions of grandeur.

Then twenty-seven years later my firstborn son told me, in one of his many hissy fits, that I was a total loser and that I had made his life a living hell. He carefully pointed out every error I've ever made in alphabetical order. The only thing he can remember in my twenty-eight years of backbreaking work and heartfelt effort is that I always blamed him, and never his brother. After writing this chapter that statement may not have been all that untrue. I never really knew which kid did what most of the time. They were masters at deception.

I guess if our kids grow up to hate us, it's from stumbling through parenthood trying to do what we think is right. It's ninety-nine percent love and one percent guesswork and I have never been good at guessing. My parenting skills were coming from someone who never listened to her parents or had taken the time to think before acting. I didn't know how to be a mother any more than I knew how to be a student, a wife, or even a responsible driver. All of which I have flailed miserably. Let's face it, most of life is on-the-job training. It took me three fingertips before I learned to peel a melon away from myself.

I'll admit I used to yell at my kids, especially when they hid raw duck eggs, in August, in the driver's seat of my best friend's new car. I even spanked my kids when it was still legal. My parents spanked me and I... okay, I'm not a good example of anything. Except a bad example. I'll be the first to admit I've made a lot of mistakes. I couldn't assemble a three-piece shelf without directions; how am I supposed to create a complicated human being? The problem is, I am the same person that thought I needed to eliminate my brother, drive my dad crazy, and was knocked out by my brother with a full-sized hammer while watching the Lone Ranger. I still have a dent in my head. Actually I have a few.

That's another problem with the world: anyone can

reproduce. There should be some sort of screening process, shouldn't there? I know if God would have given a warning and instruction manual about children to Adam and Eve it probably would have been the end of mankind. It had to be rough raising Cain.

All I can say, Pete, is that everything I did, I did out of love.

For a long time I felt very bad, but lately I've had some time to think about these entirely one-sided accusations and decided it couldn't possibly have been entirely my fault. I think that I deserve a little credit for all of those Rice Krispy treats I made, all of the sleepless nights I endured, and especially for all of the poop diapers I changed. I had excessive birthday parties every year, sold five hundred candy bars so they could go to camp, and destroyed my back going down the Slip 'n Slide with them. I believe I tried very hard. And if my life wasn't a living hell running my legs off waiting on them hand and foot, how could his have been?

After statements like "you're a total loser" and other disheartening incidents, I decided that the boys couldn't just get off Scot-free. So, I lined them all up one typically aggravating holiday, my second husband's sons and mine. A holiday where I had worked my butt off cooking, cleaning, decorating, and where no one could stay longer than the time it took to rip open their loot. Before anyone made it to the door I demanded a family photo, they agreed to humor me. I carefully staggered their little blockheads in order of height and readied the camera. Then I paused. I looked them square in the eyes and quickly put the mother's curse on each of the boys. I pointed a crooked finger at them and said, "I hope each of you has a child just like you!" Then I snickered and smiled contently, at their little worried faces.

I took the picture then and it's just priceless.

Chapter 4

I Do. But I Don't Anymore

Divorce is a necessary evil, like taxes. Avoid one or the other and you're going to do some hard time. I know that I promised God that I would stay with Dick forever, but God didn't have to actually live with him, so after six long years I cashed in that can-forgive-anything card and filed for my freedom.

I've heard of divorces taking many years to be finalized, of spouses who swore that Charles Manson would have a better chance of winning his freedom, and even of professional spouse eliminators—not that I ever looked into anything like that. If you want to hear horror stories just say the word divorce in a mixed crowd, you'll get at least one story that makes the *Texas Chainsaw Massacre* look like a Sunday school picnic.

It's easier to get through airport security with a backpack duct-taped to your chest than out of a marriage when the one with the money wants to stay in it. My neighbor who was unemployed when she filed was ready to relocate to the middle of the Sahara with a teaspoon of water just to end the fighting and tug-of-war over inanimate-or-not objects. *I thought their six-year-old grew awful fast in 1978?*

I sure wasn't looking forward to the battle after watching my neighbor go through hers. Whenever we heard them yelling, we boarded up the windows on their side of our house. It's amazing how much damage a can of beer can do at a high velocity.

Lucky for me neither of us had any money. To be honest I think Dick wanted out as much as I did, especially after he started sleeping in the Pinto on a regular basis. I personally don't know how he did it at six-foot-one. Though, some mornings he was out on the middle of the lawn covered with the floor mats.

My divorce was a horrible time of indecision. Some days I wanted to kill him, other days I only wanted to maim him.

It just so happened that the day I got divorced it was Dick's birthday. How's that for timing? Instead of getting a gift he gave me the house. It's the little things that make life worthwhile and keep us moving onward.

According to the law as it stood back in the Eighties, the displaced party could still come and go in the house until the divorce was finalized as long as the other party was not physically threatened. When some bald-headed sap-sucking sack of soggy sheep shit is removing your TV, it's a threat and it's going to get physical. And why is it not breaking and entering when you take the entire window frame and half a wall out with a crow bar in order to get in? I mean, if you are supposed to be in there shouldn't you have a key? What judicial wizard wrote that one? People going through a divorce dream about excruciating pain and physical bloodshed wrought upon the other. Protocol, is for losers.

Some days Dick was as nice as a refund check from Uncle Sam; other days he was wild, hair (one) standing on end. His normal pink color was more of a ruby and his spots were vibrant next to it. He'd stand in the front yard screaming "I want the solid silver service set my aunt Betty gave us for our wedding!" Really, if I'da got a solid-silver service set I'da melted it down by now. When he figured he wasn't going to get his request he'd take something from outside, like a leaky garden hose, a few bricks from the porch, a small tree, or a full trashcan. Guess he'd figured out not to dump them in a rush cause some of his stuff was probably in there.

Lucky for me the boys were young and seemed to take it all in stride. Daddy never really noticed them before, and now they got to watch cartoons instead of football. However, as they saw the homestead thinning out Pete helped Repete put their names on all of their stuff, hoping Daddy wouldn't take it. They didn't realize that their daddy's mind had gone bye-bye and even a set of Tinker Toys was now considered a win.

Divorce is hard on everyone, but not as hard as the marriage. At least there is hope an end is coming to the misery, depending on what court district you are filed in. I'm sure the boys felt some loss, they loved their Daddy even though he was a total bonehead. One day I saw them sitting in their happy little circus room, holding their stuffed Big Bird and Ernie wondering what they had done wrong. It was heart-wrenching. I slowly sat down on the floor with them, gave them a big hug, and carefully explained that absolutely everything was Daddy's fault. Then we all went to Dairy Queen to celebrate.

There are some things you lose in divorce that can't

ever be explained or replaced. I don't mean dignity or trust. I'm talking about the family pets. How do you split a dog? Will they issue visitation for at least the kids? Shouldn't there be pet support if he leaves it behind and you never wanted it? Poor Muffy (name changed—I never trusted that dog) must have gotten tired of me shoving him into Dick's car and then being flung out when he rounded the first corner. He finally stopped limping home for a crummy bowl of generic dog food and hit the road for better things. I truly hope he found them, even if he was Dick's dog. Don't know what happened to his bird. He was alive when I packed him up.

It's also very hard to go anywhere when your divorce is pending because you never know what to expect when you get home, or if there will still be a home there. I've heard of people bull dozing houses so the ex wouldn't get it. I think that is a little extreme. And so expensive—matches are much cheaper. It's odd but I never thought of torching anything until I filed for a divorce. Well, my brother doesn't really count.

The worst part of a divorce is the family. Not because they suffer, but because they have to get their two cents in too. It's not like you haven't got enough to fight about. They have to say stuff like, "you know, I knew you never really liked me." Then why on earth did you keep coming over? Or, "do you think it had anything to do with problems in the bedroom?" No, I love to rock the box springs with someone I hate. But, I'd prefer him tied to it with billowing black smoke in the air.

And of course everyone is worried about the poor little innocent children that nobody wanted to baby-sit before. Now everyone has to spoil them rotten with anything they ask for. Well, until they asked for a new set of tires for mom's car. People who can't tie their own shoes are suddenly psychiatrists, spewing out advice. Everyone wants you to get counseling. Hey, if we didn't communicate for seven years what makes them think some Dr. Doolittle asking, "what do you think?" will help us now. Especially when I keep yelling back, "I think he should die!"

It's amazing how quickly little kids figure out a divorce as a moneymaking opportunity, just like when mommy is drinking. They may be small but that so called underdeveloped brain has some pretty high functions when it involves money and toys. They get that little poor hang-dog look when Uncle Dan is taking money out of his wallet to pay for the Happy Meals. Soon they got five bucks, a Happy Meal, and are on their way to Toys R Us for a day of legal looting.

I don't know why but there is always that strange and unexplainable phase when for one brief shining moment you consider giving it another chance. Well, Dick wanted to try, I guess so—that was something new and exciting for him. He promised not to drink, not to be a slob, not to leave me all alone, and to work. Suddenly I was the only woman he ever loved, and that is just not true cause I've seen the way he looks at those broads on the *Snap-On* calendar. He even offered to take me out once a week, listen to me, and go back to church. I knew there was no way he was going to listen, though he did start calling upon God more often.

Let's face it, by the time you file for a divorce you should be pretty much out of options. It's not like he forgot to pick up just one case of beer cans, or ever actually mowed the yard. You don't throw in the towel just because you need rent money more than beer one month, or have just one card with the wrong holiday scratched out and the appropriate one hand-written in. No, it's from years of frustration, disappointment, and toothpaste squeezed in the middle with the cap on the floor. In my opinion, if you're contemplating murder you've run out of options.

I think one of the worst things about divorces is the lawyer. These guys are oblivious to you. But like snakes, they too are a necessary evil or the rats get out of control. I want to know why they don't regulate legal fees. No one is worth a hundred and twenty five dollars an hour unless they are massaging my feet while listening to me whine. This is a traumatizing time in your life and all they can say is, "I'll make a motion." You better make a big fricking ruckus, Buddy, because that nutcase has towed off my car!

Our lawyers may have been unconcerned because we were fighting over who would get the towels without any holes in them. I guess if we had something of real value they might have had more incentive to return our calls. I remember the first day I talked to my lawyer, highly recommended by many a vicious predecessor. He shook his twenty-four-karat gold pen at me from across a fifty-seven-foot solid mahogany desk and said, "When I'm done with him he'll be in his Fruit of the Looms with only a plastic sack to carry the bills in." His eyes gleamed with greed and ability but I wasn't sure why. I saw that every Sunday morning when we'd try to pay all our creditors.

After months of fighting, arguing, and expensive motions, I finally got my day in court. Dick didn't even show up. Ha, the good towels are mine! Unfortunately I got half of nothing, cause yep, he was out of work again. But if he found a job I would get a tad bit more than nothing in child support until the boys were eighteen or emancipated. I vowed they'd never emancipate!

I was a nervous wreck when I walked into the courtroom; it was my first experience with the legal system. I was surrounded by a lot of other nervous wrecks; everything we had was on the line. Little did we know that no one really cared but us. Everyone in the court was just doing his job, like checking out groceries or flipping burgers. Next?

The judge sat-stone faced on his elevated throne. He drove a Beamer—don't ask me how I know. Everyone kept looking at his or her watches, over and over. Obsessive-compulsive or just bored, you decide. I could hear other people's hearts pounding in my ears. When they called my case, I froze, my eyes locked in a death stare as my Egg McMuffin reentered my esophagus. The bailiff motioned me toward the hot seat. The same seat where hardened criminals, murders, rapists, and bad-check-writers sat.

My marriage flashed before my eyes, hundreds of adjusted greeting cards, greasy black hand prints on the dish soap bottle, and forty-ouncers hidden in Tide boxes. This was it. People were talking but my ear canals were filled with McMuffin—it all sounded muffled as I stared straight forward. Slowly I lowered myself down into the hot seat. Suddenly I wanted to scream out, "I'm innocent!" No eyes were on me.

The judge checked his watch one last time, cleared his throat, and uttered four little words, "Is this marriage irreconcilable?" My lawyer nodded to me. I managed to spit out a tiny "yes" followed by a small piece of Canadian bacon. The gavel fell.

Everyone was moving on, but I was still sitting in the little monkey box wondering what the heck happened. I never even got to tell them about how rude Dick had been. I never got to say why I deserved the blob of sterling silver buried under the petunias. No one threw anything, no one was held in contempt, and no one told the jury a big long and impressive story. Hell, there wasn't even a jury. My lawyer was making plans to tee off at four with Dick's lawyer and the bailiff was giving me that little move-along sign with his hand. I've heard of divorces taking years. It was hard to believe that my six years of agony and effort were over in less then five minutes. Or so I thought.

I staggered out of the courtroom in a daze. My lawyer patted me on the back as I passed and said, "Go get 'em Baby!" Go get what? A job for one, a babysitter, a car, all of the stuff Dick took with him. The list was unending. I hope he didn't mean another man, because at that moment I would have rather had a lobotomy without anesthesia.

Little did I know that I would have many more encounters with the judicial system, as my divorced life would progress into an unending nightmare of motions. Especially after Dick would remarry a youngster half our age with every lobe damaged. Nothing raises the hackles on a mother's neck like a girl who has not done hard time in a labor and delivery room instructing you on child rearing.

All I know is you'd think that as thousands of years have passed they'da got a better system or given up on marriage. You'd think that men would have wised up to some extent. Don't their fathers have those talks with boy children like mothers have with their girls? Not about periods and ironing, but about greeting cards and flowers. Why can't a man conceive the simple value in a two-dollar greeting card? It's a sure ticket to peace, quiet, and an unbegged lay. Yet for the life of them they just can't figure it out. Men can tear apart a four-million-part engine and rebuild it without instructions, they can calculate the cost and square footage on an entire house and be right within a cent and an inch, but they can't figure out if you buy the right greeting card and give it to her on the right day your life will be easier. It's as simple as yelling out "Oh yeah baby, you're the best!"

I know for a fact that the divorce system hasn't improved any over the last twenty years because I went through it recently with my poor niece. They still make excessive passive motions, the court system is still backed up worse than a shitter after a Mexican fiesta, and the lawyers are still the blood-sucking stuffed shirts they were when I got divorced. About the only thing that has changed is the pursuit of child support. Most women have given up on it and turned to welfare. The courts, however, have come up with the title "Deadbeat Dads" so I guess I can't say they haven't made any changes. A lot of fathers still don't pay their support but at least it's a name you can yell out in public.

I sometimes think that the gay movement has become so popular because these people have finally figured out men and women just can't live together. We're like two totally different species. It's like squirrels living with bunnies. They might appear to be similar. However, look at squirrels hopping from tree to tree tossing their nuts all over, can't remember where their nuts have been, leaping blind into the air always in pursuit of something nut-related. Then you got bunnies, cute, sweet little bunnies sitting quietly on the ground desiring a cozy home. Put 'em together and you got bunnies falling out of trees, squirrels jamming nuts into burrows, and a totally dysfunctional by-product of bunirrels. Men and women together cause chaos, and all because of a mismatch of nature.

I guess I'm going to have to run that one past God too, because I really think that men were not the species women were supposed to be hooked up with, even though some things hook together rather well. And speaking of God, let's not forget that little curse put upon our species in the book of Genesis; *and I will put enmity between thee and the woman...* even if you don't believe in the Bible, a curse is a curse. I mean I know people with two Master's degrees that throw salt over their shoulders and refuse to walk under a ladder.

I would stay single for the next nineteen years and nine months, such a trauma does not vanish overnight. I still refer to marriage as the M-word and look back on that part of my life with much confusion. I think that was the worst part of my life because I had to tear apart everything I had worked hard to put together. As raising my bunirrels as a single parent progressed it got a lot easier to tear things apart, yell out "ah fuck it" and move on.

Chapter 5

Child Rearing...

*C*hild rearing is an unending task. Even at their eighteenth birthday you find yourself asking, "now why did I do this?" as icing drips down their brother's face and someone stomps out the sparks on the carpet.

Each year at Mother's Day my loving family always keeps one monumental episode of my blunderous attempt at child rearing vivid in my mind. It is know as *The Beating*. In the Seventies it was okay to smack your kid on the butt or whack him one upside the head if he was being a brat. Many public schools still had what was called the *board* of education and of course the nuns had those darn wooden rulers. Pete knew them both well.

Anyway, my sister and I had set up a fun-filled outing to the zoo. We tried to do lots of fun things with our kids— we wanted them to like us, really. I drove because my car was bigger and all four of our kids fit safely in the backseat. There are about four years between her youngest and mine so her two were nestled in the middle, mostly to keep Pete and Repete separated. I couldn't leave the plywood divider in or they wouldn't have all fit.

Even from across their cousins, they managed to call names, wipe spit and boogers, extend tongues, poke and eventually have a full-blown fistfight. After may warnings of, "don't make me stop this car," they continued to carry on, almost taking out one of their cousin's eyes. Quickly I swerved the car over to the shoulder. Gravel spewed high into the air. I leaped out and yanked open the back door, my blood pressure somewhere over five hundred. I groped for a big meaty arm though they were flailing to get away. I got the meatiest one and yanked Pete's body from his locked seatbelt. With swift swats to his very stiff blue jeans I bludgeoned his butt with my skinny little arm and bony hand. I stuffed him back into the car with gusto and dug for the next largest arm. Repete came out begging for mercy—he's done nothing wrong as usual. Judi's kids sat silent with eyes the size of Frisbees on snow-white faces. I then beat his butt with what was left of my skinny little arm and stuffed him back over the two terrified little bodies clinging to each other. It turned out to be a very pleasant day at the zoo.

In my defense everyone has a breaking point. I never spanked my children when they were little, babies don't understand. But when they are ten and twelve years old, they most definitely understand what "don't make me stop this car" means, and that they are driving their parent crazy. Every kid knows what buttons to push to launch the attack sequence. Why do they do it? Maybe it is to get more stuff. As after the blood pressure drops and the blood dries, you tend to feel rather guilty for loosing your cool. Come to think of it they were usually their ultimate worst right before Christmas…huh?

Time is a funny thing. It flies by when you're at a party, eating, drinking, and being merry. It drags on when it's snowing outside and school has been canceled. Why is that? The day still has the same number of hours doesn't it?

When you're a single parent things have to change. Now you are the mom and the dad. When you're the mom you have to work, pay the bills, transport bodies, cook, clean, monitor homework, transport bodies, administer medical care, fix things, transport bodies, punish offenders, and do the laundry. Ironing is now optional. On Daddy day, *if* he picks the kids up you get to sit in the recliner for fifteen minutes after they leave and drink a beer as Dad. Then you go back into Mommy mode and mow the lawn, wash the car, check their rooms for illegal stuff, try to communicate with another adult, and make dinner before they get back home. I guess it doesn't really change that much.

Even simple tasks like going to the grocery store can present huge problems when you have kids. When Pete was about six he filled his underwear with foil-wrapped Easter eggs. I noticed because as he walked ahead of me he occasionally laid one. In front of the store manager I shook the rest out while I instructed him on the ills of shoplifting. The manager agreed not to call the police this time as he tossed the eggs into the trash with great disgust. We both did our best to impress upon him "Thou shalt not steal." Pete gazed into the trashcan, and then asked. "Can I have 'em now since you're throwing them away anyway?" Another lesson not learned.

In my opinion shopping in general is no fun with little kids. Why not just take a few elephants with you? And, why didn't they have candyless checkout lanes when my boys were little? Who wants to shed blood over a bag of Skittles because you only have enough rolled pennies for the milk? Waiting in line is hard enough for me. I don't want to have to wrestle someone to the floor for a bag of candy, and then inform the mouthy bitch behind me that it's a little too late to not be a mother!

It's also really hard to be the breadwinner and work with little kids. Daycares are scary. You never know when they are going to kick your kids out for biting and leave you without a sitter. And daycare is expensive. When my boys were little it was sixty-five dollars a week for two and that was a lot of money then. Now my niece pays two hundred and ten dollars for her one sweet baby girl. I mean for two hundred and ten bucks they deserve my two boys hopped up on Kool-Aid and Sweet Tarts with only one video controller.

I want to know what kind of a wacko wants to work in a daycare. My son's girlfriend worked in an after school program for about a year to try to gain some ground on her student loans. She never gained any and almost lost her sanity with it. Of course I was very fearful of the endeavor, as it could have very well turned her against the prospect of having grandbabies. The poor girl had a cold the entire time she worked there, all of her nice clothes were stained with markers and Play-Doh, and she couldn't understand why they all had to hang from her arms and legs like ornaments. I told her there was something seriously wrong with those kids. I sure wasn't going to tell her that was normal behavior.

To avoid the high cost of daycare when my boys were little I decided to take my kids with me, which isn't impossible if you're lucky enough to work at the zoo. Throw 'em in a monkey pen and pick 'em up on the way out. But, since childrearing wasn't considered *experience with primates* the zoo didn't hire me. It had seemed like the perfect plan.

I decided to do the only thing I was really good at:

clean. I started cleaning a few friends' homes with the boys in tow, thinking I could get ahead of the game. I would drag the playpen, pumpkin seat, diaper bag, toys, sweeper, and bucket of cleaning supplies in and out, up and down stairs day after day. While I scrubbed floors, windows, and toilets, Pete would release their small pets and pull the grandfather clock's chimes out to full extension. He helped shine their cloth-covered chairs with Liquid Gold and fed Repete dog, cat, or bird food according to the owner's pet preference. Of course we were fired from a few places. But, I always managed to find another family that didn't know Pete and didn't have time to clean their own home.

This would go on for seventeen very long years. Pete eventually figured out the difference between cloth and wood and that made a big difference on the financial rewards of running your own family business. For a brief time they were actually very helpful when I took on a large construction site of one hundred and ninety apartment units. They carried supplies, removed trash, ran the vacuums, and learned a lot of great words from the construction workers. The only downside was they were old enough to read, so Pete posted a copy of the child labor laws in the back of the station wagon, requiring me to pay them minimum wage and overtime. I agreed but told them I would have to start charging them for rent, laundry service, food, clothes, and, well, it just got out of hand when they wanted to charge me for responsive hugs. I figured it was cheaper to just leave them at home and take my chances with my amount of insurance coverage.

Right about the time I thought I was connecting with my kids, when I no longer had to monitor their every move, and I felt like I could consider trusting them on tiny things, it hit. Puberty. Of course I had completely forgotten that I was ever once pubescent and was boggled and terrified at my reproductions' new behavior. The child who used to put his toys away when asked now lived in a bombsite and threw them out the window instead. Oddly he no longer had a volume control on his vocal chords. Every word out of his mouth was loud and defensive. I was the official enemy! Now painting the dog was a statement of rebellion for the injustice of a meager allowance, and stopping up the toilet was the end result of eating a sixteen-ounce bag of peanut M&M's so his mangy brother couldn't have any. Everything was a battle of the wills. Sorry, Mom and Dad.

I became a regular up at school. The principal even offered me use of a cot in the nurse's office during the week. Save ya' some driving time. The nice nurse held my extra bottle of Valium there for me in case I forget to bring mine or ate it all in the car on the way there.

Parent-teacher conferences were as enjoyable as a trip to the OBYGN for a pap. Of course the teachers tried to be nice when telling me my kid was driving them crazy. Unfortunately all I could do was nod along and say, "I know, I know. You know, I always vote for tax increases for the school district. I think you are way underpaid. Think how I feel, I have to watch them for free." A lot of the problems they were hitting on used to seem very trivial to me. Like walking in a straight line. It's not going to help them later on in life when the cop asks them to—they'll probably be drunk.

I don't think it is fair either that your kids can give you a bad name. I've always hated being restricted or feeling unwelcome in a public place. We were restricted from quite a few local establishments. The boys were banned from Dairy Queen for an ice cream spit fight, and K-mart for a shopping cart race across the store that landed Repete over the customer service counter. A park for a small fire and the city hall for …well the boys weren't really to blame for

59

that one. After a while I was scared to go to the post office for fear I'd see our family photo posted there.

When you think it couldn't get any worse, they discover sex. Four times I took the boys over to Dick's house to hear the facts of life and each time they came home with information about replacing a U-joint or master cylinder. I was supposed to give the speech about periods and the potential payoffs of having PMS. Now I had questions like, "What is a blow job, and why do you have to be chained up and blindfolded to make a baby?" So at least Dick did give them some reading material while they were there.

At some point even the most independent single mother has to say uncle and look for outside help, so I broke down and called my brother. Yep, the same one I battled with for twenty years. Sheepishly I asked him if he could have a little talk about the birds and the bees with the boys. When he started in about dolphins' blowholes, trampolines, and a good set of tie-down straps I decided they could just find out the same way I did, from the bathroom stall walls.

As soon as boy children acquire the right information about sex the household has to change drastically. Dashing to the bathroom in my bra and panties now produced revolting groans of, "Oh my God, Mom, gross!" The same child I breastfed just realized I was a woman. I must now be covered from head to toe even in August and feel as though I have been relocated to a third world country. I used to chant while roaming the hallways in my shroud.

The worst part of being a broken family is the fact that there is somewhere to go when you get mad at one of your parents. Pete figured out real fast that he could play Dick and me against each other. To this day I am unsure of what all Dick really did or said, though I am willing to give him all the blame. Pete had definitely inherited his father's ability to spin a yarn and brought me close to handcuffs more than once. Many a Sunday, Daddy Day, ended in the front yard of his house screaming obscenities while wildly tossing yard gnomes.

When the two of you have run out of things to argue over, enter the new child bride. The stepmother is an ungodly creation. They start out as just your normal female, then they realize the loser they married has other commitments and they're only going to get half and a whole lot more aggravation. Naturally she reproduces as quickly as possible to prove... something? Mostly, that his infrequent and meager paycheck can't possibly support all of you. My ex's second wife is a book all her own. It's just not in my genre, though Stephen King may want her stats.

Every return trip from Daddy Day now expels new horror stories. "We were refused food all day" (even though mom packed their little Snoopy lunch boxes). "We didn't see Daddy all day; do we have to go see Cruella?" And my favorite: "She said you're a ____. What's that?" (Fill in the blank with a four-letter word and any hot button issue attached.) They always waited until we just get home for that one. Then I'd have to turn around and drive all the way back there to rip her heart out and shove it up her— well, you get the picture. I mean what kind of a woman would flatten tires on little kids' bikes. The kind of woman that would marry my ex.

Since murder is illegal, we were forced to reenter the irrational legal system for help in depleting my already depleted funds. Visitation rights must be altered to state that if Daddy isn't home they don't have to go; that should have been a given but it still cost five hundred bucks to rewrite the decree. Motions are made for the grandparents to get set visitation rights. I'm praying every night that someone, anyone, would take them off my hands for just a few hours; all they had to do was ask. But no, we are all back in court and the lawyer has another designer suit.

I think sibling rivalry is one of the worst things on the planet. I'm really sorry, Mom and Dad. My boys fought more than the Israelites with anyone in their way of the Holy Land! They would fight about things they didn't even want. Blood would be shed over a dried-out Twinkie. When the battle was over all that was left was some now pink-tinged cream filling smeared on the front door from the loser's attempt at survival. Fifteen minutes later someone would be bludgeoned again for the wrapper. Ah, the spoils of war.

As a parent you love both of your kids; each has special qualities. My parents told me that. So why can't they love each other? I'll tell you why: it's politics, pure and simple. It's like the dreaded election year...campaigning never ends. Pick me, oh no, pick me! He's a liar, he won't help you like I do, don't forget about the time he took money out of your wallet. You don't want someone like that for your favorite son, do you? And the best one is, don't make me withdraw from the race!

Through this entire saga one of them is learning to play the violin. Violins and stepmothers have a lot in common.

Even if one kid cries uncle and withdraws to the ex-marital opponent's ground, your woes are not over. Even though you helped him pack by tossing his sticky, stinky crap out the window you still have those maternal concerns wracking your conscience. As soon as the house is quiet and you have all the holes patched up in the walls that horrible soft side of you starts to seep through. You find yourself thinking that drinking from every bottle in the icebox really isn't that bad. It does save dishes. And he probably wasn't the only fourteen-year-old that snuck the car out to pick up a few snacks. All the fines, fires, and court orders start to seem rather silly when one of your little birdies is missing from the nest. I hate it when I'm a marshmallow because it always comes back and bites me in the butt.

Of course the remaining sibling has now hit the mother lode and knows it. This is his chance to prove his innocence and heap on guilt for years of misdirected retribution. He is an angel 24-7. Guilt drags you down like a child bride with a good grip on your ponytail. How could I have been so wrong, you wonder? Ah, but there is no longer a need to tear up your own homework or crawl around the kitchen floor with your brother's shoe making huge black marks. You are now the only child you've always dreamed of being. It's so easy to be good. The silence is golden, you're torn. Something is missing and it's just not right. It's like when you have a picnic with no flies.

It's usually good to move back and forth between separated parents four or five times in a few-year period, that way you get new furniture when they collapse from moving it. Or, you can say the offending parent kept a video game, getting a new one you never really had. This is a very good life lesson for kids too. It teaches them how to get what they want by manipulation, which is a very valuable asset later in the job market.

Though all of this I'm trying to make a nice home and quite frankly, not getting a lick of support or help anywhere in any direction. My workdays are twelve hours long, the laundry is multiplying like hamsters, the car breaks down if I look at it, and I find out that my egg basket must be removed due to some bizarre growth cluster. As soon as they throw me in the hospital the house sells and the damn cat has another litter of kittens under my bed.

A seven-week recovery period with kids should be calculated in eons. Oh sure, your family and friends try to stop by and help out, but they have lives and kids too. The kids know you can't move, everything liftable has been thrown in your meager range of motion. When they get into a fistfight now you just root for the kid that listened better that day. Kittens are pouncing everywhere, and the new owners want to know when you will be out. The next time they come by to measure for curtains you rip off your gauze and show them the hideous incision from hip to hip. They gag, smile, and say "So what, another week, maybe?"

The kids have already started packing. I know because there are all sorts of things missing around the house. Trash bags are piled high in their room with odd misspelled words on them. How long will an open package of hot dogs last in a plastic bag full of dirty socks and toys? Worse, the sandbox is empty and so are the litter boxes.

All I can do is lay helpless on the couch as Hell closes in around me. My mind wanders, thanks to the Demerol. Why does your uterus fall out the day after you sell the house? It was on the market for over two years. Shouldn't I weigh less if they took that much junk out of me? What ever happened to Mr. Magoo? Why is my mailman throwing the mail on the grass and running away? If our lives are planned and every hair on our head counted, as the Bible says, why is God ripping them out one by one? Am I supposed to be learning something here? Because I'm not. If I have millions of hairs in my head, after a couple hundred thousand, can't God see I'm just not going to catch on?

Right about now I feel like I'm on the five-millionth mile of life dragging that overstuffed suitcase missing a wheel. Bad thing is, I also know there are four hundred and forty-five million miles left to go. I look out the window and gaze into the front yard. Pete and Repete are busy throwing water balloons and an occasional rock at the passing cars. Someone is beating on the back door of the house, but guess who can't get up? I screech in each direction. "Knock that off or I'll kill you when I can walk again," and, "come in, come in, whoever you are, please just come in!" The rocks keep flying and the knocking drones on.

Trying to direct my screeches, I claw at the sofa back to rise, a tremendous head rush races through my cerebellum as I tumble off the couch and onto the floor. Thank God a few kittens broke my fall. I lay crumpled on the floor unable to move. Tiny pin claws are busy shredding away at my nipples. The knocking has finally stopped, and the boys have vanished from the front yard. I hear sirens.

I can't reach my pain pills.

Chapter 6

The Killer Merry-Go-Round

It was a sunny spring day, a Saturday I believe, because I wasn't working and all of the neighborhood street urchins were out in full force. Our house adjoined a big park and unfortunately the playground equipment was right behind our detached garage. When Dick and I bought the house we hadn't yet reproduced so the availability factor of free industrial playground equipment was quite appealing. Little did we realize that it came with thousands of wild, noisy, small-medium-and-large sized children. It also came with sand, lots of sand. In the old days they used sand to break clumsy kid falls. Now I think they have some sort of poisonous rubber nubits.

The city had just replaced some of the equipment and painted the rest in that gosh-awful road-line yellow. I had to keep my kitchen blinds closed to cut down on the glare. The boys were thrilled. I don't know why bright yellow makes kids so darn happy, but it does. They couldn't wait to get outside and try out the new "killer merry-go-round." It was bigger, faster, and there wasn't a two-foot-deep rut around it to fall into. I was inside, doing laundry, cleaning up the dead Frooty Tooty Loops, and cursing the Legos. Outside I could hear great cheers of joy over the new contraptions my tax dollars had purchased. Cheers and very shortly there after screams, screams of terror...

Within only minutes of the boys' leaving, ten kids, none of whom I knew from Adam, were all at the back door screaming, "Repete is dead! Repete is dead, he busted open his head! He's dead!" Panic set my heart into triple-time as I grabbed for something to throw on. Naturally I had just managed to step into the shower. Slipping and sliding I raced down the hallway terrified of what I would see. Kids scrambled around inside the screened in porch pointing in different directions while hopping hysterically, each trying to tell their version of the disaster. Jason's little sister stood behind the trash can, traumatized, snow-white, weeping in great despair. Repete was her one true love though he was about five months older, making it an impossible reality in his eyes.

Outside another mess of children bounced around frantically. They were scattered across the back yard screaming, some crying, and some laughing. Well, actually only Pete was laughing. "Where is your brother?" I bellowed at Pete, while shaking the laughter out of him. He managed to point toward the killer merry-go-round. I raced to the playground. It was empty. Only the killer merry-go-round lingered, still turning at a snail's pace, splashed with the blood of its latest kill.

"Repete, where are you? Where is he? Where are you?" I screamed over and over as I ran around in circles like a dog chasing its tail. Surely Pete hadn't managed to bury him already?

Back into the yard I raced, grabbing kids and examining their faces for one that resembled Repete. Nothing matched. My heart pounded as I gasped for air to keep yelling his name. "Repete, where are you?" Into the house I raced for the phone, as if anyone else knew where he was. While I was dialing a menagerie of mixed-up numbers the doorbell rang. My eyes froze, my heart stopped, my breathing halted, my pancreas stopped doing whatever it is it does.

"Someone's at the front door," a small girl said, staring in the back door with many other concerned little faces. The door? The door, what's a door? My mind was locked up, worthless, frozen like a three-year-old steak in the bottom of the freezer. The bell rang again. I stood silent, a quivering bowl of Jell-O Jigglers.

"Someone's at the front door," the girl said again, only this time she pointed to help me remember where it was. I dropped the phone and raced in the direction she was pointing, my feet barely touching the floor. I ripped open the door, expecting to see police or firemen holding the limp lifeless body of my dear little baby. Instead there stood Repete, looking a little green. From his back a steady steam of blood dripped onto the porch stoop.

"I fell," he said calmly. "I couldn't get through the back door."

"Oh my God! Oh my God!" I screamed it over and over. I like to run in circles and repeat myself whenever I am terrorized. I'd never seen so much blood, blood that belonged inside of him. The back of his little sleeveless puffy vest was saturated. Lucky for me I couldn't see how much had actually spewed from my baby's body. Quickly I guided him into the kitchen and put a dish towel to his head. It was soaked in minutes. "Lay down on the floor." He did. "No, wait, stand up!" He did. "No, lay down... no, up?" Blood flows down, right?

"But I feel sick, Mom." He pawed for my arm, his little green eyes twirling around in the sockets.

"Okay, lay down. Pete, get me a bigger towel." I fumbled to dial 911. It's amazing how hard it is to dial three numbers when you're terrified and your hands are shaking like a hula dancer's hips at a luau.

"Help!" I yelled into the phone. "Help! I need help!" Smart, as if I had been calling 911 for anything else. "Help, my son fell off the new killer merry-go-round in the park and he's bleeding very badly from the back of his head! It's a really big one, that they painted that awful yellow color." Always be sure to give the most important facts in an emergency.

"What's he doing now?" The woman on the other end of the line calmly asked.

"He's bleeding."

"Is he conscious?"

"No, but I'm very confused, should he lay or stand?"

"Conscious, is he conscious?" She asked again, with great emphasis on each syllable.

"Yes. But he doesn't look so good, so I told him to lie down, or should he sit up?"

"Tell him to sit up if he can."

"Repete, sit up." His eyes crossed, as I leaned him against the counter for support. It's a miracle I didn't pump all of his blood out of him by making him jump up and down. One of the on looking children helped with my name and our address, as I couldn't seem to remember who I was or where I lived. I am the worst under stress, especially when there is blood involved. I don't like to see anything that is supposed to be inside of the body come out, including snot. Which you see a lot of with kids.

"There will be an ambulance there in a few minutes,

just keep him calm and apply pressure to the wound." Keep him calm. He was doing fine—I was the one ready to go into cardiac arrest.

"Pete, go get Bev! Please go get Bev!" Beverly, our neighbor, was a wise woman of many years. She had raised seven kids and a few extras that were in need of mothering. I needed a mom right now but my mother was at work. My hands were shaking worse than when I sign my tax returns. No matter what I did, they shook. I'm sure they weren't helping Repete's confidence level. I didn't know how long I could hold on for Repete. I was starting to feel very ill just like I do when I see blood in a movie only this time I couldn't look away.

"Pete, get out of the damn pantry, you don't need a Ding-Dong now. Go get Bev!"

I sat quaking on the floor trying to comfort Repete. He didn't seem worried, though he may have been in shock. By now all of the little kids had run home to tell everyone in a hundred-mile radius that Repete was almost terminated by the new killer merry-go-round. Time ticked by slowly as I rocked and prayed. His short little life flashed before my eyes and I suddenly wished I had bought him the squirt gun he wanted at K-Mart the day before. We could have done without bread.

Bev came through the door like Florence Nightingale, carrying an industrial-size first aid kit. She immediately kicked into her nursing mode and assessed the damage. Then she took a look at Repete. She whipped out a thick Maxi pad and applied it to Repete's wound. "Honey, you got to keep firm pressure on it." She showed me how.

"I'm trying," I cried, "but my hands won't stop shaking and it keeps coming off."

"That's because you keep looking at it. Don't look at it any more. It's not going to do anything but bleed." Then

70

she smiled that motherly smile and patted me on the back.

Soon the sound of sirens shrieked through the air as the ambulance pulled into the driveway. We both carried Repete to the truck as everyone circled in to save my baby. My heart never stopped pounding, which I guess was a good thing. But a couple times I felt as though I had to push on my chest to keep it in its designated area. We all loaded into the ambulance and raced up a five-lane thoroughfare in heavy traffic, against the oncoming traffic all the way. Repete thought it was all very cool.

When we arrived at the hospital the nurse at the desk tried to race me into a room for treatment, due to the large amount of blood on me. I think my inability to speak, combined with my trembling hands and legs prompted her diagnosis that I was the injured party.

Repete had been whisked off immediately. They sent me to do paperwork. "I want to see my baby, where is he? I want to see him, he needs his mother! Where did you take my baby? I want to see him now. Where is my baby?" Once again I was mired in repetitive mode, ready to start circling at any moment.

"You will be able to go in soon." The nurse said in a disgustingly calm voice. "Please go wash the blood off yourself. You are scaring other people." When I got to the bathroom I scared myself. Blood was everywhere. Quickly I wiped the blood off of my face and arms. My clothes were destroyed. All I could think of was losing my Repete. This couldn't be happening. I needed to get to him; he had to be scared to death without his mommy by him.

"First you must sign these papers," nurse Noemotions stated." Do you have insurance?"

My heart finally stopped. Insurance. Did we have insurance or not? It depended on if Dick was working or not and if he was carrying it, as ordered by the courts. I forgot to bring the card. And my purse. But I did grab the beach bag. So at least we had sunscreen.

"I think so. I brought the title to my car." I knew to bring something of value. "It's worth about seven hundred and fifty bucks!" In the old days if you didn't have insurance you didn't get service. One never stepped inside any medical establishment without an insurance card, a title or deed, or a big pile of cold hard cash.

"We're not in the used car business," she said with a sneer and utter disgust.

"I can pay. I can sell the car or get a loan. I have equity in my house. I have three jobs lady. I can pay if he doesn't have it. But he should."

"You should have gone to City Hospital," she said. Compassion wasn't invented yet.

"I wasn't driving, lady! Remember, we came in an ambulance and they didn't ask me my net worth before boarding." Silence fell and she proceeded to ignore me. Repete's little life hung in the balances of Daddy's competence. I was scared to death. I wanted to hook my carotid artery up to an IV for him for free, but no one would even listen to me.

Finally an intern came out. "You can go in now, *if* you stay calm." I wondered how calm he would have been if it was his baby spewing blood from his cranium? My heart started back up.

There sat poor little Repete up on a big table in an oversized blue hospital gown. I raced to his side and gave him a bear hug and fifty kisses. The doctors proceeded to explain the damage and procedure. It would take thirteen to fifteen stitches to close up the large jagged slash across the back of his head. They would have to be done in layers. My eyes crossed when the doctor pointed out the dangling scalp meat. I may have missed a few things he said after that, but I never hit the floor.

"Don't worry, Repete, I'm right here. It won't be bad, I'm right here."

"I want my daddy." Repete said.

My heart dropped into my colon. His dad? The man who rarely showed up on visitation day? The man who paid his child support only on days that ended in z? I was crushed. I didn't care if my heart fell out of my body and was swept away by housekeeping. He didn't want his mommy. He wanted his rarely-seen daddy. I staggered off in search of a pay phone, beaten, forced to call his daddy.

To this day the hair won't grow across the back of Repete's head where the killer merry-go-round left its mark. Daddy waltzed in and saved the day, holding Repete's hand while they sewed him back together. I sat in the waiting room with Pete and the rest of the nobodies trying to find the stupid things they hide in those kid's magazines. What the hell is a fish and a teapot doing in a tree? What's that teaching a kid?

I was devastated when Repete didn't want me to be with him; I felt betrayed. I would have extracted any organ of mine he needed myself, with a plastic knife. But he wanted his daddy. I guess it's a guy thing. However, I was very glad that I got to take him straight home after his stitches were done. I would nurture him back to health as I had done before and would continue to do for the next twenty years. I stayed up all night praying and patting and kissing his little bandaged head. I was so happy and grateful that he was going to be all right.

When the hospital and ambulance bill came in, I was devastated again.

Chapter 7

Entering the Work Force

I have come to the conclusion that life would be much easier with marketable skills. Yeah, I can wiggle my ears and make my nostrils flare, but it sure doesn't work on bosses like it does on the kids. One week into my new divorced life, when my prospective employer set a timer and a test in front of me, I wished I had figured out when that damn train was arriving and not what they were serving for dinner.

Number sequence: what is up with that? What happened to adding, subtracting, multiplying, and, hopefully, no percentages? How come none of these formula questions specify Enfamil or Similac? Why is everyone else writing feverishly while I'm still trying to remember the address of my high school and what the hell is a power point?

After a few mortifying interviews and many a failed typing test, I decided I had better go back to school. But since I only had three weeks before the rent was due I opted to learn something fast and easy, like bartending. I already knew how to drink and it involved little or no math.

Bartending is a great occupation because your customers are incoherent most of the time. If they say you did something wrong you simply give the goggling drunk look behind their back to the boss. If they don't like the drink you make them, you get to drink the mistakes, and the best part is you get tips. Mind you this was before Uncle Sam figured out he was missing out on a big chunk of change and started taxing your register sales for eight percent of your ring whether you were tipped or not.

Oh sure, cleaning house was glamorous, thrilling, and barely supporting us, but there was something else lacking in my life besides money: adult company. Though after I chose bartending as a part-time career I may have overestimated the term *adult*. Either way, I entered a whole new world and found some much needed relief to endless childrearing and oven cleaner fumes.

Bartending was probably the only thing I ever learned quickly and proficiently. I was a great bartender. I know it's rude to toot your own horn but when you're single that has to happen in a few areas. Customers used to place bets to see if I could remember every drink the passing-by waitresses would yell at me, while I was tending a full bar. I never wrote a drink down and I never let them down. When I look back on my amazing ability to intoxicate people it boggles my mind that I can never remember where my keys are most of the time.

I loved being a bartender, and not just because I could drink on the job. When I was behind the bar I was in charge. Nothing like at home with the kids. People respected me because I could cut them off. Power like that is intoxicating alone. This was the only time in my life I also had a semi-respectable title, not a direction. Take that however you will, it works both ways. I tossed quite a few shiny shakers and tipped many a bottle with great style and flair, right up until my elbow joints turned to tapioca. Now I believe it is called *repetitive motion syndrome;* back then it was called *pay the bills*.

The bad thing with being a bartender is you're forced to move around a lot. Bars close, managers change, annoying customers get sick, and before you know it you're back out beating the pavement for another stage.

Alcohol has always been my friend and I'm not ashamed to say it. Drinking has really gotten a bad rap over the years. Enter all of this psychological crap and suddenly anyone who drinks a beer is an alcoholic and needs to be in a stairmaster program. My drinking buddies were my support group. Pete hates me for drinking but he'da probably hated me worse had I not. Many a shot of whisky calmed me and saved him from decapitation or worse.

Kids don't realize what is involved in being a parent. I know it isn't their fault, they *didn't ask to be born.* God, how many times have I heard that? Holding down a few jobs, the fort, and a wiry kid at the same time is complicated. You want to do it all and do it right but even you know you can't. When that cruel reality rears its ugly head it's conference time with JD. It's time to sit in a puddle of mud in the middle of a park at 1 A.M. once again badgering God on the system. I'll agree that tying one on won't solve your problems but it's a good pressure release without physical damage to anything but your own liver.

Where was I? Maybe I shouldn't drink while I'm typing. Anyway, if you don't have any God-given talents and no acknowledgeable accomplishments you have to do whatever you can to get by. I may not be a lot of things but I am a hard worker. Too bad in today's society working hard doesn't really get you anywhere anymore, unless you're in X-rated films.

I've done just about everything you can do to make a buck, legally. I slung hash in an industrial kitchen for four years until my shoulder liquefied from overuse. The pay was poor but the eats were good. I was the dessert chef and finally got to express myself in chocolate, which is truly the only medium to use. We were the only senior center that had an acne problem in ninety-year-olds. I always liked cooking, even in a school cafeteria, however, the head cook didn't see the humor in thirty chickens in various poses with towels around their necks after I bathed them. The other ladies said they would miss me and the Poultry Swan Dive competition.

I've worked in the school district in special education as a teacher's scapegoat. Why the special education department? It's a level playing field. The best part of working at school is that the kids really taught me a lot. Like how to get two treats out of the vending machines for the cost of one. I also finally learned that in math, pie need not have a flavor. Oh yeah, and the best part is you're off on holidays when your kids are so they don't have to put their own toys out on Christmas Eve because the stupid greedy bar owner wants you to stay open till 2 A.M.

I worked in an office for two days. That was like throwing a cat into a blow-up swimming pool, the damage was phenomenal. I can't seem to sit still, and cubicles remind me of the clothes hamper. I also don't know how my boss could have expected me to file when no one else in the office appears to know his or her alphabet. I mean there are times when I thought I was stupid, but when you're looking for the name "Mr. Raymond Keller" and everyone is the office says to look under a different alphabet something is seriously wrong. Especially when one of them yells out A.

I've worked in retail at a major department store but I won't mention the name because I think there are folks there still looking for me. I worked in lingerie and learned how little men really know about anything in their life especially their wife. Why would a man try to buy bras for his wife? The first thing they all say is, "she's built just about like you." A week later a four-hundred pound woman comes in with a DDD chest and says, "What the hell am I supposed to do with this little pea shooter and butt floss?" I also learned that company loyalty is as appreciated as much as telemarketers and herpes.

I worked in a body shop with my brother for two weeks in trade for some paint on my ugly car. Hard to believe that the two of us were under one roof with power tools and flammable substances and no one died. I did a lot of jobs in trade for services needed. When you have needs and no money someone is always willing to let you do their dirty work in lieu of cash. Mind you the dirty worker never comes out ahead in this arrangement.

I've waited tables, but waitressing was never my forte. It's amazing that I can remember what a hundred people drink but can't remember that someone asked for catsup or their check. I have to say that waiting tables sucks. No matter how much you apologize they will still stiff you over a bug in their food. It's not like *you* put it there.

Obviously I can't work in customer service, as it requires a little thing called patience, which eliminated a lot of job options. Apparently no one with a problem wants to hear, "Oh boo-hoo. You think you got problems. Buddy, listen to this..."

When you got kids to feed and overpriced tennis shoes to buy nothing is below your employment ability. I've washed cars for extra cash, mowed lawns, catered parties, and been many an alibi. Kids never really know what their parents go through to keep them alive and happy. Hopefully they won't find out about some of it.

Whenever Pete would get in one of his ungrateful moods I'd remind him that when I was a kid we didn't even have a color TV. He was aghast that our video games would have been in black and white. I would try to explain hard times to him by reminding him that Grandpa was a bricklayer and when the snow hit he didn't work. We lived on fried bologna and when it was gone we ate fried snowballs. He would just shrug his shoulders and look at me like most of my bosses did when my only reply was, "you said to the best of my ability." Repete was out getting snow to fry.

I often feared being a Jackette-of-all-trades without a big company to back me up. I've never had a 401K or pension plan set up for me. But after Enron, all those worries disappeared and I was so damn glad that I had managed to save by myself six hundred and fifty-eight bucks in a mayonnaise jar. It may not seem like a lot to you but I did pay into *Social Security* too. There are two words that don't go together, especially when the politicians are holding the purse strings.

I think one of the happiest days of my life was when the boys started to earn their own spending money. I know my bank was happy. Now I had someone to borrow from without filling out extensive paperwork. I still had to beg, and the interest rate was quite a bit higher, penalties much stiffer, but hey, a loan without leaving home—you've got to love that. It sure was a lot easier to get money from them when they were little. All you had to say was, "I'll give you two monies (quarters) for your one money (a ten)."

Unfortunately though it seemed that no matter how hard I worked I never could get ahead of the game. Every time I caught up on my bills the car would roll over and die. As soon as the car was up and limping along it was time to move again. After we got settled in a higher-priced habitat something would crap out on my body throwing me in the hospital and burying me back in bills. Sometimes life's a vicious circle in more than just one direction at a time; it's like that atom thingy spinning around the fig neutron.

They always say, "When the going gets tough, the tough get going." Who the heck said that, and should we trust anyone that won't leave their name? I mean, *they* tend to say a lot of highly revered statements. I just think *they* should have to leave their name if *they* are going to be quoted for decades to come.

Everyone has his or her own way of dealing with life's disappointments: my sister shops, my son exercises, everyone else I know eats. When things got tough for me I just started to laugh deliriously—they say there is medication for that now. I would look at my washer flat-faced on the floor barfing bubbles and just start laughing. The strangest things started to be funny to me. A fireman at our front door holding Repete with a fire in the trailer park field across from us, funny. My name scratched off the work schedule, funny. A bag of groceries left in the trunk for three days because they each already carried in two, you got it—funny. Our neighbor's house got robbed, hilarious, because we have nothing worth stealing! It would be like robbing a garage sale after the sale.

Though I did know better than to ever laugh in a hospital. Trust me, they will make you stay if you're laughing because a horde of wasps stung you repeatedly while standing on a ladder sanding eaves. A word of wisdom: throw down the sander, it's the noise they don't like, they will chase it until it unplugs. Always hold your laughter until you get home and the pain pills kick in.

When I call my family they don't say "hello" they say,

"what happened now?" I once had an aunt call me during a very brief moment when things were going well in my life. (* Note: this is not a standard anyone else would use for well.) After about five minutes of "no, really everything is fine," she went silent and seemed really depressed. When I questioned her despair, hoping to cheer her up for a change, she said, "Well, usually if I call you and hear what's happening to you, then anything bad going on in my life seems really minor." I assured her that if she called back in a few days I could probably lift her spirits as my boss swore he would fire me if I missed another day of work because of a sick kid. And, if that didn't perk her up, reports cards were due.

I think I've tried really hard in my life. I've stood on my own two feet and never expected anyone else to feed the kids I reproduced, not even their dad. I consider myself a good employee and a hard worker, like I said before. I will go the extra mile and do the extra task, even off the clock, if it gets the job done right. Unfortunately with our new no-boarder policy and a constant swarm of cheap labor all of those qualities are no longer deemed commendable and are now referred to as stupid.

I know what you're thinking: why didn't she go back to school and learn a real trade? Well I did. So there. I enrolled in what some refer to as a kind of "college light;" all the credit with only half the effort. These are schools that charge you four times as much to do next to nothing in half the time. Unfortunately I didn't figure that out until the middle of my second semester when I realized the two other kids in my classroom waiting on the teacher to show up didn't read or speak English. After I got my nose out of the books I was finally interested to be in, someone told me in red paint across my car, to just pay the money and take the degree.

Oh, but I couldn't do that. No, I had to fight the fight, right the wrong, and help Mohammad and Isralia fulfill their American dream. I had to file a complaint to the Dean. I had to write the accrediting boards, call the TV stations, and heap more retribution upon the three of us from the other students stopping by for a soda and to set up dates. I was determined that I had paid for a college education and damn it, I was going to get it. I finally wanted to learn and no one wanted to teach me. I was in it for the long haul, and after a gallant and lengthy battle I was given a full refund and restricted from the premises. I don't know what happened to Mo and Izzy.

I've also gone to school for hypnosis, which I found intriguing. If anything it helped me understand my own gray matter a little better. Unfortunately, I studied that closer to the end of this story than the beginning. I even, against my better judgment, opened an office in a nice little old-town area and worked very hard at making my last attempt at self-employment succeed. It was going well too, right up until the city decided to destroy one hundred and fifty homes and businesses to put a couple million in their and their construction buddies' pockets. They pulled that nasty *eminent domain* card which I think is nothing more than a license to steal. It was a long and nasty battle and once again I was in the front lines of the crusade. I dug deep into the trenches for myself and every hard-working American that staked a claim there. Unfortunately when my lease came up the owner said he'd rather just sell out so I packed up and moved on. Three months later the Old-Town Preservation Society won. My beautiful office now houses a taxicab service.

I still use the hypnosis because it suits me well. Most of the time I am in an altered state of mind anyway. The bad thing with hypnosis is there are no real regulations in the industry. A bunch of good old boys figured out how to sell the occupation: videos, tapes, and really nice-looking certificates to hang on your wall. Problem is, everyone passed the one-hour test, even though we were never tested on actually putting someone into a hypnotic state. For a mere eighty-five dollars and a few feeble attempts at study or naptime meeting attendance you can continue to enter people's minds year after year with little or no knowledge of your own. It's not a wonder people fear hypnosis, especially now that you know I am a Certified Hypnotherapist.

After childrearing, I think gainful employment is one of life's hardest tasks. In the old days companies had some respect and genuine concern for their employees. Nowadays employees are nothing more than projecting footholds on a rock wall to ludicrous financial wealth. I've heard that the CEO of Wal-Mart makes seventeen million dollars a year, while many of their employees are on welfare with no medical coverage. Does anyone need seventeen million dollars a year—especially if they shop at Wal-Mart? I want Wally to know I think that really sucks and I'm cutting back my shopping there. No one could quit Wal-Mart cold turkey, I hear it has the same effect as giving up crack.

The way I figure it the workingman doesn't have a chance; we are merely puppets on the millionaire's strings. They raise prices on one end and lower them on the other so they can still get every penny we make. Sometimes I stay home all day and don't eat; I don't turn the lights on, or use anything. It's my little way of getting back at *the man*.

What really bothers me is that at age fifty I still don't know what I want to be. Shouldn't I know by now? And even though the Republicans are inflating the job market, I'm not seeing the touted opportunities. Thousands of kids are flipping burgers with one hand and holding a sixty-thousand-dollar degree in the other, so I don't think more schooling would have helped me any. I really can't work with the public anymore because, to be honest, people just annoy the crap out of me. Especially people who can't read and follow simple instructions.

For two hundred feet, the signs entering security at the airport say, "Please have your photo ID and boarding pass *out and ready*." They even have pictures of the items in case you can't read. Yet when we reach the security agent the woman in front of me has to stop and dig through her size-of-a-small-country handbag and locate her ID. I wanted to grab one of the six signs and shove it up her… nose. I know I saw her reading them, and she spoke English to the agent, so what part of *ready* did she not understand? No wonder those agents never smile—they probably want to be a suicide bomber at the end of the day just to get away from the morons they have to deal with.

I didn't finish my application at the airport after they told me I couldn't respond verbally to any problem travelers. I guess working with duct tape over my mouth might make some travelers a little nervous.

When I look back on my employment status in the world I don't think it's a better place because of me. Somewhere out there are people with the wrong formula for making pie, damaged livers, and high-risk insurance rates due to claims that may have been partly my fault.

I guess there are things I would like to learn to do. Psychology really interests me. But I guess if you tell your patients they are being stupid, which they are, it would really hinder that *word-of-mouth* business, which I keep hearing is very important.

I think opening my own business again someday is my only real option, that way I can do what I want without all of those pesky regulations. How about this one: "Personal Bitching Sessions?" You pay a membership fee and a set fee each time you come in to bitch. Just bitch it up, bitch about anything and I will sit and listen and sympathize with you. Wait a minute... I think they already have something like that. I believe it's called marriage counseling.

Dang, I'm never going to find my niche.

Chapter 8

Gypsy Blood

I'm not exactly sure why we moved away from our nice little house on Frostwood, but we did. It was kind of a mixture of things: deranged neighbors, unsalvageable plumbing, memories that could make Chuckie shudder, and just that uncontrollable urge to move. I have that urge a lot. I have lots of very strong urges, most by now I should know better than to act on.

I don't understand how anyone can live in the same house his or her entire life. The same place gets boring. When I've run out of different color paint chips at Home Depot, it's time to move. I guess I've got Gypsy blood, I got it from my father's parents. My grandparents moved around more than salmon. A few years back I went to the cemetery to put flowers on their grave; I walked back and forth over the area for an hour. I finally called my dad and told him they moved again.

I know one reason I sold my house on Frostwood: we

needed the equity in it to eat. Another reason was upkeep. A house is a lot of upkeep for a single mother. I wouldn't mind mowing if the lawn mower would start. I don't mind washing the windows if the damn things would open without a crow bar. I do mind repairing things when I have no knowledge of the object. When you've got duct tape on almost everything, radiator hoses under the kitchen sink instead of pipes, and a bucket under anything that transports water, it's time to move. Bad thing is we had to fix it all right to sell the house.

It's amazing how much junk one can collect in only six short years. Even after I threw out most of Dick's stuff I still managed to fill a semi. Sometimes you just have to move to get away from the junk. Even I, with my limited sight of logistics, could see there was no way we were getting all of our junk into a two-bedroom duplex. My neighbor suggested we have a garage sale right before we left. The profits almost matched the equity in the house. I wish I had thought of a garage sale first. Unfortunately, that would be putting the cart behind the horse. Where it belongs.

I decided to go into a duplex because I wasn't quite ready to jump right into compacted communal living, like apartments. I don't ever want to share a common wall with anyone again unless I'm stone deaf. Some things you just don't want to hear.

The boys really needed a yard to run their sugar highs off in, and I needed my washer and dryer in a basement. Nobody wants a seven-foot mountain of dirty clothes off their kitchen—does something to the appetite. Moving days were the longest spans of time my poor old Whirlpool ever stopped running. There is nothing worse than going to the laundromat when one has two boys who think dirt is an outfit. First off, I needed to scrounge up thirty dollars in quarters, which have all been used in video games. Then I needed to hog twenty washers, which never makes anyone very happy. Then I get to sit... sit and watch the clothes go round and round...wet, then round and round dry. The boys always had races in the laundry carts, which I know is not recommended by most mothers, but it's more amusing to watch over the round and round...

Our first move was to a cute little place, which I thought was more of a *side step* than a step down, as everyone else referred to it. The windows actually opened and the toilet water went down instead of up when you flushed it. Of course after we were there a few weeks they reversed flow, but we now had a landlord to plunge and curse. The neighborhood was really nice and we were attached to a sweet little ninety-year-old woman we never saw. The day we moved in I went over to let her know if the boys were ever too loud she should let me know. I beat on the door... then I beat some more, with a rock. Then I beat on the window and screamed "yoo-hoo" at the top of my lungs. She sat silent staring at the TV. I went back home. I figured she'd be good with us.

The first year went pretty smooth, I thought. The boys settled into a new school district ready to raise some hell. The neighborhood was quiet, well groomed, and the boys even managed to make a few new friends that were more trouble than they were. Out of eighty kids there they picked a sister and brother who were both bi-polar. Every day was a new and exciting experience. I even made a friend, their mother. She would have been normal had her kids not driven her nuts.

I picked up an extra job to make the extra rent and time marched on...

However, the second year didn't go quite as smooth. The owner of our complex was forced to give up one-fourth of its units to government-subsidized housing. Most of the young men that moved into the lower circle didn't attend school or work so it wasn't a problem for them to stay up all night, cutting off valve stems, sugaring gas tanks, and slashing up seat covers. But for those of us that had to work to pay our rent it got to be a real bother.

The nice little neighborhood we lived in quickly turned into the trenches of Normandy. Outside play after dusk was forbidden. Everything was chained to something. Nightfall was a time of worry and fear. Nothing is as loud as a barrage of tomatoes and eggs on your bedroom window at midnight. Nothing is as hard to clean up the next day after it has dried all night on brick.

It appeared the vandals' favorite target was our vehicles. I assume since they didn't have one, they didn't want any of us to either. After three mornings of flat tires, I constructed a makeshift fence around my battered old car and wired it up to a little two-twenty at night. The landlord made me take it down. No fencing was allowed. Vandalism was.

The problem was ninety percent of the complex was made up of single mothers with small children, so the fear factor for repercussion was almost nil for the offenders. I tried to organize a neighborhood watch but most women were just willing to move away. My friend and her bi-polar babes moved away, and she even had a husband.

The police were about as helpful as Bactine on skin cancer. For some odd reason everything I tried to do to protect my vehicle and property was illegal or unsuccessful. I set up a fake video camera in the window by my car, but I guess the kids knew an old Nikon lens wasn't going to catch them in the act. I slept in the living room with the window cracked open and a small microphone hanging off the ledge. There were only two words on the tape the next morning and the microphone was gone along with my windshield wipers. The offenders were extremely bold and would stand out in the street laughing while our cars were towed off for valve stem replacement, again. I'm not sure what they were saying because I believe they were talking in that Ebonics, which was very popular, back in the Eighties.

After countless nights of lost sleep snuggled up next to a shotgun I decided something had to be done. I have never been one to back down from a battle, though many times I should have. The sad thing was it appeared that the police were watching me a lot closer than the criminals. I was so tired of hearing "you can't do that, it's premeditated." I'm sure the little hooligans vandalizing our property were busy planning out their night rampage, but that was apparently permissible. What was fun and games for them had definitely progressed into a war for the residents holding out. It was time to take the law into my own hands. This is never a good time.

Something is seriously wrong with the law. It protects the criminals. I don't think that is what they had in mind when they made laws. The judicial system has taken a turn into the toilet. Too many crooked greedy lawyers, pad-my-pocket judges, and ludicrous lawsuit settlements have made a mockery of the system. I cringe when I walk into a courtroom—it makes me feel...*postal*. When I was called for jury duty I wrote a letter to the judge stating that I felt our whole judicial system had become a three-ring circus. The judge is the ringleader, the liars, oh, I mean lawyers, are the magicians and then there are other assorted puppets, pawns, and pea brains. The victim is the clown. If the clown has a lot of money to pay for bigger liars he has a slightly better chance at seeing some justice. If the accused has the ACLU behind him everyone is screwed. I wouldn't be against bringing back the law of the Old West: you steal from me or hurt mine and I shoot you. Sometimes simplicity is a good thing.

Did you know that booby traps are actually an art form and should be appreciated as such? With a creative mind such as mine it was no time before the young men were warning their little friends, "don't goes near dat house, dat woman is nuts!" Of course I still wasn't getting any sleep because according to the *policeman,* booby traps must be constructed very late in the evening and dismantled before dawn. I was the midnight marauder, and for the most part doing their job for them. It was impossible to let my guard down. The bad guys were watching me, waiting for me to slip up one night. *They* were watching all of us? I made the boys run a zigzag pattern to their destiny. If captured, they were instructed to send up a flare. That was when you could still take flares to school.

Intricate diagrams hung off of the icebox, carefully plotting out the hot zones. Floodlights sprouted from every angle of the yard. They were usually broken by morning. We were living in a war zone and I was the Commander and Chief of all battle stations. The boys were my grunts.

It's surprising how quickly you can get used to living in a military state. I used to wonder why people in war-torn countries stayed there. I wondered how parents could let their kids play in the streets with bombs going off only a mile away. It's because they had flares. It's so comforting to know that if there are no bright-pink smoke lines in the skies the kids are still alive.

I thought things were going pretty well until my boyfriend lost half of his thumb trying to surprise me gassing up my car. Everyone knows not to surprise me. After that the boys refused to go near the car. Repete preferred to take his chances on foot. He would jump out the back window and crawl through the woods to a safe zone to play, especially after he ate dirt in the front yard from a few forgotten trip lines. The little guy never went anywhere without wearing his green plastic army helmet with his trusty survival knife at his side. He was a good soldier. Pete never went anywhere. He said that until they cut the wires on his Nintendo he saw no reason to fight. Repete and I kept a close eye on him; we knew he'd sell out to the other side if they tempted him with a new video game.

Did you know you could buy old hand grenades at army surplus stores? Of course they won't actually explode, but they are very impressive tied to the door handles. And MREs are not that bad-tasting, especially after a twelve-hour day.

After about four months of urban warfare we all began to falter. Sleep deprivation is a horrible thing. I almost walked into the grocery store with my shotgun early one morning in search of milk for the Coco Loops. More than once I wore two different shoes to work, and tried to sign a check at the bank with a flare. Everyone except the offenders had been wounded in battle, and our supplies were running low along with funds. I think we all know what it costs to run a war, and we didn't even have anyone diverting funds into politician's pockets.

We finally had a family meeting and decided we had better break our lease and move to safer ground. Most of the single mothers had long since packed up and moved on forfeiting their deposits to have round tires and a full night's sleep. We agreed there was no shame in staying alive. Well, actually the boys talked me into it. I wanted to go down with the ship because that's the kind of blockhead I am.

I don't know what it is about kids and vandalism. I can

see kids spray-painting their name on stuff, it's a form of art. I can see kids decorating trees with toilet paper, it's really fun. But I can't for the life of me see what joy kids get out of destroying other people's personal possessions, especially if it's not an act of justifiable revenge. I feel terrible if I accidentally run over someone's mailbox.

I doubt I would have stayed there more than two years anyway, as my gypsy blood was starting to stir, calling me...leading me to believe that happiness and sleep was right around the corner.

Gypsy blood lies. We packed up and moved again.

Chapter 9

A Typical Day in the Life of Me

I rise at 5 A.M. and stagger around stepping on Legos and the cats. Feed the cats so they let go of my legs, then curse and throw the Legos across the room—they are an ungodly creation. Make lunches to save money, peanut butter and jelly for Repete, everything else in the closet for Pete. I stand in the shower waiting to drown… it doesn't happen so I get out and continue to move around. One foot in front of the other, you know. Get dressed, anything old, which is pretty much anything I own.

Gather up cleaning supplies, clean rags, vacuum, and the fire extinguisher. I load the car.

I wake up the boys. This is when the trouble starts. Toss out bowls and Fruity Pebbles for Repete. Let Pete pick his own cereal out because I don't know anything. Carefully I inspect the milk jug for brother's lip marks, test it…. don't die and give it to Repete. Try to wake up Pete again by poking him with a broom; cannot penetrate the thick barrier of junk. He growls. We're getting close.

Root through pockets, jars, drawers, and sofa cushions for money for school stuff that never materializes. Write Repete a check for two dollars.

I try to wake up Pete again with a carefully placed football while screaming and flicking the lights fifty-seven times. He rises up, he scowls, he mumbles, and then he falls lifeless back into the black hole. I threaten to ground him until he is sixty, but realize I'm only punishing myself and quickly retract that statement. I approach the most beloved Nintendo and jiggle the wires. He leaps from the bed and screams, "I'm up!" Where would I be without video games?

I talk to Repete as he stares into his Fruity Pebbles a quarter inch from the bowl. Pete finally surfaces from the basement, always dressed in black. Is he clean or dirty? Can't tell. Good thing about black. The only thing that really shows up is icing, but he'll usually eat that later. An expeditious exchange of foul names fill the kitchen as they wish each other good morning. Pete chooses Fruity Pebbles because they are Repete's favorite. Repete wails in agony knowing he will eat them all. Pete leaves him one yellow pebble, which he touches to his tongue first.

I go through my morning ritual of warnings and threats. "Why do we have to go through this every morning? Just one morning I'd like no fighting, no names called, no sliming, no spit Pebbles. Just one! Someday I won't be here when you wake up...then you'll be sorry." Eyes are rolling deep into the backs of their heads. Pete is praying.

Pete drags a wet spoon across Repete's hair as he throws his breakfast dishes close to the sink. Repete flies into convulsions trying to remove the poisonous matter from his perfectly spiked hairdo. I scream at Pete for sliming his brother. He shrugs as he eats the yellow Pebble.

I turn my back on them, grasp the soap bottle firmly, and imitate violent acts of strangulation.

"Why do I bother to get out of bed in the morning?" I wail. Both boys shrug and head to their rooms. Mumbling my grievances to the cat, we head out to warm the car up, in August. Twenty minutes later I jump the car with the neighbor's help.

I wave good-bye to Repete as he boards the school bus willingly. I then scream into the basement for Pete to get his butt in gear or he will miss the bus. The driver is looking at the bus ceiling. After what seems an hour Pete emerges from the house eating a candy bar while dragging a machine-less video controller. Grown together. He waves good-bye with one finger, I hope because of the way he is holding the candy. The bus leaves making it safe for me to leave the house. I jump in the car and speed down the driveway. The car dies again.

Cleaning is a wonderful job. You get to do all the things you don't have time to do in your own house for other people. There are always cute little notes asking you to please wash the light fixture again (that a gnat couldn't fit its hand into), or bake a cake for their party if you have time. I always liked to leave a little note back, especially when they forgot to leave my check.

It always amazed me that people whose house was a bombsite of filth when I gave them an estimate are now capable of finding one particle of dust left behind. Three sheepdogs and six cats are running through the house, but they now noticed one eyelash I missed behind the toilet deep in the groove of black ceramic tile mortar.

It is also amazing the things people will pay large sums of money for rather than do themselves. Back in 1982, I once had a woman offer to pay me fifty dollars a week to just come in and wash her dishes. Of course the entire kitchen was piled high with every dish and rusty pan she owned crusted over in rotting food. I pointed out that at fifty dollars a week she could buy a dishwasher in about six weeks. She said they didn't get the dishes clean, nor would a blow torch and pick-axe after solidifying for a week. I didn't take the job. I doubt anyone did and I bet the dishes are still piling up.

If one wants to make money cleaning houses, one has to be fast and efficient. So I would follow a strict system, starting at the back of the house, circling the room from top to bottom, and then vacuuming my way out. I figured this one out on my own long before they wrote books on how to clean. Cleaning up just came natural to me, I guess because my life was always such a mess. After I finished my first house in record time I would drive like a psycho to my second hoping to finish and get home before the boys do. This is a pipedream.

I get to the second house and, lucky for me, a kid is home sick. I try to work around the little bastard and all of his mangy little friends playing hookey. They ask if I would mind stopping my work to make them Kool-Aid even though they see the gallon of Windex in my hand. I ask if blue is okay? They opt for sealed cans of soda. I can hear the little vermin down the hall talking about me. Foolish little children. Carefully I shine their dress shoe soles with Pledge. I finally surrender to the deafening music and half-ass the living room during a Cheetos fight, and then move on to house number three.

Locked out.

I race down the highway. I'm so excited that I have extra time. Being poor, I always eat my lunch in transit, providing I didn't leave it at home like today. I rummage for money and come up with seventeen cents. Lucky for me the boys had a pretzel fight in the car.

I will try to clean as many paint-and-plaster-filled bathtubs as I possibly can at the one hundred and ninety-two-unit apartment building I took on in a moment of insanity or drunkenness. While scraping paint and plaster, I listen to the dizzy office lady ramble on about how someone just has to move into the unit half-constructed because of its eventual view, even though there are twenty units clean with grass instead of mud surrounding them. Neither of us listens to the construction workers denying any part in trashing the twelve units we just cleaned. I stare at my razor knife and wonder which one of us should I cut first? They notice and leave. I continue my mission.

My vacuum cleaner screeches, blows smoke, and a foul, melting rubber smell emits. The belt breaks. It can't manage to eat one more screw, nail, or chunk of plaster. I buy belts by the gross, yet I am always out. I curse Mr. Hoover, strangle the hose, and head off in another direction. There are always plenty of small green felt dots attached with Gorilla Snot glue to be removed. The manufacturers stick them all over the damn mirrors; they have no purpose other than to piss me off.

I suddenly realize it is after five—time flies when you are having fun. I panic and throw all my junk into the car. I always leave something behind. Frantically I drag a thousand pounds of trash to the dumpster, cursing the union laborer who left at three. Crazed, I yell back warnings of death to anyone who goes near those clean tubs. I am the only person still on the jobsite. I speed out of the complex, zigzag through traffic, blaze through orange lights, and hit the entrance ramp at 60 mph.

The highway is a gridlock.

Quietly I sit in the smoldering heat with the windows down and the heater on high. My dad says this will keep the car from overheating in traffic. It also helps to intensify the vapors from Windex, Comet, and oven cleaner rags while I talk to God.

As I round the corner to our duplex I can see signs of life, but thankfully no flames. Sixteen kids are playing in my driveway. I know none of them. The front door is open. There are only a few blood spots on the front stoop, hopefully not from mine. The lawn chairs are scattered dead in the front yard, and the neighbor is yelling something but I can't hear her over the TV from our unit. Inside everything is on. No one is there.

The boys arrive from different directions as soon as I chase away all of their new friends. Again expeditious exchanges of foul names fill the air as they begin to rat each other out. The cat is on top of the kitchen cabinets hissing violently while the hamster gorges on Coco Loops mangled on the floor, the kitchen faucet is running, and the icebox door is wide open. Thank God nothing bad happened while I was stuck in traffic.

Quickly I whip up some dinner while the boys lie about their homework assignments. The phone never stops ringing but it's rarely for me. This is good because you can't hear what anyone is saying; we rent a duplex on the runway at St. Louis Lambert airport. All right, right next to it, but they are trying to buy us out because there are tire tracks on my roof. I now know why they showed me the unit at 1 A.M.

Dinner is the normal snatch-and-grab to get more than your brother, even if you don't like it. Everyone is talking at the same time and no one is listening. There is something odd in Repete's mac and cheese. Pete suggests something ghastly then laughs frantically. Repete locks up, gags, and spews noodles out his nose. Dinner is officially over.

The cat has finally come down from the cabinets and is now only twitching. Repete has surrendered to torment and locked himself in his room. Perfect, because now that Pete has no one to pester, he resumes his video games. Semi-silence befalls the house except for the 747's taking off every five minutes.

I quickly hose down the kitchen, pay a few bills (only the ones with threats attached), and then throw in eight or nine loads of laundry. If I'm lucky I will get to watch *Little House on the Prairie* in peace.

Repete sneaks from his room to notify me that one of his flying squirrels is missing again. Flying squirrels are tricky little creatures. They don't actually fly—it is more of a vicious leap toward you and then a quick soaring motion away while attached to some part of your flesh. Flying squirrels are very small with big claws, big teeth, and a very bad attitude when approached with containment devices. Quickly we all don net laundry bags and hats, garden gloves or mittens, and are armed with badminton rackets and colanders. Capture time: two hours and fourteen minutes. *Little House on the Prairie* is over.

Repete has finished his shower and Pete has entered the bathroom. The water is running steady—too steady? After about fifteen minutes I smash my head to the floor and look under the crack. Aha! Just as I suspected: he is sitting on the floor reading comics. I threaten to come in and wash him. He quickly jumps into the tub with his socks on. Repete is doing his nails.

At last everyone is bathed and homework might be done. We move into the living room for movie time. We watch *Police Academy* or *Ghostbusters*, again. The boys must stay on separate sides of the room at all times. They are not allowed to go to the kitchen or bathroom at the same time unattended. The usual arguments ensue during any breaks.

All I can think of is sleep but the time ticks off as slow as a federal audit.

The phone has finally been taken off the hook so every kid in the neighborhood is now beating on both doors. In a frenzy I savagely write on hunks of cardboard signs that say "GO AWAY!" I attach them to the doors with steak knives. The kids know me and leave without further incident.

At last it is bedtime. I sweep up the popcorn, wipe up the Kool-Aid, and put the curtains back up. And yet another expeditious exchange of foul names fill the basement as the boys tell each other goodnight. I toss out a strange male cat and put the hamster back in his cage, turn off the lights, put the phone back on the hook, and climb into my inviting little bed. Tomorrow night is Friday and I will be tending bar till 1 A.M., and Saturday night too. Thank God.

A fight breaks out in the basement. Pete has violated the code of boundaries and entered Repete's room to swipe some Kleenexes. Gauze will be needed for the blood shed over a nose blow. Everyone is screaming in an opposite direction as I race down the steps only to find a carefully placed Lego. It would appear that Pete's box of Kleenexes has been emptied since we moved in. Why has it not been replaced? Because he loves to hear his little brother scream every time he needs one. Preferably when we are all half asleep.

I quickly whip up a sermon on the rights of each other's property and privacy. No one is listening as both boys throw out rude accusations. I drag Pete back to his room by the neck of his black T-shirt and beg him not to terrorize his brother. He laughs and agrees.

Carefully I make my way back upstairs, limping from the small Lego man that feels like he is still embedded in my heel. Again, I fall into bed fighting my covers which are severely knotted from my vicious exit to the basement. Eventually I give in to defeat and lie on the lump. I have no energy left. Our mama cat stretches out across my face, as shadows fill the room and silence settles in the basement. I begin lamenting my usual request to God, and beg for mercy. But soon I am interrupted by one of the idiots I am casually dating. He calls and asks if it's too late to stop by for a quick visit. I rip the phone from the wall and pass out.

In all honesty I have to say some days are better than others. On the weekends I don't have to wake the boys up early or try to get them do anything. But they don't go to school on those days either. Maybe they're all the same.

Chapter 10

Dating: A Lot Like Divorce

I f you don't have enough agony in your life you can always start dating again. It's kind of like sunbathing with poison ivy. I know not all men are the same. Right. I also know that out there somewhere is Mr. Right waiting to turn into Mr. Wrong.

Unfortunately, dating is another one of those necessary evils. No one wants to grow old all alone and be called *the crazy old cat lady*. Also, there are other needs in life... but I won't get into that as my mom will read this book.

I'll admit it: men are attractive to me. They have interesting bodies, nice muscles, and bigger pay checks. Unfortunately, it's their underlying qualities that slowly seep out after they can no longer manage to maintain their "party manners" that makes me want to eliminate their species from the entire planet. Men for the most part are just little boys that never grow up. Even the most sophisticated man on the planet will still have the desire to blow stuff up, race someone in rush hour traffic, and just once—sleep with a broad named Bubbles or say, someone, with a cigar fetish.

Somewhere between being stuck with a hundred-dollar dinner tab and walking home at 3 A.M. I decided to turn the tables and drop my party manners. One has to deal with each species on its own level. To avoid some litigation I started asking the important questions up front. Questions like, do you mind if I run a criminal background check, past marital status, and credit report? Do you have a deep freeze and can I check the contents for body parts? What kind of a relationship do you have with your mother? She doesn't stay in your attic, does she? Do you have any fetishes about dolphins, trampolines, or tie-down straps?

I've learned there is no rhyme or reason to the male. I've dated some fine-looking men, with ape brains. I've dated some ape-looking men with ape brains. Unfortunately I've never come across a fine-looking man with a fine brain, but I'm not saying he's not out there somewhere. I've dated men that didn't even have any party manners— they just started out rude and stupid and couldn't understand why they got the phone number to the nut ward at County Hospital. I've dated men who expected me to buy *them* dinner. Why would I want to feed three boys? I'm old-fashioned: I think the man should pay, especially if he makes seventy grand a year to my ten. I've dated men who forgot they had a wife, kids, communicable ailments, and a boyfriend named Randy. I've dated men who I'm still not sure to this day were men. In my defense, some of those were very carefully calculated set-ups by friends who are no longer friends.

Men are odd creatures and if you're going to try to figure them out you're going to put yourself back in the nut ward for another Blue Cross vacation. If I have learned one thing in fifty years it's to accept men for what they are. Men. Three little letters, not much more.

I find it kind of odd that there are hundreds of books out there to help women understand men, but very few to help men understand women. Why is that? Could it be that the profit margin writing for a demographic that doesn't care if their butt crack is showing isn't very profitable? Yeah, some women will buy the books for men and try to slip little facts in during *Cops*. "Hey, listen to this honey, even this doctor says 'you have to preheat the oven before you shove the turkey in.'" Personally, if you're talking to your man during any TV program, or even commercials, you're talking to the wall. Men have a special filtering device to tune out our voices no matter how high an octave we can hit.

Even if you accept men as a lower life form, you still have to make them mind. Men need rules or they'll pee right out the front door. Bad thing is men find rules more of a guideline, kind of like a chalk line. True, you need it but if it's off a hair no one is going to notice. Look at third world countries where their women are buried under a blanket and have no voice or control over their men; their countries are in chaos. Men need strict supervision, rules, and the fear of retribution from a strong woman. Nothing strikes terror in the heart of a bad boy like the thought of losing half of his stuff, especially his toys or anything camouflage.

I'm a pretty easygoing person, but if there is one thing I can't tolerate with men it's cheating. Most men think of cheating as *an error*, especially when they get caught. They look at you with those big bulging puppy dog eyes and say those four utterly stupid words "it didn't mean anything." To most men it probably doesn't—sex to men is like getting an ice cream from the neighborhood dinger man.

It's a treat, it's not illegal, and as long as you can afford to pay you should get as much as you want. The bell rings, run out and get some. Whereas I see it as more of a life and death issue: don't if you want to keep your dinger, man.

Nowadays, all of this casual sex makes it even easier on men. These young girls don't realize what they are doing. Moms used to say, "Why board the cow if they can get the milk for free." Nowadays women say, "Why take on the whole hog for a little bit of sausage." There's a big flaw in that theory because men don't care if you just borrow their sausage. What's next? We don't need the chicken because we can recreate the eggs? Anyway you look at it farm animals haven't gained much respect over the years.

There are a lot of painful things in life but I think dating is the worst. Nobody wants to get hurt yet we keep putting our hearts out there to be pulverized. Everybody says they hate to play games dating, but let's face it: it's all a game. The man tries to get what he wants by buying up property, houses, and hotels to impress the woman. The woman tries to get what she wants: her name on the property, houses, and hotels by returning acts of kindness. They keep moving around the board impressing and pleasing each other. Now and then he will be awarded a get out of jail free card just to keep him in the game. The woman changes the rules to suit her needs. This is legal. He finally folds. He's confused and it's too much work to keep impressing her. He gives her Park Place and ties the knot. Shortly thereafter he finds himself sitting on Mediterranean Avenue, broke and cut off.

When you're single for nineteen years and nine months you have a lot of time to meet a lot of different men. When I say "different" I mean lock him up different, like a fellow who likes to drive his convertible naked at midnight. Why? Because it feels so free and of course he wants you to experience it with him. How about a man who likes to go to carnivals and buy up a good supply of funnel cakes to freeze for the winter months? Don't they have recipes for those? Oh, and a man who knits. Now, I'm not one to dog anyone on their techniques for relaxation but please don't take it to the show on a Friday night.

Do women actually marry these men? You know how sometimes you meet a couple, and the woman is smart and just gorgeous and the guy is an unemployed barnacle-sucking nutcase, you can't help but wonder, man, he must be hung. If you ever have time to ponder it, try to figure out why the women you know are with the men they are with. It usually loops back around somehow to *the crazy old cat lady* syndrome, especially if you're not impressed after you see him in a Speedo.

I've never understood the reasoning to go out on a blind date either. As if life isn't a big enough surprise. I have to say that I've only had one blind date—his dog was really cute. I've never trusted my friends after my ex, especially when I still owe them money. Yet there are still those friends determined to make your life worse than it is. Why is that? If they say, "I've got someone I want you to meet."

I say, "I've got a thirty-eight, loaded."

It is hard to meet a potential partner, especially when you're working three jobs. Let's face it, meeting guys in a bar is just asking for trouble, especially when you work in the bar. Suddenly he doesn't want you to wait on anyone else, as if you are already married. Trust me, tips really start to plummet when patrons have to make their own drinks.

Eventually you have to catch him when he's sober (not easy) and explain, "I don't think this is going to work out, you're slung on the bar like Dick was in the recliner." You lift an eyelid with a swizzle stick and lean into his ear.

"Buddy, I'm looking for a bit more this time. We're through!" He rises five inches, stares, mumbles and tumbles. For a couple bucks the bus boys scrape him off the floor and shove him out the door, and you're back on the market.

After a couple hundred bad dates, one starts to question their own ability to choose mates. Choose anything. You find yourself wracked with indecision choosing a new flavor of cereal or cheese at the supermarket for fear it will morph into something else a few days from now. You won't even tell your kids, when asked, if you think their friends are cool. Not that they ask much after trying to fingerprint their nine-year-old friend that slept over.

You come home from your second job saturated in peppermint schnapps someone's iron constitution rejected only to find your kids sitting on the couch alone. A note from the babysitter says in two words she's done watching your kids. There's another stray dog between them ready to give birth, lamps are on the floor, and the toilet is running as always while they quietly eat ice cream out of the dripping half-gallon cartons. And to think on the way home you had just vowed that your job and kids were enough to fulfill your life.

This is the point in life where all reason abandons you. After a million or so mistakes you figure anyone has more sense than you. Why not let someone else think for me? Other people appeared to be succeeding in life. On the advice of a friend I tried out one of those dating services. For five hundred bucks you'd think they had more going upstairs than yourself. I've never been offered fifty cents for my opinion.

Dating services used to be a last resort, but since e-dating I've heard it's not just for nerds anymore as it was back in the Eighties. The problem is they don't give lie detector tests during the questionnaire stage. I even went to a "Christian" dating service, hoping for a little more honesty, but since there isn't an actual "Thou shalt not lie" commandment, the results were pretty much the same. There seems to be a really big gray area for most people, and *as close as possible* could be a continent away for many.

The worst part of dating services is the difference in the photo and the actual person. Glamour Shots can do some amazing things, while others will put in a photo of themselves from ten years ago. Let's face it: sooner or later you are going to see them and know they were airbrushed and are on Social Security.

I like how people try to sell their best attribute, like "I have a beautiful smile—it's right under my toucan nose." I want the truth first; I don't mind a big beak (but preferably a little lower on the anatomy). And good grief, warn me about it; a shock like that could cause a heart attack. And here's a tip, don't wear a necktie with a toucan on it. Duh.

Dating is even more complicated when you are a single parent. The biggest challenge now isn't if you like him but if he likes your kids. They all say they love kids at first, and they do. Most have a few scattered across the country that you'll find out about later. They'll buy them some toys and treats to get to mom, and the boys were always good with trading me off at a price. But then one night the guy up and decides it is payback time. Quite frankly, I think I'm worth more than a bag of gummy worms and a few plastic Transformers.

I did run into *one* man in my life that was totally honest. He frankly stated he didn't like kids and didn't want any around. He would be willing to pay for a full-time nanny if they didn't live with us. Why was he still talking? I've got two kids standing by me pinching each other, making fart noises, and begging for quarters. Maybe he thinks they're returnable. Am I supposed to choose now between this gorgeous, rich, world-traveling man, and my kids? I always messed up when pressure was applied.

Dating has definitely changed a lot through the ages, and to be honest I never really kept up after awhile. Some changes are just plain bad, especially when they are taken to the extreme. Today everything seems to be to the extreme. It's like suing because you got fat shoveling Big Macs into your own face, or burned by hot coffee. Would you have paid for cold coffee? Does someone have to actually tell you it is hot or that it's impossible to burn off eight thousand calories a day? I want to know where common sense went.

Woman's lib was a good change. I didn't *need* to be bound up in a bra anyway. The right to vote and wear pants, all good. But then some overzealous broads decided we could take care of ourselves. They crossed the line. All that did was let guys off the hook from their only real purpose in life besides donating the little swimmers. Buying dinner. And yet we think men are stupid. Who cooks, cleans, does the laundry, raises the kids, works full time, pays the bills, mows the lawn, and then feels guilty because she can't get it all done in an eighteen-hour day? Why, so we can say we can *do it all?* Men have no problem with saying they can't do laundry, or cook, or deal with the kids, and whose day ends at five-fifteen on the couch with the remote? Who's playing golf or hunting on the weekends, ladies?

During the Eighties men were really eating up all of the new cultural changes; they jumped into woman's liberation with an open zipper and an empty wallet. Why buy your own place when you can move into her ex-old man's house? Hey, it even comes with a fully-stocked icebox. No shame in free! But, it seems to me that no shame and no respect tend to go hand in hand. Like my dad always said, "If you don't work for it you don't appreciate it." Guys in the Eighties were like kids in a candy store with a free pass. And you thought free love was just a Seventies thing. Fortunately for us, the girls of the Nineties put them back in line and under the yoke where they belong.

Shacking up, as my mother called it, was popular when I got divorced. Women didn't need a piece of paper to support some grown, able-bodied man. Women were strong; they started doing men's jobs. I'da loved to make fifteen bucks an hour but not to jump into a live sewer line—that is a great job for men. Walking girders a thousand feet up, dangling from a rope off a bridge, all good jobs for men, especially married ones. I guess I wasn't much of a woman's libber. After they got me out of that confounded brassiere I was pretty content. Come to think of it, after I ditched my padded bra was when the respect issue took a real nosedive.

The Eighties were a confusing time for me, especially being all alone. You can't really sit down with your kids and discuss your dates. Especially a guy who wore a trench coat through dinner, chewed like a tree chipper, lit up a doobie after dessert, and then didn't even offer to pay for your cab before the police took him away. That's when you realize you need a break from dating, when the only thing that bothered you was no ride home.

You start to think that maybe there really isn't anyone out there for you. Maybe there is something wrong with you? You decide to lower your standards another notch and consider dating guys that wear fanny packs. Then you realize you can't go any lower because the next step is men with handbags, and so on. It was at that moment I changed my whole theory on men and went from finding Mr. Right for keeps to just hanging out with *Mr. Not as Bad as Some* for a free dinner and a movie. I decided to just let nature take its course. Sooner or later the right guy would come

111

along and I'd be too busy to notice.

When I look back on my dating experiences it kind of runs along with my ownership of vehicles. A lot of junkers, one I couldn't afford, and some that seemed dependable but obviously had been driven too hard by a previous owner. However, preowned are much better than right off the showroom floor. You don't have to baby 'em for the first five hundred miles because the first wife has already broken them in. Second, third, or fourth wife models—steer clear they've been driven way too hard and are probably diesels. Nothing can break 'em.

Nowadays older women seem to be seeking out much younger men, I believe they call them cougars. We used to call them child molesters. True you can train younger men as they are not set in their ways yet, but who wants to start all over with the toilet seat issue at thirty?

I once asked the boys if it bothered them that they didn't have their dad around full time. They both said no, they couldn't live with him either. Then Repete said he had learned a lot from the variety of men I dated, one taught him to hunt, another how to fix and build things, and another how to evade taxes and prosper even in a really bad economy. I felt a lot better after he shared that with me.

As the boys got older it was funny how our roles changed. Instead of me asking what time they would be home they were putting the same questions to my dates. It was kind of a warm and fuzzy feeling, thinking they were watching out for their old mom, even if they were really just trying to scope out the possibilities of a party as soon as we left.

I've learned a lot dating, probably more than I learned in all my years of schooling. I've learned that dating can be a lot like divorce, especially if you're into joint ownership or as we used to say, sharing stuff. I love to watch those TV courtroom shows where some bozo bought a house, a car, imported leather furniture, and a two thousand dollar pedigreed dog with an obviously psycho partner after dating them for three whole weeks. The only thing you can safely split up is the living room set—anything else is going to cause irreversible damage to the item. So they stand there and argue who chipped in the most, and you know the judge just wants to say, "how about thought—did either of you chip in any of that?" I mean how well do you know someone after three weeks? Good enough to sleep with 'em, sure, but not enough to share a dog!

I've also learned after a few damaging blows to my checkbook to let them have all the stuff in their name. You get to use it and enjoy it but you don't have to pay for it, nor do you have to move it every four weeks or so. When he loses his job, and he will, you don't have to even think about the creditors until they yank the sofa out from under your ass. Nothing damages your credit rating faster than letting a guy leave with a new truck your name is on too. Trust me, he will not make the payments, especially after you adjust the side mirrors with a baseball bat.

Oh, and never borrow against your life insurance to help a boyfriend out. That should be a no-brainer, but just in case there is someone out there as stupid as me, don't do it. If a man can't take care of himself he's not worth having. I recently told my niece that it's just as easy to love a rich man as a poor man. Actually, it's a whole lot easier! I told her she might as well go for the gold or at least a thick gold-overlay because rich or poor they will eventually all drive her nuts.

If I could do my dating years all over again, I wouldn't. I'da went straight to the pound, picked up a load of stray cats, and called it a day after I signed the divorce decree. Hey, I've been called worse.

Chapter 11

Hey, Let's Move Again

R ight about the time I think God has finally given up on trying to teach me anything, another lesson is right around the corner.

The small office I had cleaned for years was finally beginning to grow. The owner bought another building and my paycheck was growing right along with them. It was the first time in my life raising the boys I didn't have to work more than two jobs. Though stripping and waxing spacious industrial floors alone at 4 A.M. isn't really living the good life.

Pete was hanging with Dick and Repete with me; it was just safer all around to keep them a minimum of thirty miles apart. I had rented a really nice townhouse in a really nice area, which was a really nice change of pace for us. I'd finally bought my first car from someone other than my dad, which had always forced him to buy a new one. Gee, I felt like such a grown-up. Of course I was scared to death because this sort of thing just doesn't happen to me.

This would be our fifth move, this time back into the city. We decided to leave the quiet country life for a few reasons. One, Repete wanted to play basketball and apparently in a small town the coach chooses the team based on your family's status. Two, some holy roller's possessed child was shooting all of the cars on the apartment parking lot up with his new BB gun. There is no arguing with one of God's disciples, even if her kid's head is spinning around while you're trying to show her the videotape of the violation. And three, the bar I was working at accidentally burned down due to some bookkeeping discrepancies. I didn't keep the books, I just didn't want to be called as a witness for who did.

A few months after we moved into the nice new townhouse, my rear end dropped out. Not on the car. To avoid a huge hospital bill from a lack of insurance I went to the doctor's office for emergency hemorrhoid surgery.

Back in the Eighties you didn't get to walk away from a big hospital bill you had incurred. As a matter of fact, you didn't get to walk into most hospitals without insurance. Back then they could ask if you had insurance. If you said no, the person at the front desk would say, "then we can't help you, and please take your blood trail with you."

It's hard to believe that the United States government made hospitals be compassionate to all Americans despite their inability to pay. Think about how compassionate the IRS is. If you owe them money they'll take the roof from over your head and the meat from out of your mouth; everyone else should just let the bill slide.

My doctor recommended against my cheap-sided judgment, but he knew better than to argue with me. I should have listened to him. Do you know how bad a shot of Novocain hurts stuck into your jaw? Multiply that by a

115

million! The rest of the procedure was pretty much a horrible blur. When I went back for my check-up I did notice a large bite mark in his leather examining table. Someone is missing a tooth in the same place I am.

I can only remember two things clearly. One, myself saying over and over, "I'm saving a thousand dollars, I'm saving a thousand dollars…" Two, hearing the nurse ask me if I was capable of driving home or if she should call me a cab. While hanging on the counter, scribbling all over my hand and checkbook, I informed her, "Hey, lady I didn't do this here under a local to spend the difference on a fricking cab!" I tend to be a little short when I am in severe pain.

It's very hard to drive sitting on your hip. Either one. I did a lot of praying on the drive home, even threw in a Hail Mary, and I'm not Catholic. I don't mind dying but I don't want to take an innocent person with me just because I'm cheap.

Repete carried me into the apartment and I passed out on the couch for two days. Otherwise, I had a pretty quick recovery, but life's always been a pain in the ass so I may have gone back to work not knowing the difference.

One morning while I was cleaning the new office building, a man I hadn't seen before sat in the cafeteria rocking on a chair with his feet up on the lunch table. He was a large man, missing some fingertips and both of his thumbs. Apparently his brain was in one of them. Who puts their dirty work boots on the table you eat on?

I'm always in a great mood when I'm cleaning because I'm just having so darn much fun, especially since I am cleaning up after fifty men. "Would you mind taking your dirty feet off the table?" I asked.

"And who are you?" he retorted with a smirk on his face.

"I'm the cleaning lady," I said with as much sarcasm as

I could muster. I displayed the mop and bucket in my hands, just in case he was deaf and not just stupid.

"And just who are you, buddy?"

"I'm Dale, I was a meat-cutter for twenty years," he said with a stubby wave.

"Not a very good one." I replied. I've always had an answer for an asinine person. I find it unbelievable when people say they had no reply to a rude or stupid comment. The problem is, most people think before they speak, holding in the classic comebacks.

Stubby then stood up and pointed to me with a nub. "I'm also the boss's brother and am taking over the maintenance on all of the buildings, and I know you're going to lose your job, little lady."

I didn't have a comeback. One week later two morons with one rag and a bucket replaced me.

Naturally we could no longer afford to stay in the nice townhouse due to a huge drop in my income. Repete informed me that since he had made the basketball team he would not leave his new school. He would move in with a buddy, sleep in the park, or live in a box. I knew he was serious because Repete never demanded much of anything, well, except for real Fruity Pebbles. I agreed I would do everything in my power to stay in the school district. Had I not had to purchase real Fruity Pebbles things may have gone differently. Unfortunately the only place we could afford to live was the city park. Camping wasn't allowed.

On the advice of a friend I wound up purchasing a used mobile home. They're not my friend anymore. The mobile home broker found an open lot in a very nice mobile home park that was still in his school district. So, we packed up and moved one more time, into a box with wheels.

However, it turned out that the landlords of this particular park were into a lot of *side jobs* to make extra money. When a trailer would move out they would bust out the concrete pad for the shed then inform the new tenant that they had to pour a pad for the shed lying on its side in the yard. Fortunately for the new tenant they poured concrete pads and what a deal at only $400 for a five–by–six chunk of rock.

They also picked up extra cash bonuses from the mobile home dealers and brokers by freeing up lots via eviction. It seemed every day someone was moving out and a new trailer was being moved in. I never really thought about why, but when I called there wasn't an open pad for a sixty-mile radius. I assumed my broker just got lucky.

Upon moving in we were given a list of restrictions a quarter-mile long and told that they really didn't bother with most of them, it was just to keep the riff-raff out. Little did I know the riff-raff was the landlords. We made it one year with only a few warnings for minor violations. A trash can left out thirteen seconds after pick-up, Repete out four seconds after *their* set curfew. Amazingly, someone claimed to have heard Repete's stereo blasting while I was at work and he was at a game. However, the best one was for a total stranger parking in front of our house on the wrong side of the street while we were gone. I usually can control that sort of thing.

By now I had taken on a job as a cook and went back into the bar business. I was still cleaning a few houses on the side so that Repete could have a one-hundred-five-dollar pair of required tennis shoes and a really neat sweat suit that snapped up and whipped right off for a grand entrance onto the court. I was also still buying Pete's clothes, as Dick was a huge fan of the Blind Resale Shop and, well, polyester pants in high school just don't cut it. Daddy said they were good enough.

Most of my days started at 4:30 A.M. and ended at 2:30

A.M., with Mondays and Tuesdays off to sleep. Any time in between was used to run Repete to games and practices and to shuffle the boys back and forth between parental houses. I swear I passed myself on certain roads driving them four to six times a day.

Living in a mobile home isn't like living in a regular house. There's a little thing called heat tape that you have to plug in or your pipes will freeze solid. It costs one hundred and fifty dollars to have them thawed out. Also, the life expectancy of a mobile home's sub floor is about the same as a gerbil, providing they aren't already rotted when you buy it. It's a funny feeling to stand in front of the mirror and watch your self shrinking.

Have you ever seen the movie *Bridge on the River Kwai* where they put one of the prisoners into a little metal box to bake in the sun all day? Well, that is what it feels like living in a mobile home with an old air conditioner. I'm also a little claustrophobic and almost six feet tall, so seven-foot ceilings make me uncomfortable, especially when the window starts at your shin and ends at your chin. I spent a lot of time out on the front porch steps. Of course these are all things you can learn to live with as long as your kid is on the basketball team.

Apparently spying and informing on neighbors is a rather popular pastime in a trailer park. I never understood the theory of ratting out your neighbor unless they were doing something illegal. I'd rather just talk to them or slug 'em. I sure didn't enjoy hearing her four little girls singing *Jesus Loves Me* at the top of their screechy little lungs every fricking day, but I wouldn't have reported them for excessive noise. Little did I know their Sunday-school-teacher mom was compiling a long list of infractions against us. So much for that "love they neighbor" crap.

After a long hot day of cooking for people with no

teeth, I came home to an eviction notice on the front door of my trailer. It seemed one of our visitors had parked their car three and a quarter inches over into her driveway space. She had a photograph with a ruler by the tire. I had thirty days to move my doublewide or it would be confiscated for rental property—another sideline business of the landlords.

After a phone call to the landlords, I was definitely evicted. I've never been able to stay calm or hold my tongue when someone is hosing me. I wrote two words with a Sharpie on the eviction notice and proceeded to battle the injustice. I wrote letters, I picketed, I employed the help of a state representative, and I did some major undercover spy work. With the help of many other unjustly evicted tenants we got enough dirt on the landlords to fill a stadium. People came out of the woodwork to help hang the heartless landlords. I forwarded all of the information to the owner in Georgia and some other interesting tidbits to the IRS.

Unfortunately, renters don't really have any rights, especially in a trailer park. For some odd reason you are looked upon by the court system as a subspecies and tossed aside like a voter after an election. I lost my plea and sold my home for the payoff to avoid confiscation. I found a hauler the twenty-ninth day of my notice. As they removed tie-downs and split her down the middle I stood vigilant with a box of wooden matches. No way were those double-dealing landlords taking my home and renting it out.

The Sunday school teacher begged my forgiveness after she read the big sign on her side of my trailer that said, "LOVE THY NEIGHBOR." I told her not to worry about it, but please get those damn kids some singing lessons.

I'm not sure what it was that God was trying to teach me on that one either, unless I was a tool for his use. I did manage to get the landlords fired and hopefully saved some other people the agony of their money-motivated evictions. They say everything happens for a reason. I'd like to think I lost my home for a good cause. Then again, God may have gotten me for screaming *Jesus Loves Me* along with the little magpies while I mowed my lawn.

Oh, and I got my picture in the newspaper a few times, which was kind of nice. I also got legislation started for mobile home owners, to require that they be given more than thirty days' notice, and that substantial grounds be required for eviction. I learned that when renting, it doesn't matter if you are renting the building or the land, you're subjected to being screwed either way. Leases are for the landlords, not for the renter. Most importantly I learned that if you are going to buy a house on wheels make sure you can pull it with your little Celebrity station wagon.

We packed up and moved again.

Chapter 12

Santa Sucks and Other Hassledays

I hate holidays. I don't mind Groundhog Day unless the little fur ball sees his shadow and I don't mind Arbor Day cause most people don't even know what it is. What is it?

Holidays have been taken to the extreme just like everything else. You used to just have to illuminate the outside of your house on Christmas. Now there are purple lights for Halloween, pink for Easter, and red, white, and blue for all those patriotic holidays. People, isn't untangling lights and falling off the ladder once a year enough?

I think it's all a plot by Corporate America to suck our wallets dry every month. As if there weren't enough legitimate holidays they had to add more. Administrative Professionals Day is April the 12th; just so you don't forget. United Nations Day is October 24th. Should we all go out and found a new little nation or something? Then there are the *up card sales days* like Grandparents' Day, Secretary's and Bosses' Day—isn't everyday the boss's day? May the 20th is Shavuot (you figure that one out). Did you know that February 24th is Mexican Flag Day? Honest to God, it's on my Chinese-made calendar hanging here in my U. S. of A. office. If you are in America what flag should you be flying every day? There is a Canadian Flag Day too. What about Kwanzaa—it just appeared one day. Now, the Blacks had to see though that one. "Damn, Wanda, do they really expect us to buy all new decorations because we're *African* Americans!" The marketers even admitted that Kwanzaa was made up. But then so was the Easter Bunny—man, I wonder what they were smoking in *that* think tank?

I saw on the news the other day that a school in Florida canceled all of their holidays because a Muslim parent wanted a Muslim holiday celebrated in the school also. So as to not offend the Muslims they took away all of the little kids' fun. No holidays. And once again, I have to go back to the fact that this is America and we *have a history.* Muslims or Muslim beliefs did not found it. And correct me if I am wrong, but weren't all of the 9-11 bombers Muslims? What day should we celebrate, Jihad Day? Why don't we all just wrap a sheet around our heads and hand over the keys to the White House while we're at it so as not to offend anyone for being Americans? I'm not against diversity, but why do I have to diversify? I'm already about as different as they come!

To be honest, I think it's all a ploy by government workers too, to get another paid day off of work. Somewhere in the basement of government building on long, long coffee breaks they are thinking up new holidays. Well, I simply refuse to celebrate any new holidays. If it wasn't on the calendar when I was little, my clan and I are not celebrating it. And I'm not giving up any of the original ones either.

I won't even go into the issue that the real meaning of Christmas and Easter have been buried alive in commercialism. Nothing drives me crazy like Santa bowing at the manger, compliments of the peacemakers. Or the atheists demanding the season be renamed the "Winter Holiday" so they don't feel guilty for rejecting God. I say reject Him and see where it gets you, but leave my holidays alone! This girl will continue to say "Merry Christmas" until they cut my dried-up tongue from my big blockhead. No one is taking Christ out of my Christmas. And as for the Easter Bunny, well, I'll let him slide because I really like speckled eggs and purple Peeps.

The worst part of holidays is the expense. It grows every year. I think that's called inflation? Anyway, it's not that I don't like to get presents—I just don't like to buy 'em. It's hard to buy good gifts when you have no money and I hate to give gifts with an excuse. "I know it's not what you wanted, and I'm sure it won't fit yah, but it was on sale. Feel free to take it back and get a small ice cream cone with the money."

It was always so hard for me to produce a great Christmas like I had when I was a kid. My parent's had money. It wasn't too bad when the kids were little because I could rewrap stuff they hadn't seen in awhile. That works on old people too. But when kids learn to read advertisements they know what they want. I couldn't garage-sale them either because Pete checked for price tags and UPC codes. By age six he had a closely monitored inventory of both of their possessions for the do-over factor.

Sure you can threaten them with getting nothing due to bad behavior, but no matter how bad they are you know you aren't really going to put hot molten lava rocks in their sock. You know you have to produce toys and lots of them.

I remember one Christmas when the boys were about seven and eight years old. It was the Christmas that would change my life's mission. As always I was on the downside of the financial ladder to nowhere. Repete was still young enough to be excited with just about anything you wrapped up. "A bag of Cheetos, cool!" However, Pete wasn't so gullible and was getting really hard to trick.

On the advice of a friend I decided to have a home toy party to earn some gifts for the kids. It sounded like a great idea—the only cash I needed was for some snacks for the buyers. Cheetos, cool. I sold over five hundred dollars worth of toys and I got to pick out all sorts of cute stuff, but unfortunately nothing they were advertising on TV. I thought I had done pretty darn well for the means I had and was really excited Christmas morning to see their joy as the rip-a-rama began. Fifteen minutes later the living room looked like a bombsite as the boys sat panting on the floor.

Then as if God himself came down from Heaven and said, "Nancy, stop waiting, I'm never coming to get you," Pete's smile turned to a frown as his eyes scanned the floor. He then uttered the three deadliest words I'd ever heard. "Is that all?" My heart dropped like your handbag off of a sky lift in an amusement park. No recourse.

Pete had wanted some overpriced multipurpose transformer thingy he saw on TV. As always they only made a hundred so they were impossible to find, and unfortunately I used all the money I made for groceries and rent that month. I had hoped he would have been so happy with all of the other toys he might overlook the fact that Santa didn't bring the Transformer. Yeah, like the IRS would overlook your honeymoon as a deduction.

I tried to explain that Santa had to pay his elves to make the toys and maybe he couldn't afford to bring it too. Repete immediately chimed in "I bet the elves are union." I agreed. Union wages are high. Pete didn't buy it and went to his room with his substandard loot to sulk. I was crushed.

Every year that followed I started shopping for the next year's Christmas gifts on December 26th. Christmas hung heavy on my mind like twinkle lights on an aqua trailer in June. That made Christmas a twelve-month mission instead of just the usual three-month push. Nothing would stop this Santa's helper again from delivering the goods, not long lines stretching to China, moms with sharper fingernails, or security guards. I was obsessed. I had dreams of turning tricks for a Snoopy snow cone maker.

I had lay-a-ways at every area K-Mart store because they only demanded two dollars down and ten percent a month till Christmas. I probably spent five hundred bucks in gas driving all over town to pay on them each week. As long as I kept the initial total down low enough the ten percent was doable. Like I said before, I am a financial wizard.

Finally a neighbor kid helped my boys figure out I was more than just Santa's helper—they were crushed. I was so relieved. I felt like a load had been lifted from my shoulders. At least now I could reason with them as to why they couldn't have the entire Toys R Us catalog. Too bad they still couldn't understand.

It wasn't just Christmas that drove me to the edge of insanity. No, for every holiday I would decorate extensively and purchase enough candy to rot the teeth of an entire country. I would dress up for Halloween and be in the kid's school haunted house. I'd tie twenty rubber snakes to my head for the Medusa, or don my wedding dress for the Bride of Frankenstein. There was already some green stuff on it from the wedding.

I had rituals for each holiday especially my world-famous cut-out cookies. I made heart cookies for Valentine's Day, Santa and reindeer for Christmas, ghost cookies for Halloween, bunny cookies for Easter, shamrocks for St. Pat's, and rum balls for me.

Then one Christmas I had a really bad idea: since I was making tons of cookies anyway I might as well sell some for profit. It is amazing how many women hate to bake. My sister took orders at her work, neighbors and friends of friends called, orders poured in like red Kool-Aid over white carpet from a jug with no lid. Before I knew what hit me I was up to my neck in flour and sprinkles. I had to purchase additional bakeware, cooling racks, and an extra fire extinguisher. I baked day and night, freezing them in shirt boxes in my mother's deep freeze. Frantically I rolled, cut, and packed to make the December 15th deadline. I decorated all the boxes and delivered over eight hundred cookies to hungry customers.

When I finally had time to sit down and do the math I figure I could have bought all of those cookies at an uptown bakery for much less. I might have been able to buy the whole damn bakery. I gave up after the calculator had a meltdown and so did I.

Not all of my holiday missions were unrewarding. I once won twenty-five dollars for my Bride of Frankenstein costume and I was voted best room mother at school by my boys and all their mangy little friends. Of course rewards such as these only drove me crazier in the never-ending quest to produce a bigger and brighter holiday than the last.

I thought nothing of doubling our electric bill at Christmas so our house would glow like a nuclear power plant worker. Isn't that what budget billing is for? I bought fireworks with the money I was supposed to use to pay the hospital for one of my many organ removals. What were they going to do, put it back in if I didn't pay that month?

Who's going to pass up fireworks when the sign says buy one get four free? I'd fly a hundred flags for Memorial Day and have a family BBQ for any summer events. Of course the burgers were eighty-percent filler, usually old holiday crackers, so most people knew to bring their own meat. The boys loved getting ready for a big event, especially if it involved smashing stuff like the crackers.

It's terrible when you have kids to impress. The little buggers have really high standards as the years go on. If you put out a giant lawn pumpkin one year, you'd best have two for the next year, and a fifteen-foot ghost. You buy one electric deer and in a few years you've got a whole damn herd stretched across your yard, pulling a mechanical Santa on the lawn tractor. I even made and wore an elf suit for many years. It was very cute when I was younger and in shape. I retired it when I was called a troll.

I think the Chinese are to blame for all the excessiveness; they make all of these other holiday decorations. They ship over all these adorable little figurines. Who's going to turn down a cute hand-painted bunny door hanger for only a buck? Not me.

Somehow, though, it didn't really matter what I did or how well it turned out because those three little words haunted me after every single holiday: "Is this all?" Of course by now I have blown it way out of proportion as I do with everything. Had I just said when Pete asked if that was all, "I guess so? Boy, Santa sucks," the years that followed could have been a lot easier. But no, immediately my mind would start planning for the next holiday's conglomeration of emblazonment. I hated it. No one wants to be lying on a beach thinking of how to run twinkle lights off of your car battery. Okay, my sister might, as she is a total Christmas fanatic. Judi puts up fourteen Christmas trees, one in every room. She starts decorating before the stores do, and I believe earlier I stated that she was the normal one.

I also save every tidbit and snag from everything all year long to save money. Old Christmas cards can be made into new ones, gift bags can be used a hundred times, candle nubs can be melted down into a mold (but you have to buy wicks, old shoestrings don't work). Birthday ribbon can make Christmas bows, coffee cans can make cookie jars, and crushed Easter egg shells, glue, and glitter can make the biggest damn mess you've ever seen.

I was one of the first people to ever wrap my gifts in newspaper, long before it became the chic thing to do. For me it and regifting was just the cheap thing to do. I also wrote in my uncle's birthday card one extremely desperate year, *I'm not giving you any money because you don't need it and I do.* I am still reminded of that. It seemed like a good idea at the time. Little did I know it would be put right up there with *The Beating.*

Since the boys have grown I dream of skipping the holidays just once. I spend Christmas week on a tropical beach somewhere. I lie under a palm tree that doesn't drop needles. My hands are not frostbitten, and I sip on a bottomless Pina Colada. Of course I still set up my manger and wish Jesus happy birthday but the rest of it just passes me by. Of course I never do it. Instead every year I dig out the five hundred Rubbermaid bins and curse my way through a thousand hours of decorating, shopping, baking, and wrapping. I send out two hundred cards to people who never send one back, and I make cookies, hundreds and hundreds of cookies to feed to the birdies in February.

Even after the kids have moved out I still hang decorative crap all over the house, obsessive compulsive or syndrome—you decide. I have lovely sets of embroidered hand towels for each holiday, which no one is allowed to touch. Worse than that, I keep buying more, especially for Easter. I fear I have some weird bunny fetish. Along with bowls, watches, stationary, art supplies (though I seldom make anything), and Chapstick.

It boggles my mind how far I have gone to make my kids happy on holidays. I used to think it was appalling that Jehovah's Witnesses didn't celebrate any holidays, not even birthdays for their kids. However, when I look back on all the work, the millions I spent on gifts, all the eggs I colored and hid, candy I bought, balloons I blew up, costumes I made, and pumpkins I carved I should have never slammed the door in those people's faces. I should have converted.

Chapter 13

Getting Away From it All

Vacations can be a wonderful thing for some people. It can be a time of relaxation, family bonding, exciting new adventures, or a real pain in the ass. Almost all of my feeble attempts at *getting away from it all* were a huge pain in the ass. I don't mean to sound vulgar, but "butt" just doesn't describe my vacations.

To this day my family will fondly reminisce and laugh about our first camping trip. The brand new tent flew off the roof carrier. As we watched backwards in horror, speeding semis reformed the poles. We pitched something that resembled a tarpped jungle gym. My poor mother got her hands burnt from trying to heat and reshape the poles, my dad's puffy face never unpuffed, and someone put the BBQ chicken flames out with the pee bucket. The desire to camp is etched in my mind like the desire to eat hot pizza right out of the oven—even though I know the cheese is going to stick and burn the dickens out of the roof of my mouth. Forty years later I still try to go camping and hate every minute of it. I'm either a die-hard camper or a total idiot.

When you're poor you take poor people trips. You drive instead of fly, you camp instead of staying in a hotel, and you eat out of cans instead of restaurants. Even cut-rate vacations sound like an improvement over what you are doing at the time. It's something different, like scrubbing tubs over toilets.

Everyone likes to take a vacation. We watch advertisements for them on TV and actually think it is possible to have fun the entire time. It's what they don't show that we need to see. We need to see the snorkeling family get stung by one of those pointy fishes, the boat leave without them because they forgot to set their watch back, and someone blowing chunks for eight hours in a hurricane! I want to see a family with severe sunburn, five thousand mosquito bites, four butts in three seats on a charter bus, and people sleeping with clothes pins on their noses due to foot odor in a ten-foot-square room. I've never seen people laughing with ear-to-ear smiles all the time on any of my vacations—well, except for a few people on that Blue Cross one.

And, I want to know where are those pretty colored fish, the ones on all of those stupendous brochures that sales agents tout. What fish? We saw four in the entire Gulf of Mexico. You do tend to see a few more when the six-foot waves you're floating in bring up your really bad included-in-the-tour lunch. But, even then they are at best pale yellow, silver, and a sick green, which could be some sort of sea slime. The water is never marine blue either; it's more the color of an over-chlorinated pool after someone peed in it. I can go to the pet store and see more color. Enough stuff can go wrong on a vacation without our being lied to by the graphic artist.

Something always happens to devastate my vacations. It's like a requirement. Just like my sister *requires* a trail ride on every trip. On my first trail ride the horse bolted from a bee the size of Texas and bounced my eyeglasses off. Then the trusty steed behind me pulverized them with his big fat hoof. The rest of the vacation was spent squinting through glue cracks and white medical tape. On our trip to Florida my brother slapped me on the back so hard he knocked one of my contacts off my eye and right out the window of the car. The rest of the vacation I spent like Popeye. I finally figured out to take two pairs of contacts, extra glasses, and a white cane anywhere I went.

Unfortunately, my luck didn't get any better just because I could see. Sometimes one is better off not being able to see what is about to happen. Like when a passing speedboat catches your fishing line. Until all of the line is out and the pole is rocketed across the lake like a javelin, it's a lot of fun thinking you finally caught the big one. A word of warning, let go of the pole.

One fun-filled family getaway I was sent to the hospital with my neck packed in ice for swallowing a bee. It seems that kids are not the only ones who like all the powdered sugar in the bottom of a box of Lemon Cooler cookies. And, to think that my brother almost got the box away from me.

It's always something. I lose something, I forget someone. Customs singles me out because my suitcase is locked. No problem—an ink pen viciously jabbed into the zipper rips it right open. I am then left to arm-bundle my junk through the airport while dribbling a trail of panties, jelly boobs, and the douche bag behind me. Nothing that's not embarrassing ever drops out. Why is that?

I have to say that one of the worst vacations during my

single years was with my then-best friend Sandy. She moved away. This was somewhere in the hundredth year of child-rearing. We decided to go to Gulfport with a bunch of her friends and the National Guard on a maneuvers weekend. They weren't much on maneuvering, I have to say up front. We found a sucker to take the boys and skipped out of town fast before they could realize what they were doing.

We drove her car because it was slightly better than mine. Little did we know until about three hundred miles later that mine was better. We left in the wee hours of the morning to avoid traffic and headed off down Highway 55. Sandy didn't want to leave before sunup as she had worked till one the night before. But I assured her that it was the right thing to do because my father always left before it was light out while we all slept. Bad thing was, I forgot my dad wasn't there to drive. I did get a few catnaps in but the horns kept waking me up.

As the sun rose so did the temperature on her poor old Duster. We stopped for a cool-down and lunch out of our economy-packed cooler. Thirty miles down the road the old Duster was starting to blow some steam or smoke again so we pulled over and let her cool down. After ten cooling stops and about forty miles gained we decided to find a service station to find out what the hell was wrong.

By now we were questioning our friendship, as we were both about as hot as the steaming engine. I had remembered some words of wisdom from my dad: that little tip on running the heater to pull heat off the engine. This didn't help us much, but it did get us about four extra miles per stop for the Duster. It was about 110 degrees outside that lovely August day.

We had slowly inched our way into Mississippi and, no offense, but they don't have much to look at besides trees on every side. We took the first exit we saw and ended up in a very run-down minority neighborhood, where we were the minority. We decided we needed to remove the thermostat from the radiator, because my dad had said they could stick and can cause intermittent overheating. We both agreed we had to be firm and stand our ground, as we knew what a service station could do to traveling women.

We filled our pockets with devices of defense: a mini can of pepper spray that hopefully Pete hadn't emptied on Repete, and a metal nail file. Sandy walked up to Mr. T. and barked out her orders to remove the "retardor cap it's stuck!" He smiled a golden toothy smile and drove off with the poor little Duster. We sat quietly on the side of the curb trying not to look white. It was easier for me than Sandy as I tan—she just got pinker with more spots as the sun blazed on.

After about three hours Mr. T. returned with his bigger brother who seemed to think our situation was extremely funny. I'm not exactly sure what he was saying, as all their parents' money must have gone into his brother's teeth. We nodded along as he spit and slapped his arms and thigh in a very rhythmic motion. I kept a firm grasp on my pepper spray deep inside my pocket as Sandy clung to my back poking my spleen with the file. Still spitting Snoop handed us a bill—we wouldn't be eating much the rest of the trip. I whispered to Sandy to get in the car, start the engine, pick me up, and leave just my side door unlocked. She was gone before I was done talking.

Both men just stood and stared at me as I handed him all of my cash. It was apparent I wasn't getting any change back because no one headed in toward the register. I told him to keep it as the Duster peeled out raising a cloud of black smoke. Sandy raced to my side then past me as I yanked on the locked door screaming out words I'd rather not put into type. Two hundred feet away from the station she realized I was still running alongside her and slowed enough to unlock the door. We drove like a bat out of hell back to the interstate for a good forty minutes until it overheated again.

Lucky for us we had picked up a few extra gallons of water at one stop so we cooled her down, filled her up, and inched our way to Gulfport. To this day I have never experienced such unforgiving heat. Our eleven-hour trip took seventeen and a half hours. Hell no longer scares me for I have stood on the face of the sun in Mississippi.

When we pulled into Gulfport we were no longer speaking, saturated in perspiration, and determined we would never set foot in the Duster again. Naturally since we had missed the check-in time by over six hours, our room had been sold. We got back in the Duster.

We drove up and down the strip until the Duster overheated again, added some dents, and then started walking. We crossed into Biloxi with blisters on our feet looking for any room with a shower. At this point the ocean was starting to look good enough but it was apparent that we both feared our actions upon each other—actions that may later be regretted. People were out on the strip laughing and having fun. I wanted to kill all of them.

Finally we found a room on the top of the Holiday Inn that was not being used because the AC was broken. We begged they let us use it, as all we really wanted was a shower. The manager finally agreed to rent it for full price, and offered to give us a window fan to use. I demanded a discount! Sandy slapped me upside my head so I gave her a vicious monkey bite on her upper arm. The desk clerk broke it up. We showered and went to bed.

The rest of the vacation pretty much followed suit. We'd plan something and it wouldn't work out. We'd plan a day at the plantation gardens and it would rain enough to raise Noah's Ark. We'd agree to meet the gang at Murphy's Bar and Grill, and they'd all be at Milley's Bar and Grill. Pre-cell phone days—you were just screwed. We'd walk out onto the beach with plates full of yummy nachos and walk back with excessive gull pecks and empty plates. We'd eat shrimp at a cheap roadside stand. We'd spend the whole next day in the bathroom regretting the two dollars we saved.

As if the drive down wasn't bad enough; I tumbled down a flight of steps, was stung by some bees, and lost my credit card. Sandy had a little better luck. She was only burnt to a crisp the first day out. Including her eyelids.

One morning we got up slightly hung over. Okay, most mornings we got up hung over, but it was only to ease the pain of the adventure. As always, half asleep, I guzzled down a big glass of water then filled the sink to splash my face. Oddly enough the water was a peculiar brown color next to the white porcelain. I called the front office and they informed me not to drink it as there was a little problem. And yet, another day spent in the bathroom. I should have bought stock in Pepto-Bismol before we left. It was the *longest* vacation I ever went on, but fewer days.

Fortunately for us a few of the guard guys managed to fix the Duster so we did have transportation home. We left at night just to be safe, no sun, no overheating. I drove first as Sandy said she had a terrible headache. She snuggled in the backseat for a nice long nap while I ran with the truckers. I was on a mission. Occasionally I would slap myself in the face to stay awake. Occasionally I'd beat the crap out of myself for even trying to *get away*.

Ten hours later I crawled out of the Duster somewhere outside of St. Louis as the sun was just coming up. Sandy finally woke up and agreed to drive for the last twenty-eight miles. I wanted to punch her in the head but my joints were locked in a sitting position, so I slugged her in the kneecaps and we headed home.

For our second trip we borrowed someone else's car and only went as far as we could walk back in four days. It appeared to be a pretty good plan but then we decided to take the boys with us and well, it was downhill from there. The friend who was supposed to watch them wised up and moved away.

We started off the trip with a flat tire in a torrential downpour. A flat tire to two women and two kids is like a land mine to a marine. I know how to change a tire, but they put the lug nuts on so tight you can't get them off without one of those power wrenches. I see the theory but the way I figure if it just fell off, it would still be easier to change, even if you had to put the wheel on a few times.

Having fun on a vacation with kids is another pipe dream. No matter how much you plan or spend it will suck most of the time. They will never want to do the same thing at the same time. That would be just too easy and bring joy to the other sibling. They will dispute every word that comes out of your mouth and act as if you have purposely taken them to Hell to be punished. Perhaps if you have a male figure on the trip, with a club, it may be different. However, two women alone with two boys is a recipe for disaster. When we walked out of our house the boys were looking at us like Pit Bulls sizing up bunnies.

There are a few things you should do before leaving for an auto trip with kids. First you need to shave their heads (averts hair pulling). Everyone should wear a cup. Females should wear three. If they say they will ride in the back of the truck or station wagon it is a blatant lie. Forty miles into the trip everyone will be in the front seat with you. Leave the plywood in—they can talk though the air holes. If they object, always offer the trunk or roof carrier as an option. No matter how much of their crap you drag along they will lose interest in it in less than one hour so only take handcuffs and gags. Sedatives if you have access to some. Only buy one flavor of soda and one kind of snack; trust me on that one. A full can of cream soda bounced off the back of the driver's head can cause devastating detours. Never take bubble gum or leave home without Jack Daniel's.

Once you have reached your vacation destination assign sleeping arrangements before anyone enters the horrible rusty aqua trailer you rented sight unseen. Make sure that everyone realizes you are out in the wilderness where screams cannot be heard and animals will destroy the evidence. This will avoid additional repair bills and keep the boys guessing for at least a while. Give this speech while holding the ax.

Fill every available container with water just in case. Chop down any trees or brush in a one-hundred-yard radius of your campfire pit. Tie cow bells to the outside of the exit doors. Keep the car locked at all times and the keys around your neck.

Never rent anything: boats, jet skis, go-carts, or horses. Someone will be whining the rest of the trip that the other guy got to ride for four extra seconds even if it was just disembarking time. (This explains why they wanted stop watches for Christmas.)

No amount of restitution can compensate the slighted child except some form of amputation to the other. Let them walk and swim, that is why God gave them legs and arms.

Don't waste your time on cultural museums. Kids don't want to learn anything. Roadside attractions are better for kids. A giant alligator to climb on beats a million years of

Egyptian history hands-down. Never, go to a live alligator farm with male children.

Never roast marshmallows on fully extended wire coat hangers; they tend to bounce with any form of movement, and by morning your campsite will appear to have been a flyby zone of Raptors. Keep a spatula in your hand at all campfires for easy removal of hot marshmallows on bare legs. Never leave the campfire without adult supervision—something will explode when you return. It may be something you need to get home.

What is it about boys, fire, and explosions? I can't really blame my boys because they were taught by the best, my brother, Uncle Pyro. One year down at the lake my brother found a ground bee nest and proceeded to instruct my boys on how to rid the world of them. First he poured a can of lighter fluid into the hole, and then he carefully tucked in a brick of firecrackers (lucky for us it was the Fourth of July). He then added just a dash of white gas and a few bottle rockets for the visual effect. Truth. The boys stepped back a few yards guided by my fist grasped firmly on their collars as Uncle Pyro dropped a match into the small hole. After the smoke cleared and our hearing came back the hole was ten inches in diameter and the bees, two small bushes, and the neighbors' kitchen fly, were no more.

"Cool! Look for another bee hole!" Pete and Repete yelled.

Wear earplugs and drink heavily until departure time.

Take pictures of the accommodations you are staying in so that the owner can't blame any *extra* broken windows, gouges, or holes on you. Take a large airtight container to store tennis shoes and rank socks in while you sleep. Old holiday popcorn cans work well. Still, put the containers outside in case someone knocks the lid off sleepwalking. No one wants to die in their sleep like that.

Don't let anyone eat pork & beans!

If you are a slow learner like me, let them each take a friend along just once. I assumed that once they were teenagers it would be safer, as you no longer have the fear of returning a swollen or fried baby to some once-trusting parents. If the parents of teenagers are offering to pay good money to take their kids with you, the liability fears drop significantly. But, it doesn't hurt to get a liability release form signed. All parents of male teenagers will eagerly sign it. I've signed many.

Some of the preparation rules will have to be altered unless their kids like the Kojak look. You will have to allow their friends to bring games, magazines, and music but be sure to remind them that, when away from their parents, it can accidentally get knocked out the window while still in their hands if it becomes a problem.

Everything else you do should be referred to as a "game." *The Lock Down* game, *The Can Houdini Escape* game, and my personal favorite, *Who Can Get Home First if They Are No Longer Riding in the Car* game. By referring to all forms of containment and retribution as games it averts the parents and Family Services from getting all over your back later on down the road. "Oh, for Pete's sake, we were just playing a game!"

However, at this point of trying to get away from it all, you have unknowingly abandoned all forms of rational thought, honestly believing that a friend for each will eliminate fighting. Thinking a vacation will be battle-free is like a fantasy with the *I Can't Believe It's Not Butter* dude. Before you back out of the driveway you will have a vision, and following through on this procedure will totally avert the desire to ever vacation again.

I've learned it's easier to have fewer expectations when leaving for vacations: plan for the worst and be pleasantly surprised when it turns out bearable. It's not just me. My friend recently e-mailed that she was taking a trip with her sisters and mother to Hell. When she got back home she said, it was only Purgatory. I've been there too.

After I had experienced enough journeys *through the valley of death* and my second-to-last friend abandoned me, I decided to stay home and only do day trips. When Six Flags opened up in Missouri I took all the boys. The ride there was brutal but once we got out of the car they vanished. My heart leaped for joy. My wallet and I had a wonderful time napping in a small restricted area right behind the Screaming Eagle.

It was an awakening, and the birth of my own little *mini trips*. From then on I'd turn the boys loose in amusement parks or malls and when I picked them up four to eight hours later I felt like a new person. This might sound like the acts of a careless mother, but believe me the other people in the mall were in more danger with my boys there on the loose.

Of course before you release them you must give them the *be good or else* speech. Remind them that all they own was bought by you, that you gave them life and can take it away, and that you will not bail them out of jail or post bond ever again. Remind them that there are two of them being released and if there is only one when you get back you will make it none. I usually frisk them too, just to be safe.

When you need to get away, you need to get away. That's the problem with parents today: they think if they don't include their little darlings in every activity they do they aren't being good parents. Parents and kids both need time alone. My kids always loved to see me go away. Still do.

Chapter 14

Making a House a Home

I've always thought that making a house nice and homey was very important for my children. If everything else was unstable around them they could at least come home to a nice, clean, place that felt comfortable and safe. But now that I look back on it, it was a total waste of time.

No matter how much effort I put into decorating and fluffing our surroundings for that warm and cozy feeling, Pete's room made us all want to move out. The top of his dresser reached the ceiling with sticky crap piled on it. The bed legs were suspended three inches above the floor from sticky crap stuffed under it. We never had a bug problem in the rest of the house; they all hung out in Pete's room, as it was a veritable smorgasbord. The closet looked like a chunk of compacted trash with sleeves, and anyone scrapping for aluminum would have hit full retirement funds on the empty soda cans wedged into spots a gum wrapper wouldn't have fit. It was the way he liked it.

I must have spent a couple hundred thousand dollars over the years on anti-stink devices. I had extension cords with just six Plug-Ins on them. That kid's feet could knock a buzzard off a shit wagon and it's never gotten better with age. I always passed out if I got in too close to inspect them for some sort of disease. His pediatrician moved away with one of my friends when I made an appointment to go in for a diagnosis. I tried to explain to Pete that even though socks have two sides like T-shirts you can't wear one side one week and the other side the next week. I'm also sure part of the problem was their size; the kid wore size fifteen shoes in the eighth grade. That is a lot of space to grow stuff. I know what you're thinking: *and you divorced his father.* Not everything is genetic.

No matter how much I begged, badgered, or bludgeoned, Pete would not keep his room clean. I tried giving incentive allowances but he'd look around and say it wasn't worth it. I have to agree. I threatened taking things away, but I couldn't find them. I cleaned his room when he was gone as promised. By the time I regained consciousness, from the smell, it was a mess again. I even hid some of his favorite things in hopes that he would clean it up to find them. He'd just go out and buy another one. That is a trait he inherited from Dick. Dick couldn't see a pile of papers, junk, and trash on the living room floor if you knocked him into it with a lead pipe. He'd grab a broom and pole-vault over a pile of his dirty clothes before he'd think of picking them up. How can anyone put a cigarette out if the ashtray isn't even visible under the mound of butts and ashes? I once asked Dick, "Do most homes have a five-inch mound of ashes on their coffee table?" He replied, "Not if their wives empty the ashtray." See why he had to go?

Repete, however, is just the opposite. He was a neat nick like me. His room was nicely organized, carefully planned out and preplanned for rearrangement on a regular basis. His clothes were color-coded on hangers and his bed was usually made unless it was Sunday and he was washing his linens. He did have a few anti-stink devices but only in defense of wafting fumes from his unwanted neighbor. Sometimes he would change socks three times a day.

My boys were the true example of night and day differences. Pete never wanted to be outside, probably because the video wires wouldn't reach that far. He was a bookworm, and a seriously addicted Star Wars junkie. He always had food on his clothes and proudly referred to it as shrapnel. I called it speed-eating. Nothing was ever his fault.

Repete was a sports jock, an outdoorsman, and a true social butterfly. Repete was always impeccably clean, and ate with the manners of a dignitary. If I didn't know better I'da thought Repete wasn't even Dick's. Nothing was ever his fault either, their only similarity.

I guess when you have more than one male child God likes to mix it up a bit so you don't blow your brains out five minutes after the second delivery.

Wherever we moved I gave the boys' free rein on decorating their rooms. We'd paint, paper, put up decorative shelves, new curtains, and purchase the appropriate superhero bedding and accessories so that their room was their own special place. The first time Pete moved into his dad's I was appalled at the living conditions given to his own son. There were no walls to paint—the basement had never been finished. Nails sprouted from bare two-by-fours and bed sheets in various stages of deterioration hung around a ten-foot area. The rest of it looked just like the mess he had at my house. The basement's perimeter resembled something out of a Vincent Price horror movie and smelled so vile from assorted leakage you couldn't even smell Pete's feet. Pete was good with it because he had a TV to play video games on in his... room? Mind you, he sat in a pile of tires to play them.

It's hard to live in a house where two people are so very different which is precisely why Dick had to be relocated years before. I'm building a case here. Sometimes I feel sorry for Pete—he got the worst of both of us. He loves to sit in a recliner and tell wild stories while playing video games just like his dad. Only Dick was spinning yarns while watching football for endless hours. Video games weren't invented yet. Pete is also a shop-a-holic and slightly psychotic, like me. Pete suffers from depression too ☹. Sorry, Pete.

Actually Pete was blessed with many wonderful talents: he can draw beautifully, play music by ear (which is really funny to watch), and sported a 159 IQ in the fifth grade. He has a heart as big as Texas and is extremely entertaining, especially when he slides down the stairs on his belly as the *Stepworm*. Sadly, he never followed through on using any of his talents other than the Stepworm for parties and social gatherings. No matter how much I begged or badgered he'd only put his effort into beating Tetris and Donkey Kong. Every day was a battle of the wills, but after many years I finally admitted defeat, especially after they came out with the Super Nintendo.

After being schooled on my many shortcomings as a mother, Pete packed up his boxes of stuff, unending wires, and (honest-to-God) trash and moved in with Daddy for what was supposed to be the last time. Together they would let nature take its course.

I have been schooled more than a professor at Harvard.

If I tried to write on what I did right, well let's just say I couldn't fill a one-page Post-It according to Pete. I don't mind being called on true errors, like forgetting to pick the kids up after school, or flushing the toilet while they are in the shower, but I hate to be accused of things I didn't do. That really makes me want to do them, especially if I'm going to be blamed anyway. Regardless of proof, Pete cussed me out again, and left to find greener pastures.

Repete was in Heaven after he meticulously fumigated and sealed off Pete's room. He and I hung together and spit-shined everything we could get our hands on. After time I found out that Repete may very well have been innocent on quite a few occasions of misdirected retribution. Maybe I needed glasses for the eyes in the back of my head too?

When I first started out I had very high standards for each of our homes. I'd even take on another job if it meant being in the right place with the standards I believed the boys deserved. I always planted flowers wherever we moved, even if it was just a small patio garden of potted plants. I always hung lots of family pictures, the kids' awards and the little brass handprints. I carefully placed out objects of endearment and memories. By our ninth move I was stabbing Wal-Mart buck bushes in the ground and tossing out stuff like a dealer at a blackjack table. Sometimes I'd just leave the whole box labeled "family treasures," out, on a lace doily of course. It was just going to get packed up anyway when the next travesty hit, causing us to round it up and ride on.

There is something about a single mother with two boys that brings out the worst in landlords. Maybe it's the holes in the walls? And there is also something about single mothers and vandalism. Some punk kids with parents in Tahiti vandalized our car almost everywhere I moved. I used to key my own new car just so the little brats didn't get to do it first. Of course once the little darlings found out what a psycho, whack-job, nutcase I was when riled they usually directed their energy elsewhere in the neighborhood. Unfortunately they had to hit me once, before they realized how viciously unstable a financially strapped single mother can be.

One thing that I was always a stickler on was that we would have family meals together, even if I did have to hose the walls down after the boys were done. When I was growing up we always had dinner together. It was a great time to communicate, make plans, bond, and kick my brother under the table. Maybe it was inherited but, I am still hell-bent on bonding around the table. Though, I could achieve better bonding results by dousing us all in Super Glue. Maybe the boys thought I said, pounding?

Every Sunday I would make an extra-nice meal for the boys and myself with lofty hopes of growing closer together. As long as there was food on the table things were pretty good, but as soon as the plates emptied, names would start to fly along with any rinds, skins, and non-edible items. As the years passed I conceded to drive-though meals taken to a park. It saved my dishes and fed the birds before the boys shot 'em with BBs. A Last Supper of sorts.

It's amazing how during the many phases of your life things that were once very important suddenly lose their sheen when you've packed it up eleven times. Toward the end I was selling off stuff faster than an auctioneer at an estate sale. I sold a beautiful twelve-piece place setting of fine china for fifty bucks and a case of paper plates. Crystal vases, hand-knitted linens, and a blob of silver went at garage sales for pennies on the dollar just so I didn't have to move them again. With just Repete and me we didn't need a lot of dishes because now no one was hiding them under the bed or down the side of the sofa. The two of us had learned to be efficient on a minimal amount of stuff.

Even after each child picked a place of semi-permanent residence I found myself keeping an extra room fully stocked for Pete's weekend visits as he had to sleep somewhere. Repete could tell instantly if his mangy brother had stepped foot in his room. Alarms and booby traps were installed which made even me think twice about delivering his laundry on a weekend day.

My icebox was filled with the appropriate snacks for when Pete would sit in front of my TV all weekend and play video games. Repete would leave reluctantly to spend the weekend in Playtex gloves and a facemask at Daddy's. As each boy would waltz through the revolving door I would try to make amends, with extensive bribery, for all of our numerous faults as divorced parents. The boys sucked it up like a frosty cherry slush on a hot summer day. We were the poster family for dysfunctional.

Why is it that people act like a dysfunctional family is something that was created in the last decade? Hell, families have always been dysfunctional, people just didn't go on national talk shows and brag about it. If your spouse was having an affair it was kept quiet, if your daughter had three babies by six different guys you sent her away, and if your uncle was only ten years old you called him your cousin. Nowadays people can't wait to spill their guts to the world on how they messed their lives up. Hey, and if you really want to see dysfunctional families, read the Bible. Seven hundred wives, what the hell was King David thinking?

By the Nineties the boys were into girls, cars, and music. I was nothing more than a... well, a mother, the same thing I had always been. Their home was nothing more than a place to stash their crap and grab a snack. Even so I continued to do my job faithfully. I would set up Christmas trees, hang lights, Easter eggs, and ghosts in the trees (not all on the same holiday). I'd sprout flags and red, white, and blue bows out of the potted plants and stick cut-out hearts everywhere. I always decorated our home with festive signs of each holiday. Chevy Chase had nothing on me when it came to celebrating a good old-fashioned family Christmas. Repete and I had ten thousand lights on a trailer!

When they bothered to come home they were always welcomed with their favorite baked cookies, special events planned, and a whole lot of attention. I washed their clothes, bought them new clothes, took them to lunch, took them to dinner, and took them to the show until it was no longer cool to sit by me. Then I just gave them money to go with their friends, sat alone, and dreamed of bonding with them.

I sat through rain and sleet with PMSing mothers at hundreds of sporting events. I went to all of their school affairs and returned home alone waiting for my darling babies' arrival...While I waited I baked more cookies and made up little signs to hang around the house to enforce their greatness... Around 2 A.M. I froze the cookies, pitched the signs, and went to bed.

I helped them buy vehicles, I put gas in their vehicles, I helped them repair their vehicles, and I even loaned them my vehicle. I bought an ugly station wagon so that would stop. I even let them park in the garage or driveway. That's the kind of mom I was.

I bought homes with pools they didn't swim in, yards they didn't play in, and extra rooms they rarely stayed in. We built clubhouses, sandboxes, and workout rooms. I housed many a creature so that they would know the joys of having pets as a child. We had dogs, cats, hamsters, gerbils, flying squirrels, more cats, fish, turtles, large river frogs, more damn cats, and a snake (but only for a very brief stay: in the front door and out the back). Together we built them elaborate pens and cages they were never in.

I hung all their creations on the icebox until the hinges started to give way. I wore a giant paper daisy pin and macaroni jewelry to public places with great pride. I fell over so many bicycles it's a miracle I still have shins left. I tolerated hundreds of other people's rotten kids because I was the only mother that allowed them to play inside my house. I made fifty green Rice Krispy Christmas trees individually decorated at 3 A.M. after work, only to have them called torpedoes.

My kids played me like a fiddle and I sang along like a canary in a cheap gilded cage. One little smile, one little hug, one little "thanks, Mom" drove me onward like a bull running in a fresh water stampede. Until one night, with a glass to the wall, I overheard a conversation to, "heap on some guilt...throw her a bone," and something about an excellent reproduction of my signature. I had been duped.

I really thought I was making a good lasting impression on them. Building something between us that made us one. I thought they would look back on their lives and feel loved and protected. I thought that someday they would remember me as a great mom. And what of all of this effort do they remember today?

"You always blamed me, you never blamed him." Good God, what a waste of time!

Chapter 15

Cursed or Just Unlucky?
You Decide

I've decided to condense my misfortune into one itemized chapter. Otherwise I would have had to name this book *War and No Peace*. I'd hate for you to miss any of the highlights. I've also shared with you some of my painfully experienced knowledge. Hopefully you can learn from it. Unfortunately most of it still hasn't sunk in all the way for me yet.

You'll see that I've haphazardly categorized and subcategorized a few of my best mishaps, sucky luck, and bizarre beliefs so you can be inspired quickly and easily. If this part of the book seems confusing...welcome to my world.

I've had such bad luck in my life that I rarely even notice disasters anymore. If water is pouring out my front door, I just go around back without blinking an eye. If smoke's blowing out of the hood of my car, I just turn on the wipers. I do stop for flames. If I'm alone, I have no desire to move when everyone else is panicking in a public place. If someone screams, "bomb!" and bodies scatter, I calmly put my head between my knees, thank God, and kiss my ass goodbye.

I'm not sure of the cause for most of the problems in my life. They say you make your own destiny but I don't believe that. Who would do this to themselves? Well, here. You be the judge.

Friendships: Not pretty. I have a way of repelling people, though I have not yet figured out the actual repellent agent. All but one friend I've ever had has moved away. (I wonder about the one that hasn't.) Every time I find a person I like and start to build a friendship they pack up and move away. Oh sure, they have a reason for moving: a husband is relocated, better job offer, a warrant; the point is they have all still moved away. I even warn people now: unless you want to relocate you might not want to take this relationship any further. This pretty much stops the phone from ringing after I begin listing each friend's destination. Hell, even my pen pals move away and send no forwarding address. Come to think of it, I've had mail recently returned to me, by the post office. I sent it to the boys.

* Never climb on things if you are unlucky. Broken ribs are very painful.

Health: I wish my mother had taken an extended warranty out on me because I've been throwing spokes worse than a Honduran-made bicycle. Just to list a few ailments: I've got acid reflux and I've never done hard drugs. IC, Interstitial Cystitis, which means my bladder is full of cracks and holes (my liver I could understand). I've got IBS, irritable bowel syndrome, which means don't eat anything if you got to be somewhere early the next morning. Asthma: don't breathe either. No hormones from a total hysterectomy at age twenty-four; the only surgery I really appreciated. It was period to the periods by taking out the nursery but leaving the playpen in. However, the playpen doesn't assemble as quickly as it used to, which might have something to do with the absence of hormones.

* Cleaning-chemical fumes do have an effect after many years. Follow the precautions on the cans.

I'm blind as a bat, my teeth are bad, and I have a normal body temperature of 97.1 and am freezing cold 24-7. I am ADD, dyslexic slightly and. In 1997 I was rear-ended by a real super cool '79 Mustang reaching mach speed between two stop signs. Four of my neck vertebrae were sent flying and never seen again. The chiropractor is my best friend. I was dragged behind a boat for an extended length of time before anyone in my family noticed I was no longer skiing. My left arm is now two inches longer than my right.

The only time I had a big boob some know-it-all doctor cut the fibroid out instead of my request to transplant half on the other side. They grow really fast and after all it was benign. I like to grow all sorts of odd bumps when I haven't anything else to do. All have been surgically removed and most were undiagnosable. Doctors do a lot of head-shaking around me. My left side has bursitis in my shoulder, tendonitis in my elbow, carpal tunnel in my wrist, and arthritis in my thumb. Guess which hand I use? I've had eighteen years of blood-vessel-busting severe headaches, but when the boys finally graduated from high school they dissipated. I suffer from depression ☹.

Weight Loss: My advice is to stay single, and don't go

to a real college. You will never make enough money to get fat. Don't get married. Men make you fat. Have male children. They will eat everything not nailed down leaving no food for you and run off every ounce of meat you put on. (Though I advise against this method.) There are hundreds of diets, methods, and pills on the market if you're already fat. The best method I have found that never fails is, don't eat. It costs nothing and it works every time. I like to diet after I lose a job.

*Never buy anything without three extended warranties.

Employment: Please refer to the previous chapter, "Entering the Work Force"—no use reliving it all again.

Income opportunities: You know how some people can be made an offer, jump in, and walk away with a pile of money? I'm not one of them. Let me tell you right now, there are no envelopes to stuff, but I can sell you a flimsy pamphlet (i.e. book) for thirty-five bucks that tells you how to scam other people. You don't need the postal worker's book to take the postal worker test—I got one you can borrow. You do need a friend at the post office. Assembling crafts at home I'm pretty sure makes the same book the envelope stuffers do, because they look a lot alike. Base pay after rejected work, supplies, kits, shipping, and "other charges" just like on your hospital bill is somewhere in the area of thirty cents an hour. Not bad if you live in a third world country.

Pyramid schemes are illegal no matter what your sister, boss, or preacher says. Putting out flyers and phone books should be illegal and under the sweatshop category. If you have to send money first, don't; it gets very expensive. The lawyer is a liar, the money chain letter won't work due to human greed. Why send the two dollars to each person on the list when you can put your name on for free. I'm sure

I'm the only person out eight bucks. Refuse to buy uniforms until you are sure it is legitimate employment, it is a hideous wardrobe you won't get any wear out of.

*Don't gamble if you know you are unlucky, salt in the wound.

Love: If you really love someone and all is right with the world, he will cheat on you. If you're only with someone because you haven't time to find someone else, he will be the most loyal and caring man on the planet. If you are with no one because you have put yourself in a time-out, men will crawl out of the woodwork to ask you out. If you finally know in your heart you have found your soul mate, don't marry him. He will be taken over by a poltergeist within a year or less. If you are unsure if he loves you, test him repeatedly. It's all a test anyway and men accept this system. If you have to make him ask you to marry him and buy your own ring... I can't believe I even told you that.

*Never invest if you are unlucky. Bury it, but remember to make a map. Leave a Post-It in a very obvious place for when you move. Some people won't let you dig up their back yard later.

Homeownership: Never buy a house with someone else, especially if you can't make the payment alone. Never put the money down on a house with someone who has no money; he will after you're forced to sell. Put everything in writing and sign it in blood. Never buy a house that is a fixer-upper unless you can actually fix things. Never buy a house with a friend if your friends move away. Never buy a house on a busy street with big old trees. Never buy a house with plumbing especially with a creek nearby. Never buy a house if you are single. Never buy a house built over an old lady's bones—weird shit happens. Never buy a house! Let someone else buy it and just crash there.

*Never drink when signing any binding legal agreement.

Renting: Never invest your money in property you are renting; this includes cleaning. Do not take your children with you to avoid eviction. Never rent a trailer pad, it is not considered eviction if you can take your seventy-foot home with you and live on the side of the road. Never have a joint lease with a psycho boyfriend, or a friend that moves away. Never move into a two-bedroom then sneak in two kids over the age of six—it's a double move. Never sign a lease, never *don't* sign a lease, never rent month-to-month. Leases are for the landlord. Never assume you have a roof over your head when renting. Move south and set up a tent on the beach.

Education: Pay the money and take the degree.

Vacations: Don't borrow a car that is in worse shape than yours just because it is bigger. Don't assume it has a spare tire and jack. Don't travel further than you can walk back. Don't eat anywhere where the sign says "Eat." You may save money but it's a long time before you can get back on the road. Don't get in your car and drive until you hit the ocean, turn and hit the next ocean, and so on. Your job won't be there when you get back. Never go out West. Don't eat Spam. Always pack fully stocked extra luggage, check one, carry on one, and mail one to your destination two days before you leave. Never take teenagers to Disney World. Never take teenagers in canoes. Never take teenagers on vacation. Stay home and send the teenagers away.

*Never take in a boarder without a full background check; even little old ladies.

Vehicles: Always check the trunk before purchasing a vehicle from a private owner. Never purchase a vehicle from a private owner who is leaving the country that day. Never purchase a vehicle from a private owner with only a post office box. Never purchase a vehicle with an agreement that they will repair something before pick-up, especially a small knocking noise. Never purchase a vehicle if it takes thirty minutes or more to "warm up" or if they have it running when you get there to see it. Never pick out your kid's car—the curse still applies. Always get a written statement from a salesman and make him swear on his mother's life with two witnesses.

*Only buy used cars from your father.

*Never deliver something wrapped for someone you barely know, even if they give you gas money and it's on your way.

*Never give your ex husband a break, unless it's between his chin and shoulders.

Men: Avoid men who need a lot of maintenance. Most men need very little though they rarely smell as good. Steer clear of men over the age of thirty living with their mother, unless you want another kid. Don't let men talk you into reproducing, it's a trick, observe the animal kingdom for verification. Get everything in writing with witnesses. A side-by-side icebox is a good trade for sex, ask any wife. Don't let him talk you into anything without running it past your lawyer first. Beer is an appendage of a male, if you can't accept that you might want to cross over to the other side. Send yourself cards and flowers. Men for the most part are liars; don't trust them further than you can toss them. If you are a trusting person by nature, date very petite guys.

* He will not change.

Child rearing: Don't reproduce. If it's too late, never buy or allow anyone to give you Legos. Never buy or allow anyone to give you Dr. Spock's baby book. Follow your heart and federal law. Don't waste your money on toys, get big boxes out of dumpsters. Save the money for your retirement when they grow up and leave you all alone. Duct-tape your toilet lid down for the first five years of life. Give 'em a bucket to use until they understand the theory of plumbing. Pets teach kids nothing, except reproduction at the most inopportune times. Always have Ipecac syrup and fire extinguishers handy. If you have more than one child try to space them out, about thirty years, to avoid sibling rivalry. Accept the fact that you will always love them more than they love you. Pray for mutes. Try to have girl children—if you don't try to do a switch-a-roo in the hospital. Trust me, boy children are just little *men*.

*Don't try to be a stepmother. Don't try to be a friend. Do be a spoiled girlfriend, you're going to get a bad rap either way.

Hobbies: Never go into a hobby thinking it will make money if you are cursed. You will know. Never take up hobbies because your friend suggests it if you know you are incapable of doing it. Do not take up hobbies that may be an unfortunate one-time event, like rock climbing or white water rafting. Adult diapers are a good investment for these sorts of hobbies. Don't try to do crafts if you have no artistic talent. People will laugh at your finished product. Don't keep trying to garden and grow things if everything turns brown. Buy plastic, no one can tell from a distance.

*Don't buy lottery tickets. Give the buck to charity, it will look better if you ever get to Heaven. Odds of sixty-six million to one are not good odds, but the chances you will answer to God are very good.

My Credo: Stand up for what you believe in and always tell the truth, unless it's going to get you fired. Principles won't pay the bills. Fight hard for the causes that inspire you until somebody gets hurt, and then pull out fast. Don't write too many letters to the White House—you will be put on a watch list. Always get even first and then repent. Remember, your family will never leave you no matter what you do. If you really mess up, just move away. A stupid look is as good as a long explanation. Change your mind often; variety is the spice of life. Trust in God, love your country, and give to charities even if the CEO is making a couple million a year—God will get him later. Talk to God often or He may forget about you and leave you here forever. If at first you don't succeed, give up.

*Always follow the instructions on lighting a gas grill. Do not get close and look into those little holes in search of the flame. Make sure the cat is clear.

In closing this heartwarming chapter I would like to say that not everything is bad all of the time. I've had some good times, even with my kids. Once we were out shopping and found a twenty-dollar bill on a parking lot just blowing around. We were all so excited. That was a good thing because when we got back from chasing it, I had a flat tire to have fixed.

Once I sold a house and actually got some of the money I put down on it back. That was a good thing because the next house we purchased cost three times as much.

One summer in nineteen years Daddy actually came to take the boys on a trip for two weeks of vacation visitation time. That was a very good thing until he called two days later to say he was bringing them back home due to some sort of mental breakdown. It was hard to hear with the child bride screeching like a banshee in the background.

*Never leave town and trust your ex to keep the kids for the time he says. Family Services do not like children sitting on a front porch for twelve hours while you race home from Florida.

I've also had a few lucky medical breaks, though medical people tend to define the word lucky with a lot less expectation than I do. They considered me lucky that my broken rib did not puncture my spleen when I dived off a five-foot fence. The fact that I *almost* had a nervous breakdown was also considered very lucky. I guess I'da hit the jackpot had I made it all the way? They considered my egg basket growth lucky, as it had not yet spread onto any other vital organs. The large blood clot that followed the surgery was classified as unlucky which I considered lucky because I got an extra week off before I had to go back to scrubbing toilets. I also consider the results from my psychiatric testing not resurfacing later in life, as the doctor had warned, very lucky. They had no comment.

*Never try to do a cartwheel when you are over forty.

And never, ever, write a letter to your mother-in-law if things are not going well.

Chapter 16

The Bag Lady

My parents own some lake lots. For the first ten years it was a fun place to go with the kids and it was cheap. All we really needed was some food, well, actually a lot of food for the boys, and a tent. Everyone else in the family has a trailer on one of their three lots. I was usually lucky to have a roof over our heads at home.

One Memorial Day weekend we headed off down to the lake with one of my boyfriends in tow and false hopes of having fun. I have a theory about Memorial Day weekend because it always rains: tears from Heaven in honor of all of our fallen soldiers. I used to think that God hated picnics and camping as much as I did so he flooded them out each year. I think the soldier theory is much better.

Anyway, we headed off down to the lake in the boyfriend's new car, with AC and tunes that actually worked. Not that you could hear the music over the boys bickering in the back seat. About five miles into the trip the rains came, not that it hadn't been a foreboding sky when we left. It was. We'd leave in a hurricane if we had plans; no one wants to tell their kids "we're not going." It rained so hard we had to pull over at one or two points. Yet, we drove on with lofty thoughts of sunshine any minute. The lying son-of-a-dog weatherman had promised sunshine for most of the weekend. Never believe a lying son-of-a-dog weatherman, especially on Memorial weekend.

When we got to the lake it was a hassle to get in as always: names don't match, car plate discrepancies, visitor passes instead of family passes, head count is off. However, after we were all frisked, our car searched, and everyone fingerprinted we drove onward through what was now just a light sprinkle. There used to be a very low concrete bridge of sorts over a spillover into a creek that fed into the lake. Above the mini-bridge was a mountainous gorge about equal to Pike's Peak. As we approached the bridge we noticed water running over it. I panicked. The boyfriend carefully proceeded to drive into the water stating it couldn't be more than a foot deep. It was more than a foot deep. The car died dead center and we all sat there staring at the boyfriend.

While I was shooting daggers toward the driver's side of the auto I noticed a wall of water coming down the mountain toward us. That was the first wall of water I ever saw. It's quite amazing to see how quickly a wall of water can move. It actually looks like a wall, too. I just gazed stupefied at it while it made its way down the pass and on to the side of our vehicle. Mud water slammed into the car knocking us sideways toward the spillover creek, which was now rising quickly. I panicked. The kids bounced around in the back seat like pinballs. The boyfriend frantically ground his starter down to a nub. Everyone screamed.

By now water was up to the top of the door and we were becoming a bit buoyant. Water was slowly seeping inside. The boyfriend continued to grind frantically. Quickly, I opened my window and instructed the boys to climb out and sit on the hood of the car. We had gathered quite a large crowd of yelling onlookers. Three buff biker dudes waded out into the rapidly raging water and lifted Pete and Repete onto their shoulders and carried them to safety. I climbed out the window next and told my boyfriend it's been fun but I'm not going down with your ship. Obviously he was, as he clung to the wheel, grinding, begging, and bawling.

People began to make a human chain, steadying another burly dude with tattoos and a Confederate doo-rag on his head. Carefully he made his way out into the rushing current. Frantic I wrapped myself around his head and clawed at his eyes while he battled the raging water. People pulled and yelled as he struggled to carry me to the blessed, semi-dry land. The boyfriend sat alone, his panicked little face stared at me in terror, as he continued to grind on. What is it about men and cars?

The water was now pouring over the hood of the car. The surge was too strong to wade into. Another boyfriend down the drain. I decided to run for help when Pete turned ghost white and screamed, "Holy shit, all of our food is in the trunk!" No food and my boys could lead to cannibalism. I started running. I've never run so far and so fast in my entire life. Naturally the rain picked back up to help weight down my clothes and make it more slippery in my ninety-nine cent pair of China-made thongs. They broke after three falls and twenty yards. Soon my mascara had run to my chin and I expect someone may have called in a Bigfoot sighting. I kept running. I fell into a creek and I slid down a muddy hillside full of bad bite-bites. It was almost impossible to see through my contacts now covered in triple-thick waterproof mascara. Every now and then I would have to stop, blink repeatedly, and try to get my bearings. Then I would run some more.

When I finally reached the street their lots were on I started screaming with what little air I had left in my lungs. Everyone stood silent and looked confused. Finally, I believe my sister recognized me. When I saw myself in the mirror later I understood why no one else did. It seems a lot of mud had splashed up on me by passing cars that I assume thought I was out for my morning jog. Otherwise I'm sure they would have offered me a lift.

Wheezing, I staggered into the campsite, garbled out a few words, then collapsed into a nice muddy section of grass. The men folk raced off with tow chains to see what was left of the boyfriend. Turns out, the water quit rising and the same burly dudes that carried us all to salvation helped pull out the once-beautiful Cutlass Supreme the boyfriend owned.

When they finally got his car towed to the campsite the inside was completely flooded; the glove box was flooded; the trunk was flooded. Fruit drinks and frankfurters were floating in the trunk due to the water wall jolt that knocked open the cooler. The suitcases weighed four thousand pounds and dribbled water all the way into the cabin. The tent was floating in *a can-of-rotten-corn* smelling water. Cheap generic rotten corn. The smell never went away. The boyfriend figured it was wash down from the cornfields on higher ground. Whatever it was it stunk like rotten corn. To this day I cannot stomach the smell of a can of corn.

We tried to dry things out but it never really stopped raining. Every time anyone tried to put on dry clothes the sky would open up with tears, tons of tears. We mooched our way through the weekend for any supplies that didn't survive the flood. Which was pretty much everything we brought. I'm sorry, but I can't eat a steak that smells like rotten corn floating in mud water. Call me crazy. The only good thing that came out of it was free bait. Yep, seems a few minnows were on the water ride and were thin enough to fit through the cracks.

Since I didn't have any dry clothes I cut three holes in a Hefty thirty-three gallon trash bag and tied a rope around the middle. They are actually very warm. I wore a trash bag for three days and was given the honorary title of *The Bag Lady*. At a later camping trip I was given as a gift, by my Aunt Jean, an industrial drum bag to use as an evening gown. Twenty years later my aunt still loves to tell the story of *The Bag Lady* camping trip.

There were no campfires that weekend. For some odd reason they don't burn well in a torrential downpour. There were no s'mores or the yummy smell of stick-roasted weenies, just that damn rotten corn smell everywhere we went. Naturally we all drank heavily to sustain us through the weekend. We weren't smart enough to go home. The kids had a great time. Rain doesn't affect children. They swam. They were going to get wet anyway. They hiked to collect frogs, trying not to drown in the grass. They made small paper boats and floated them in the yard. They fished. There was no need for a bucket. You could just let your bait and catch swim around next to you. They fought; there are no weather restrictions on bludgeoning your brother.

At night the boys bunked with Uncle Richard in his tiny trailer. The boyfriend and I slept on an old sofa sleeper inside my parents' cabin; one can't drive tent stakes into water and expect it to stay put. The bad part with sleeping in the cabin is everyone comes in to use the only port-a-potty. So, while you are lying on a quarter-inch piece of foam that barely covers an iron bar that runs straight across your spleens you get to enjoy wafting aromas and be awakened by a thousand apologies.

About midnight, when everyone's bladders were empty, we got another unwanted visitor, a cricket the size of a Clydesdale. E'e, E'e, E'e, relentless E'eing droned on. I buried my head under the pillow, but apparently he had a Dolby Digital Sound system. E'e, E'e on and on...It was soon apparent that one of us had to die. I rose and turned on a small light so as not to wake the boyfriend, who had finally stopped crying over his new *carn*. I sought out a fly swatter and followed the blasted E'e's. With swift blows I beat the entire cabin and everything in it, gouging deep into every corner with great gusto. I listened... silence finally fell. I went back to bed.

As soon as I had the iron bar situated right where I liked it... E'e. I flew out of bed and graduated to a broom. I ransacked what little remained of the cabin desperately trying to silence Jiminy. I listened. I swatted. I listened. I threw things, I cursed, and I listened again. I moved around the one-room cabin like a cat on a moth. The boyfriend began to snivel again, probably because he was hit with the broom a few times. Silence finally fell, well, except for the dripping of broken bottles. I waited a fair amount of time; he'd tricked me before. It was hard to see in the dark but I think he was lying dead in the middle of a box of pancake mix. Ah. I went back to bed fifteen minutes before my mom came in to start the morning coffee for everyone.

The boys were extremely unpleasant the next day, as it seemed Uncle Richard had snored like a grizzly bear the entire night. Uncle Richard stated he wouldn't have snored if he had not had to breathe through his mouth, due to a clothespin on his nose. I believe he said the boy's foot odor was *caustic*. I know that smell; exactly why I chose the iron pole in my spleen.

No one was in a good mood the next day. My brother's trailer leaked, my dad was digging trenches most of the weekend, and my sister had to sleep with her husband. Everyone was soaked and all the women gave up on even trying to apply makeup. Hence, we were all in an ugly bad mood. It was hard to grill because the torrential downpour kept putting out the fires we barely got started with wet charcoal and five quarts of lighter fluid. When we finally got something cooked to eat, well, it all tasted like lighter fluid. We should have just drank the lighter fluid. The boat sunk in the yard.

Oddly enough, no one headed home early. We all stayed there and toughed it out because we are stupid. When it was officially time to call the weekend over everyone staggered off to his or her vehicles, haphazardly chucking in moldy soggy crap, while praising God that it was over.

I had to drive home as the boyfriend was in shock. It was his first trip to the lake and he didn't believe me when I said it was par for the course on a Memorial weekend. Of course we had to drive with the windows down because the rotten corn smell had intensified in the humidity. It smelled like corn casserole. It wasn't a problem to drive with the windows down because as soon as we were all finished packing up the sun came out in all its glory.

Okay, the windows down were a bit of a problem as it caused a slight *sea spray* out of the vents and off the dashboard. I felt kind of bad for the boyfriend, though I had offered to take my car before we left. I was more in fear of damage from the boys. My car has been flooded many times, as the boys usually forget to roll up the windows. I just tried to think of it as a free interior cleaning. The boyfriend didn't talk much on the way home. He'd occasionally squish around on the seat and pat the dashboard, start sniveling again, and open another beer. The men folk donated, with great sympathy, a twelve-pack to him for the ride home. I had to stop halfway for another one.

We never go anywhere on Memorial weekend without a box of Hefty trash bags. The kitchen size make nice T-shirts, the small basket size can create some stylish rain bonnets, and they all come in a variety of potpourri scents now which really helps with that rotten corn smell.

Chapter 17

More Child Rearing...

I can't believe that parents today want to home-school all of their kids. The first day of Kindergarten was like passing the parole board for me. Yes, school presents a lot of challenges and problems as they mature and their imagination develops, but it has to be better than doing *life* with no hope of even an outside work program.

School has many phases, and most of them are annoying. When the kids are little it's little things like fifty hats and pairs of mittens lost, when they get older it's sixty-dollar books misplaced and detention for whistling at the teacher.

It's hard to believe, but lunch used to be a big problem for us. Normally food and the boys went together well. But, my boys hate beans, any kind of a bean. Their preschool loved to serve beans, green beans mostly. Green must be a terrifying color to little kids. Every day we'd have a battle going to school because there might be a green bean on their tray for lunch. It didn't do any good to tell the teachers they didn't have to eat the green beans because *everyone* has to eat their green beans. I even requested they save my boys' green beans and I would eat them when I picked them up. No, each person had to eat *their own* green beans. Changing daycares didn't help because every school offered green beans on the curriculum. This reminded me of the great spinach battles my father and I had growing up. I finally yielded to end the lunch trauma. I decided to take the boys with me to clean, all the time dreaming of the first day of Kindergarten.

When they finally entered the educational system things started to look brighter, but not for very long. Pete is a very intelligent boy, and was bored with school most of the time. To stimulate his brain and destroy mine they introduced him to the violin. "Twinkle, Twinkle, Little Star" is now a death march to me. They introduced him to all sorts of extracurricular activities, most were detrimental to the surrounding neighbors and me.

Another problem with schools, and I've noticed it hasn't gotten any better with time, is *the bully.* I was lucky because back in the Eighties kids just beat on each other with their fists. No one would have thought of bringing a gun, knife, or a bomb to school. Unfortunately bullies were still a problem. Some second-graders can really pack a punch, especially if they were held back a few years. No parent wants some punk beating up on his or her baby especially when they are small and not yet trained in the art of Kung Fu.

In the old days a parent could touch someone else's kid. Heck, we could touch our own kids with no fear of being sued. I recall one particularly mean bully on the boys' bus—the bus was another problem but I won't get into that right now. Little Jeffery was a big fat bully. He liked to punch on everyone but especially on my Pete. Every day Pete would get off the bus with red marks all over his face. Pete tried to hit back in self-defense but *he* was instructed there was no fighting allowed. How come the kids defending themselves are always the one reprimanded? Another brazen blunder of the justice system.

Almost every day poor Pete would get off of the bus pink and puffed, with tears welled up in his eyes. I talked to the bus driver, who said, "They are all beating the hell out of each other. I have to drive the bus." I talked to the principal, who was apparently afraid of Jeffery Sr. so his only suggestion was to drive the kids to school myself. Unfortunately I was at work when they were on the bus so that wasn't an option. Out of frustration I was forced to take the law into my own hands once again.

When the bus arrived and Pete got off puffed from punches I boarded the bus and yelled out, "who is Jeffery?" Sixty-seven kids pointed to a red-headed little punk twice the size of Pete. I walked to the back of the bus and grasped him firmly by his Polo shirt collar then raised him out of the seat. "If you don't want your mom to see your face on a milk carton in the morning, quit hitting on my son! Do you understand?" Jeffery swallowed his tongue and nodded in agreement. Everyone on the bus cheered and the bus driver tried to slip me ten dollars on the way out. Two hours later I received a phone call from Mrs. Jeffery to inform me that her husband would be by after work to kick my butt. I told her to "bring it on, babe! I'll put your whole family on a fricking milk carton!" He never showed.

Poor little Repete had a lunch bully. You know that kid who makes his income off of your kid's milk money. He also takes everyone else's food, pocketing his own lunch money to secure an early retirement. One morning Repete took all of the good stuff out of his lunch bag and tucked his PB&J inside his coat pocket. When I inquired why he refused his cookies he hung his head in despair and mumbled, "Why take them—I never get to eat them." It seemed Eddie the lunchroom pillager did. Repete, being *scraggly* as he often referred to himself, wasn't about to be thumped each day over a few cookies. So, I went up to school. I talked to the lunchroom monitors, the teacher, and the principal to no avail. Most suggested I just pack extra so he could share. I was already putting in close to a dozen. If I could afford to feed the whole school, would I be cleaning for a living?

The next night I mixed up one of my world-famous batches of cayenne pepper oatmeal cookies. Repete left the next morning with a devilish grin on his face and joy in his little heart. When Repete got home from school he was still grinning. He said Eddie never left the water fountain the rest of the day. He also told Repete, "Dang, buddy your mom is a really bad cook!"

Repete replied, "You think so? We love our mom's Cajun cookies!" Eddie and Repete became friends after it all; however, he never took any more of Repete's food and refused all of my dinner invitations.

As the boys got older the problems got worse. Repete went into sports and then we had to deal with the bully parents. Many a fight broke out in the bleachers as parents encouraged their kids to *kill* the opponent. I hated sitting in the bleachers with possessed parents. It was bad enough that it was usually raining or freezing cold but you also had to listen to the criticism of all players except their flawless prodigy. I never knew what the outcome of a sporting event would bring for me or the kids: a black eye, a broken foot, pulled muscles, or the best one, amnesia.

One night in high school Repete's friend dropped him off at the front door and skedaddled out of town. Usually they come in to forage for free food so I knew something was not right. Repete entered the house with an odd look on his face. He then picked at his T-shirt and asked, "Why am I wearing this? I wouldn't wear this." I knew something was seriously wrong because he wouldn't wear something that didn't match to perfection. He then questioned how he got home, and thirty seconds after that he repeated, "Why am I wearing this? I wouldn't wear this." I called the doctor, and tracked down his buddy who informed me that he might have taken a severe blow to the back of his head by one of the boys on the basketball team with some anger management issues. We went to the hospital. All the way there I was questioned about how he got home, what happened, and why he was wearing a mismatched outfit. In the examining room he deducted two years from his age and forgot which President was in office. The doctor informed me that his short-term memory was knocked out but that it would return with time. We went home with the same questions, over and over...

The first thing I did when we walked into the house was to rip off that darn shirt and put something on him that matched. We then played *this is your life* for the next six hours. Through the night I slept on the floor by him and woke him every hour to check his pupils with a flashlight. As if they are going to do anything but slam shut when a Maglite hits them? It took him about a week to recover, and the kids at school had lots of fun taking him to the wrong classes and reminding him that he owed them money. I have to admit, I had a little fun myself telling him he just ate. I thought it might bring down the grocery bill a little.

Pete never participated in sports. He found other things to drive me crazy with, usually art and science projects. Sometimes he would dismantle one of my appliances in search of the mystery. Sometimes he would put them back together and sometimes he would make them into other items.

Pete always seemed to get the psycho teachers too. One year we were all at our wit's end with one of his teachers. No chair could be tucked tight enough to the desk, no book could be returned to the shelf properly, no word could be enunciated clearly. I went up to school. I tried to talk to the teacher but I wasn't sure which one of her I was talking to. I then talked to the principal only to find out that she had a little brain tumor going on and was going to teach until she was no longer able to. I felt we had reached that time. Of course once the word was out about her condition the kids had great fun tormenting her. Pete made it through that year with low C's and D's. I'm guessing he had the most fun.

I never stormed into school demanding my child was innocent, because usually they weren't. I can't stand parents that think their kid can do no wrong. The brat could be standing there with blood all over his hands, a joint in his mouth, and three drug-dealing thugs behind him awaiting his instructions. The parents will still say, "I'm sure there is some logical explanation for this. He's a good boy."

Once in high school Repete came home and informed me that a teacher had slammed him into a locker. My first question was, "what did you do?" However, by seventeen Repete towered over me, so my vision was not a pretty one: a big bad burly man beating down a young boy. I went up to school and straight to the teacher's classroom. I knocked on the door and waited to confront him. Out came a tiny woman half my size. As always I realized Repete had left out a few details to the story. When I asked her if she had slammed Repete into a locker she sweetly replied, "Oh yes. Oh, he gave me that *look.*" We both cringed—I know that *look.* The look that says you are a total idiot, and should not be allowed to walk the planet. I patted her on the back, apologized for my son, and left without incident.

School was eighteen long years of problems: green beans, bullies, parents, violin concerts, and soggy sporting events. It was lost lunch tickets and broken school property. It was missed busses and after-school detentions with no bus service. It was confiscated toys, lost books, ripped-up coats, bumps, bruises, and busted bones. It's a miracle they learned anything. It was every childhood sickness known to man, twice. I used to tell the school nurse, "They got it *from* here why the hell can't they bring it back?"

Another fun part of school was always parent participation. It's not that I didn't want to be a part of my kid's education, I just didn't want to work another job with no additional pay. It always seemed that the single parents did the most at school. I guess because of the huge burden of guilt we were carrying. Two-parent homes figured they were doing it all right, no use doing more. Either way I always tried to help out with a few extra activities. Every year I was a room mother busy baking cookies, cupcakes, and green torpedoes. I went to most of the PTO meetings, which I set as Pete's violin practice time. I always went to parent-teacher conferences in fear of early release from the system. I took expensive gifts, groveled, offered a free house cleaning, and promised they would do better with God as my witness.

I know what you are thinking right about now on the instructions issue. If you are a Christian you're thinking God gave us the Bible to follow. Well, I agree it's a great book but oddly enough I've never had anyone coveting my goats or maid servants. Hell, I was the maid. I do try to refer to it. However, in today's society raising kids is a lot more complicated, which leaves me to use my imagination and improvise. Unfortunately my imagination is a bit twisted and the last time I tried to improvise they tried to lock me up. Even twentieth century instructions, written by specialists in the field for child rearing, never seemed to apply to my boys. The little darlings.

I guess if I had birthed girl children it might not have been so trying. Either way I made it through it all and they graduated. This was before the *No Child Left Behind* program. Back then they were all pushed through the revolving doors and shot out the other side, ready or not. Probably why I had to go with Repete to close on his house, and I had to take someone with me to close on his house, and we had to pay a lawyer to make sure one of us was right before we closed on his house.

The apple doesn't fall far from the tree.

Chapter 18

The Fillers of Life

After my divorce I felt so liberated I decided to try a few new things. The first one was Sam. The second was dancing…I did better with Sam, he had a lot fewer steps, though dancing was more…creative. I like to classify extra activities as fillers; they fill up that void or empty space in your life. I don't know why I tend to have void spaces. Suddenly a welcome rest will turn into an attack of total emptiness and it seems to happen off and on throughout my life. Feels the same way between my ears sometimes.

I've tried a lot of different things, nothing great like skydiving since I have a fear of heights; I tend to keep as close to earth as possible. Sounds kind of odd coming from someone rearing to get to Heaven, doesn't it?

I've always thought that someday I would be something better. Hey, even I have an occasional thought of hope. Gee, how many times have I told my kids "I want to be

178

something too, you know!" And how many times have they responded, "but you're our mom." What makes every child think that their parents' only mission in life is to have and worship their kids until their end of time?

I've often seen myself being a great dancer, ever since my sister and I took tap and ballet lessons. I felt I had talent, and I think had she not jumped on my back to help me do a Chinese split I'da probably stuck with it.

I've always envied great couple dancers; they look like one as they move across the floor. Dick couldn't dance, not even drunk. If you can't dance drunk, you can't dance. And, if your partner can't lead it's pretty hard to follow. Thank goodness ballroom dancing is no longer required and you can just kind of move around the room flailing, spinning, or even have a good spasm if you take a notion to. Still something inside me thought I could be the next Paula Abdul if I'da had the right partner. So without any thought, I signed up to learn swing dancing. As for freestyle, I don't mean to brag but I've always been a pretty good spaz.

The problem with swing dancing is there are lots of steps and you are supposed to be doing the same ones at the same time, only on different sides. That may sound easy but it's not if you are left-footed. I did manage to learn the basic steps with my instructor. Unfortunately I was unable to ever reproduce that with another human being. Go figure.

I also took line-dancing classes during the country craze, something made me think I could do better all alone. However, I forgot about my inability to stand in a line for very long. No matter how hard I tried I was always swimming upstream. If everyone was slapping their boot I was kicking, if they were turning around I was running into someone. After much frustration I finally conceded to just being a spaz, though I still tend to do a little ballet after a cocktail or two.

I tried making crafts with my sister. I even took some art classes. We made some really nice looking stuff; it's just that no one wanted to buy any of it. Sure, we sold a few things to family but after the cost of materials, space rental, gas, snacks, and coffee for my addicted sister, not to mention all the crap we bought from other crafters we came out way behind. I think my sister might have done better had she not hooked up with me because my attempts at entrepreneurship usually crashed and burned faster than a SCUD missile out of its Russian shoot. I've since learned not to do any extra activity where the mission is to make money or bring me fame. Not that I really thought I was going to get on *Dance Fever*.

I like to garden a lot but the earth doesn't seem to like me. I can grow some great rocks and weeds. I've actually learned to appreciate weeds as beautiful plants, and rocks are very low maintenance. The first time I tried to put in a garden to save on food costs it was another SCUD. My cantaloupes started out okay and then they all fell over so I pulled them all out, and my corn was so bad the squirrels wouldn't even eat it. It had kernel rows like the teeth of an Ozark hillbilly. The zucchinis were cucumbers—I have no idea how that happened but I was really hoping for zucchinis like in the picture. Rabbits ate most of the rest. I have to say I've gotten better in the last thirty years. I can grow some pretty good tomatoes, if the root rot or cut worms don't get them first.

I like to plant flower bulbs too, but all that cone up-cone down is so confusing; it takes three years before I get them in the ground right. And well, planting from seeds never seems to work either. Usually the dang seeds are so little they blow away while I'm putting them in leaving me the only house in the neighborhood with zinnias down the cracks of my driveway. Of course the ones I managed to plant in the bed never grow.

Sitting in the sun seems to be a good activity for me. It requires no classes or investment, and no thought, making it perfect. Since my average body temperature is around 97.1, the heat is always very welcome. I actually like to get into a hot car in the summer, lay my head back, and just sit there in my own little sauna. I don't do that anymore, not after some Good Samaritan almost busted my window out trying to save me. Apparently I sleep with my mouth gaping wide open.

I like to walk too. Again, not much thought required. When I get out into nature and smell the fresh air and wildflowers and see the towering trees and vast meadows, I love to just let my mind drift away. I can walk for miles. Though it usually does take some thought to find my way back home.

I like to collect things while I'm walking too; don't know why. I have more shells than the Atlantic shoreline. Someday I will make something out of them, maybe a new shoreline? I have lots of rocks too. It says something about your personality if you get really excited about a rock. I have more rocks than the LaFarge Quarry. I also like to gather up dried pods and grasses, not to smoke, but to make wreaths and fall displays for my house. You have to be very careful that a pod is not in fact a nest of some sort, because then you may have some unwelcome houseguests for a while.

Repete and I also went though a stage of bicycling after Pete moved in with Daddy. I have to say that bicycling feels a lot like work. We had really cool-looking mountain bikes, with water bottles and gel seats. All they lacked was a motor. Of course Repete didn't have as much trouble as I did since there's a little twenty-two year difference. We would head off down the Katy Trail early on Saturday morning, peddling along, bonding. When I'd finally catch up with him I'd beg to turn around and go home because my back, arms, legs, and butt were numb. Easy-going, Repete would spin around and disappear in another direction. Thanks to some cute girls with tire trouble on the trail, I caught him again. Wheezing, I begged him to please tow me the rest of the way or leave me there to die. We tied our shoestrings together and joined our bikes. Repete was in training for football anyway so I told him to think of it as dragging a linebacker to the goal post. (I don't really understand football but he fell for it.) I felt kind of bad when a passing mother told her children, "Now look at what those two stupid kids are doing. If their mother knew she'd never let them bike again!"

I also like to drive—it's a lot less work. During the four hundred and fifty years of child rearing I drove a lot. I used to get into my car and speed down the highway late at night while the kids were sleeping; my friend was there with them—I wasn't that bad of a mother. I would race around what is known as the Golden Triangle out in St. Charles County. It's priceless land even God wants to build on; hence the name. It's about twenty to twenty-five miles on each side and takes about forty minutes if you're not doing the speed limit. And let's face it: at 2 A.M. who is? If you roll the windows down and sing real loud to *Holding On to Nothing but the Wheel* it's quite soul-stirring, especially naked...or so I hear.

The only bad part with my mini road trips is that I still felt really fenced in as I never had enough time to drive any farther. But I always swore if I ever got the boys raised and on their own I was going to get into my car and drive until I hit the ocean, turn and drive to the next one, turn and drive to the next one...

I started to get into politics in my younger years before I understood the system which is, if you are not going to be a *politician,* don't bother with politics. Once you cast your vote you are like a used Kleenex to them. Also, after you walk your legs down to tiny bloody nubs campaigning for someone you believe in, they usually change their beliefs when the bribes start to ooze in.

Politicians today don't even try to hide their misdoings, it's like you get extra points for them toward the presidency. Of course with our new pliable Constitution it's easy to make anything work to their advantage. The bad thing is *We the People* have forgotten we have a voice and that our government was set up to be run *by the people.* We have to speak out and demand change. We can't just continue to pull the cart along. We should be bucking and kicking them out on their pompous butts, judges too. Who made them God?

I once met a first-year state representative who had high hopes of changing the country and swore to fight for the little man, he even helped me out on one of my many crusades. Ten months later I saw him and asked how the legislation was going through. The bastard sold out for a case of cognac and a box of prohibited Cuban cigars. I still fight for political issues but usually not on the side of the politicians. I really had high hopes that this guy was going to be our country's first honest politician but if he had I'm sure they wouldn't have let him live long. He may have been privy to that notion too. Mostly I think he served a term to secure that full-pay retirement program they don't pay one damn penny into. Politics, the judicial system, and violins have a lot in common.

I don't understand how some people can be so obsessed with money. I'm not all about money. For many everything has a price. Our leaders have even put a price tag on our country. I couldn't believe it when I heard they actually sold off American land to the Japanese. Didn't they bomb us a spell back? Of course they have restrictions, like it can only be used for golf courses or a seven-acre buffet. That makes me feel much better.

As for money, I like to have some when I need some food or gas, but I don't need a pile of it to make me happy. Well, one might need a pile for gas now. However, I can't understand people whose only hobby is making money, unless of course they are a counterfeiter. I can't for the life of me see why Trump, Gates, and all those other money machines want more. They are billionaires, for crying out loud! I don't even want to win the lottery, not that with my luck I ever would. I can just see all my long-lost friends traveling back for their cut. And family—I don't even want to go there. I know one thing for sure: my kids would be calling again. I do believe that money can buy happiness; it sure seems like it for the people who are taking it away from me.

Religion I shouldn't really put in the filler category because it actually means a lot more to me than an extra activity. Actually God means a lot to me. I need someone in control. I just find religion very confusing, frustrating, and for the most part just another big money-making enterprise. That term *not-for-profit* has to be the biggest misdirected meaning ever construed. I mean if the CEOs of charities are making 450K a year, I'd say that's mighty profitable. All they are doing is cutting the pie bigger for them so there is nothing left over to pay taxes on. I can't believe that the average pastor makes over seventy thousand a year plus a pile of benefits. What about that humble, simple life they preach to us? I hate to be preached to when I know the preacher is giving me one of those, *don't do as I do, do as I say,* sermons. Then he goes home in a Hummer and I go home in an eleven-year old Sunbird with the muffler wired up.

Mind you I'm not talking about TV preachers, they are far worse. I once got a letter from a TV preacher after I mistakenly called in for a free booklet. In his picture the preacher sported at least a three-carat diamond stickpin on his lapel. The ring on his hand made Liz's rock look like a sand pebble. He promised a big return from God if I sent him a sizable donation. The more I send the more I get back. That's never happened to me, the only time I sent a TV preacher twenty bucks I was twenty bucks short from there on out. I sent back his free booklet instead, and wrote on it, "lose the stick pin and put your hands in your pockets if you want people to give you money. It doesn't look to me like you need more."

I've tried a lot of religions and seem to gravitate toward Lutheran. Maybe because I was raised that and feel more comfortable there. I do prefer the Evangelical Lutheran Church in America Synod, which is more relaxed. I don't want to condemn anyone else to Hell when I'm not all that sure on the actual rules and system. Well actually, I guess I already have, in a few moments of anger. I'm not a blind-faith person; the Bible has been translated thousands of times by thousands of men. There are many words that can't even be translated into English, and we all know how men hear things. We yell out, "you want to go to the grocery store?" and they unzip their pants.

Dick was Catholic. Naturally in the old days you had to sign your kids' birth certificates over to the Catholic Church lest they be dammed for eternity. I took all the courses but had some bad faltering spots, especially that meat on Friday thing. I hate fish, and no matter how hard I tried every Good Friday I'll be damned if I didn't start out with a nice piece of crispy bacon. After we divorced I went back to being a Lutheran because they are carnivores year-round.

I've spent a lot of time trying non-denominational churches, too, which are kind of nice. I never really figured out their *rules* and no one seemed to care as long as I dropped some green in the basket. They sure are a lot more uplifting and interesting to watch, especially when someone starts speaking in tongues. First time I saw it I thought she was having an epileptic seizure. After the security guard got the emery board out of my hand I was going to shove crosswise into her mouth, the phenomenon was explained to me while I was escorted to the parking lot.

Yep, I've tried a lot of brands and think I will stay with the Christian ones. I figure Christians all believe in the same God and most importantly, Jesus as their Savior, so they are my choice. Men for the benefit of man established the rest of the dogma and rules, well except for the Big Ten. Christians definitely have the best theory. I mean who in their right mind would turn down a free gift of salvation? It is a gift—would you hand back a Christmas gift, birthday gift, or heaven forbid a make-up gift? It's a gift with no strings attached. Life doesn't give out many of those.

I've got a good relationship with God—it's probably better for me than Him. I do tend to get a bit pesky at time, talk too much, and need to slow down. Or so I have been told.

What I can't understand is people following bizarre cults, dancing with snakes, living in a ratty-confined commune, or chanting all day long. I'm done singing after two hymns. I really don't understand this radical Muslim sect either, especially for women. They tell a suicide bomber that if he dies for Jihad he will get sixty virgins when he gets to Heaven. Sounds more like a whorehouse than Heaven to me. And what about the women? If you go to Heaven and all you got to look forward to is being pestered by a bunch of horny men, might as well stay on earth at least you *know* there is chocolate here.

I've also done a lot of writing throughout my life. I wrote for a large community newspaper for a few years as an "Opinion Shaper." I entered a contest and was selected out of over one thousand article writers to be one of the honored twenty-one. That went along pretty good and it was nice to voice my opinion publicly versus just to the family pet. However, after 9-11 I had a slight disagreement on my freedom of speech and how I chose to describe our attackers, so I resigned from my post. I've also written a million letters to manufacturers, false advertisers, institutions, politicians, the White House, newspaper editors, and my mother-in-law. Never write your mother-in-law a letter.

I have a lot of things I'd like to try still but as I age they sound more like work than an adventure. My life seems pretty full, but that might be because it takes me a lot longer just to get ready to go somewhere. I also don't tend to get bored like I used to and don't feel like I have to search for something that is missing. Well, unless I've misplaced it again.

I have taken on some charity work now, which is a lot like work, but they can't fire you. Though come to think of it, many organizations I applied for never called me back after my first day. Charity work can get really aggravating. Everyone has the attitude they aren't paying me so it doesn't matter if I do it right. Nobody wants fifteen cans of lima beans on top of their loaves of bread, or their toilet to flush every time they turn on the garbage disposal, even if they are poor. I've never heard the phrase "so fire me" uttered so many times in my life as when I started volunteering at an area food pantry.

I've also volunteered at a shelter for abused women, nothing funny about that. However, instead of letting me work the phone lines as I was trained to do, they put me in the childcare room while the mothers had classes. Me in childcare—think about it. Well, I guess that is funny. A fifteen-foot-square room with ten displaced children acting out their frustrations with throwable-size furniture and very hard wooden building blocks. Now I know why they locked us in. It wasn't so the kids wouldn't leave, it was so I wouldn't leave. Why would you give very hyper, distraught children scissors and glue? My beautician moved away.

I usually fill some of my empty time with continuing my education. Usually the subjects I take courses on are useless. Though I did try to learn another language a few years back. I can now order at Taco Bell and pronounce the items correctly. I cannot respond to anyone that speaks Spanish to me with anything other than "no comprendo." I'm not giving up though; every now and then I get out my tapes and book and repeat the words I know and practice counting to thirty. Anything after thirty sounds more like Chinese. The other day my cousin wanted to know where the butter was on a buffet, so I asked the entire Latino kitchen staff where the suitcases were. Laughter is a universal language.

I think I'm going to stick with the sunbathing and walking, because they have caused me the least amount of trouble. Unless I get skin cancer or can't find my way back next time.

I read too, who'da thought from reading this? Reading is a great filler of time, especially if it has a lot of big words in it—you get to read the dictionary at the same time. However, I have been restricted on my reading material as some things just fire me up like a weed-eater. No more political scandals; everyone in my family is tired of me harping on the ill actions of politicians. I like to read murder mysteries, but I always read the last chapter first due to my ADD and ADHD. Then I'm bored by the third chapter because I already know who done it. The cats don't like to sleep with the lights on either.

Oh, and I am also an Olympic shopper. I think there should be a sporting event in the Olympics for that. I think they should take our top shoppers and let them all race through a Wal-Mart to see who can get all of the items on the list for the least amount of money first. I think they used to have a game show like that? *Supermarket Sweep*, I believe was the name, but they just snatched and grabbed to see which one could get the most. The trick to shopping is to get the most for the least if you ask me. I have timed myself on a few occasions. I think I could take home a gold or at the very least a silver medal.

As I age I'm not too sure what to *fill* with. Grand-parenting would be a good *filler*, but I don't have any grandbabies yet. Hint. I guess I could take up some senior activities since I did get my application for AARP the other day. But I'm not really ready for napping to be my *sport*. I could take up playing bridge, but that involves math doesn't it?

I like to make and eat chocolate things. It not only fills the time, it fills the tummy. ☺

Chapter 19

The Little Birdies Leave the Nest

For what seems like an eternity you have kids attached to your hip, back, or wallet, and then one day you look around and they are all gone. God, what a relief.

I want to know who coined the phrase *empty nest syndrome*, because I thought syndromes were supposed to be a group of symptoms that together are characteristic of a disorder or disease. My house is finally *in order* and those deadly stank socks that could walk on their own have been completely eradicated. I'm seeing clean and quiet, something I haven't seen since I left my mom's house. How can that be bad?

When my last little birdie was shoved out of the nest, I felt emancipated. I felt like I had done my job and now it was my turn. Little did I know they would fly back and forth on occasion to pick apart the nest for apartment fixings, and still expected me to wash feathers and stuff worms down their throats when they were low on funds.

I think wanting your kids to leave home is a natural process. You want to know that they can stay alive without you should your number ever come up. You want to know if all you taught them had any effect. Can they actually operate a washing machine or still just watch? Do they know where peanut butter and jelly comes from and that you have to pay for it before you leave the premises? Have they ever figured out leaving the door open in extreme temperatures costs you money? How about money: does it grow on trees or not? These are things they have to know when you can't go on anymore, when your back says uncle and your mind says bye-bye.

When I hear about parents that have thirty and forty-year-old kids still living at home I want to just slap them upside the head. The mothers are still doing their laundry, buying and fixing their food, fixing those Easter baskets, and hanging up Christmas socks. The kid is raking in seventy grand a year and mom is still driving him to the doctor. I mean at some point doesn't everyone want a broken bone to heal?

The bad thing with the kids being gone is that now you are expected to be something. Everyone looks at you like, *well what are you going to do now*? I didn't know what I was doing for the last twenty-five years—why do I have to suddenly *be something* now?

It's rather scary to swiftly have your identity stripped from you. You are no longer a multi-tasking personal servant—you're just a person. It's like being forced to take early retirement from a company you've been making widgets for, for the last twenty years. All you know is widgets.

You find yourself alone at the kitchen table with fifty pancakes, three pounds of bacon, and no one slugging it out for it. You race downstairs at 4 A.M. to throw in a load of jeans but all that's on the floor is one pair of panties, two socks, and a dish towel waiting to be a load. You can't stop buying food in jumbo packs or Sweet Tarts at every checkout lane. Panic attacks shoot through your body when a school bell rings as a vision flashes back of the boys left on the school lot over the weekend. You try to sit down but you can't. You must keep jumping up every few minutes.

Everywhere you look you can't find a mess to clean up. Everything you put away stays there, you open the icebox and there's food in it. You check an hour later and it's still there. You lay a dollar on the counter and it never disappears.

So you go back to school again to try to find out who you are and what you should be now that no one needs you anymore. I always sensed a look of put a bullet in my head now when I sat down to talk to a student counselor. Immediately they wanted to sign me up for Empty Nest 101, Basket Making, and Bird Watching. I'm alone, not senile. I always figured they were a real counselor, so why not unload on them for free. Might be why I always got that look. Right about the time they started to nod off they'd jolt and remember they have paperwork for this sort of thing. Quickly they would dig out a mountain of surveys to help me decide what I want to be when I grow up. While they were shoving me toward the door I kept trying to explain that I've taken all of these tests before, especially the ink blot ones. Suddenly the closed for lunch sign is up at nine-fifteen.

I'd like to meet the guy that makes these surveys. I bet he doesn't know what he wants to be either, why else would he be asking all these questions? When taking these tests you must to be very careful because they can be very tricky. They have hidden meanings. Would you rather draw a picture or build a flowerbox? What is more important, happiness or money? Would you rather help people or hurt people? You've got to carefully consider how you answer some of them or you could end up being a politician.

It's not that I never considered finding myself in the four hundred and fifty years of child rearing, it's just that I was usually too busy trying to find the car keys, a homework assignment, or a restraining order. Some things just have to take precedence over others. Every now and then when life piled up on me like a full bucket of rock from a backhoe, I'd sit down after the kids left for the day and Jack and I would discuss the meaning of life and what I should be. It always started out good but by the time Jack was empty I didn't even know I was alive. Hence when I regained consciousness I was still me.

Any free time I did seem to find was usually spent on fighting for a cause. I fought for the environment and to enact recycling and to this day can't throw away a soda can, plastic bottle, or newspaper. I wanted my children to have a healthy planet. Neither of my boys recycles anything unless they are at my house, then they leave it on the counter for me to put into the obviously labeled recycling bags that have been in the same place for seven years.

I've fought for animal rights, renters' rights, landowners' rights, children's rights, and the right to turn right on a red. I've spoken out on over-taxation and under-representation, and I've written more letters to government officials and businesses than my boys got reasons for not calling.

My parents always said I was a fighter just like my dad. He once stood on a trashcan to duke it out with a guy twice his size. Heck, I even got into a fistfight over a bag of potato chips in an Aldi's store. Somehow a lack of conveyer belt space for the impatient woman behind me turned into a food fight, one of my babies being hurt, and a knock-out for her where there was plenty of space on the floor. I'm surprised one of my career survey results wasn't "prizefighter."

I live and breathe principles. I'll gladly forfeit a limb, mine or theirs, if someone steps in front of me in line after I've waited my turn semi-patiently. I can't tolerate wishy-washy people who can't take a stand on anything. I may not always be standing in the right place but I always stand firm on my principles. I'm a true-blooded blockhead.

I've exercised my right to picket, protest, and vote on everything. Neither of my boys vote unless it's concerning the next American Idol. I would like to think that somehow I've made a difference in this country that I love, but I'm in grave doubt that I have. My taxes have quadrupled, our politicians continually top the feats of debauchery by their predecessors, and you still can't turn right on a red in the city. Or so the cop said.

I can't help but wonder why I put so much effort into the things I did when I could have put some effort into me. I wouldn't be sitting here right now drinking a highball, eating popcorn, and wondering what stupid stuff I did to take out and what stupid stuff I did to leave in. What do I want to do after this is rejected? Naturally I will recycle all of this paper I've once again wasted in my pursuit of literary fame, but what should I do next? It's all so confusing. I may have to take a break and discuss this with Jack more intensely.

* * * * *

It's amazing how fast twenty-four hours can pass. Another plus of alcohol: if you have time to kill it can wipe it out in a blink of an eye. You know how sometimes you're very nervous waiting for an important appointment? All you have to do is have a little cocktail and relax, stop worrying about it, sit back, and before you know it you've missed the appointment.

Oh yeah, back to the little birdies. I'm sorry that I get side-tracked so easily, but more people need to observe the sides of the tracks. There are many interesting things there.

I have to say that having kids had to be one of the most confusing and least gratifying jobs of my life. I know many of you right now are gasping for air and clutching your heart while fumbling for a nitro. But, honestly, as I sit here all alone, one son not having spoken to me in over three years and the other too busy to check in once a week—well, it's the truth. I'm in awe at how easily they have tossed their faithful old mother aside. And they haven't even read this book yet.

It's not that I don't love my kids. I do. I just think that having kids is way over-rated. It's a lot of work for a long, long, long time. There are no retirement benefits, no incentive bonuses, no time off, no real vacations, and no pay. I mean, who in their right mind would apply for a job like that? "Yes, I'd like to apply for the slave job."

Yet they are all you can seem to think about only a few weeks after they are actually gone. I mean the real last time they move out, when they finally buy their own house and are tied to a hefty mortgage is a pretty safe bet it's the last time. Oh, the quiet is nice for a while and not doing laundry every day is really wonderful. Talking on the phone without four hundred call waiting clicks: heavenly. Strange kids they don't even know the names of not sleeping in your basement or garage for weeks at a time: much safer. I mean there is a time when you think you have just died and gone to Heaven. After all the years of dreaming of having time for yourself you finally have it. I used to dream of

195

fixing my hair every morning. I used to wonder if I'd ever have ten painted toenails in the summer. But, as I sit here and type I look like a sheepdog after a tornado touched down. I sport six-and-a-half painted toenails because now I forget what I'm doing versus don't have the time to do it. I guess I need to find someone new to blame for my tacky appearance.

So then, what do we empty nesters find ourselves doing now? Now we're dreaming up ways of coaxing the kids to come back out and visit us. I light up like a Christmas tree when the boys stop by to borrow something. I even try to give them extra stuff they didn't ask for. I follow them around like a puppy just waiting for that little pat on the back of assurance that they haven't forgotten me completely. I race to the kitchen and start to make them a seven-layer sub, and then pack it up in a Zip-lock bowl because they don't have time to eat it. Lovingly I pack a few cans of Coke in the bag. And twenty bucks.

As they drive off down the street I start plotting the next reason they should come out. I don't care if they return my new gas grill and I really don't care if they pay back the loans. I don't even care if they bring all of their mangy friends next time and trash my house, just so they come out and see me. It doesn't matter if it's the step-kids or my kids, or for that matter a friend of their friends with news updates that they are still alive.

When the phone rings our hearts skip a beat, our eyes gleam, as we beat each other up to reach it first; it might be one of *your* kids. It's *his* kid, close enough.

Overwhelmed with joy we both grab our hearts to keep it inside the chest cavity. We hang on every word, repeating it to the other. "He wants to know how to shut the water off for the house."

"Shut off the water, good, good. Don't tell him too

much or he won't call back."

One explains the procedure while we both nod and smile with delight. "He thought the main was under the kitchen sink," he whispers, "I don't think he has a big crescent wrench."

"Didn't they take it last week, with the floor jack?" I whisper back.

"No, that was my torque wrench, the ladder, and my new set of sockets," he says, slightly despondent.

I'm overwhelmed. I can't stand the suspense while he searches for the wrench. Quickly I race to the freezer to check for pizza rolls; they might be forced to come out for another tool. Pizza rolls and cheese sticks, maybe? I scrape the thick frost from the boxes to make sure it's not a deadly vegetable inside. "Did he find the wrench?" I yell back while continuing to dig through the big box labeled *Kid Coaxers*.

"Not yet." He yells back, nodding with approval. "He has to go out to the garage. I could run one over to him. I'm kidding. I'm kidding, don't throw anything. I won't even remind him that the Home Depot sells wrenches."

My mind races. Didn't I buy one of them a pair of gloves or was it a hat? It could have been a pacifier it has been so long. Now where did I put it? I stumble into the kitchen covered in frost. "I've still got all these snacks we bought last Easter when they didn't come out and eat; do you think they are still good?" My hands are trembling with anticipation and frostbite. I fumble for cookie sheets.

"Don't thaw the pizza rolls," he says in despair. "He's still got my crescent wrench too."

He finishes explaining the procedure and is quickly left with a dead dial tone. Standing motionless he looks my way and raises an eyebrow: God only knows what he is thinking, he's a man.

"What else did he say? What are they doing this weekend? Did you invite them out? Are they all right?" I hang on his arm like a baby chimp on its mama. "What did he say? Please tell me what he said."

"He said, 'bye'."

Slowly he hangs up the phone as he melts back into the sofa. The hunting channel resumes. I toss the junk food back into the freezer and sigh. "I'm going online for awhile," I mumble. It was close, very close. One almost came out.

"I better go get another crescent wrench in case he loses it again, or if I need it."

"Good idea. Pick up some more pizza rolls, those things in the freezer are petrified."

Okay, maybe it is a syndrome.

Chapter 20

Emancipation Day

After I got my empty nest syndrome under control I realized I had forgotten to do the one thing I had always wanted to do, besides be the Queen of England. It was finally time to get into my car and drive with only the oceans as my boundaries.

When my lease expired on my second apartment I decided to fulfill my one dream of roaming the country unrestricted. See yah, Golden Triangle! I put what little stuff I hadn't sold off into storage. I packed up Little Red— I always name my cars. I have found that they don't break down as much if you treat them like a member of the family. I headed off with my Igloo cooler, Smith & Wesson, and a rubber monkey riding the dashboard for luck. I was totally free and ready for an adventure of a lifetime. As to not break precedence I put no thought into any of it.

The East Coast is very far away and the Smoky

Mountains are very high up for a person with a fear of heights.

The road is a great place to meet the world. You may think you've met a lot of people in your life but you haven't until you have spent thirty days on the road. You find that even a thousand miles from home you have a lot in common with other folks. For instance you all walk funny when you get out of your car after ten hours. Everyone worships a clean rest stop and will discuss the unclean ones at great length while working their kneecaps back into their sockets. No one can describe road construction without using four-letter words and that an out-of-state license plate is like fly paper to a fly for thieves, direction seekers, and radar traps.

I form a bond very quickly with other travelers, with anyone really. My mom looks at me like I'm nuts when I start chatting to people in the supermarket. If I overhear them talking about something of interest, why not join in? Anyone can jump in on a hot-button political issue and who isn't proud of his or her major surgeries. You're not going anywhere with a price check anyway. Why not visit?

Traveling alone for a long period of time can present a few problems. Like trying to play road games by yourself. I see something blue. The sky? Game over. Of course it's always fun to watch license plates while you're driving. We used to make a game out of who could find the most different state plates when the kids were little. We had to replace *slug a bug* when they saw a Volkswagen because they were beating the crap out of each other. God forbid I drove by a dealership; hell, we'd end up in a ditch.

As a writer I decided to keep a little journal on my trip. It's very hard to write while you are driving. I kept little tic marks for all the different license plates I saw; just doing my own little poll of who goes where. If you drive for eight

200

to ten hours a day you start to do all sorts of weird things to help pass the time. Like mooing at all cows, they say that is some sort of an honest-to-God disorder and my whole family has it. I just think it's fun. At least we don't *oink* at pigs. We yell "sue-eee" at the top of our lungs.

Eating on the road can be fun until you get out at a rest stop with catsup packs and fries stuck to your ass and paper napkins trailing your flip-flops. After a few hundred burgers and only the rubber monkey to dine with you have to break down and eat in a real restaurant. I like the Cracker Barrel because it combines my favorite two sports: shopping and eating. The Cracker Barrel is a traveler's stop, so you're not just one out-of-towner in a nest of locals. That can be scary, especially in the South.

Travelers stand out from the locals like a horse in a dog show. We also tend to gravitate toward each other with that telltale, *been-on-my-pony-too-long walk*. They usually all smile and nod after checking out your out-of-state plates. And heaven forbid you are from the same state eight hundred miles from home—it's like a family reunion!

Everyone starts naming off towns and people they know. After you are all amazed that you don't know anyone they know in an eighty-four-thousand-square-mile state, you start the *have you been to* routine. Unfortunately I never ran into any Missourians on this trip. Well, I never ran into anyone, so I guess that is another lucky break I can add to my short life list of lucky breaks.

After only two days on the road I was eager for acknowledgement from anyone. I was in dire need of a real conversation. The monkey had a cup over him because we weren't seeing eye to eye anymore. I poked air holes in it for him. I like meeting new people and I always speak first because, like my therapist says, I can't keep my mouth shut long enough for anyone else to speak.

"Hi, where you from? I'm from Missouri, did you see the big accident back on 157, wow, never saw that many chickens loose before. That was a good stretch between Murphy and Madison and it was nice and smooooooth. Are you on vacation? I'm..." Questions and statements can spew forth from my trap like Old Faithful. It feels so good to talk to someone that could talk back if I gave him or her a chance.

It always seems like they are in a big hurry after I approach them. I guess they need to get back on the road. It's nice to chat for a moment. I no longer feel like I'm eating my chicken and dumplings alone because the woman across the room talking to the security guard and pointing to me is now what I like to call road family. I wave and smile again—what a friendly bunch! Hopefully I will pass her later on down the road, giving me another opportunity to strengthen the bond.

Eating isn't the only thing that's hard to do on a lone wolf road trip. Sightseeing leaves a lot to be desired. People start to move away if you keep nudging them and saying, "look at that, look at that," every time the gator comes out to get the chicken leg. Sometimes it's better to take a tour because tour groups tend to tolerate stragglers better than, say, a rich family from New York City.

The bad thing with taking a tour alone is usually no one is really watching out for you except the bus driver. By the time he notices you're gone, you're gone. I once headed out alone on a walking tour through an old Georgia plantation. It started out all right as the tour guide led us through the vast open fields and up to the beautiful plantation sitting out in the middle of four hundred acres. After her speech the guide gave us free run of the plantation and I was instructed to please just follow the signs by the family from New York City.

I think someone changed some of the signs on me because I headed out to see the old cotton mill and ended up in the gator swamp without any more signs to follow. I was never much in gym class in school but I really surprised myself how fast I could cover four hundred acres that day. A word of warning: Georgia has a flying insect in the swamp areas that could be mistaken for an Apache helicopter.

Not only do I tend to attach myself to strangers, I tend to pick up whatever accent the area is using. I can be Cajun raging with the best of them, cross a county line and without a thought slow down to a southern "howdy partner" drawl. I don't know why that is. It might be another syndrome.

A really big issue when traveling alone is where you choose to spend the night. Just because the front of a hotel is pretty doesn't mean the room is. I'm all for saving money but I don't like to stay in rooms where all the stuff is chained to the wall. Including the spare rolls of toilet paper. I also don't consider a room with two hundred cigarette burns on everything a non-smoking room. I've learned you should always ask to see your room before you give them a credit card. Just asking to see *a* room won't work. And don't settle for a picture of the room because they are just like those colorful reef and fish brochures in the Caribbean. Sometimes you are forced to stay in accommodations that may be a tad below your standards, due to highway hypnosis or a stop on your credit card. If you run into problems don't be afraid to speak up, or write letters to the corporate office when you get home. I've gotten many a refund and valuable coupons for *other* establishments after tormenting them for many months.

Sometimes the hotel is nice but some of the other travelers aren't too desirable. If three wild Hispanic dudes at the pool yell at you and grab their crotches, don't try to communicate back in your rusty high school Spanish. Get back in the car and drive fast and far. You can buy new clothes and toiletries in the next town.

Signs on road trips are also very important to pay attention to. A *run-a-way truck ramp* is not the place to pull over for a picture of the canyon. Signs that say, "do not enter desert" are also very important to observe. Scorpions are mean little buggers. As an American we just assume there is a Quick Trip on every street corner, but when the Nevada highway patrol takes the time to put out a big sign that says "there are no supply or fuel stops for the next 100 miles" you had best take that as gospel even in the States. They don't call it Death Valley for nothing.

I think the worst part of taking an extensive road trip alone is the loneliness. Funny that didn't dawn on me before I left. It's hard to take pictures of yourself, the damn rubber monkey can't spell you on driving, and there's no one to argue with or blame when you get lost. Oh, and I hate it when I won't stop to go to the bathroom. I'd sure expect anyone else to stop when the urge hits me. Unfortunately I tend to set little goals for myself, like I will drive one hundred miles before I stop again. These are usually the only goals in life I can actually achieve so I struggle to drive with my legs crossed just so I don't fail at everything.

You really can't see much of America when you do all the driving. A lot of my photos have the dashboard in them. I like to photograph the *Welcome to Our State* signs. There's just something rebellious about crossing state lines. Probably because when my kids were little my divorce decree said I had better not unless I wanted to wear an orange jumpsuit and be a cellmate to Bonnie "the Bulldog" Bronson.

It's very nice to have a friend or relative to visit on a road trip too. It gives you a break from hotel rooms and they actually want to talk to you. I visited a friend on the East Coast for a week, but that was too much of a flashback from child-rearing years since her kids were still kind of small. If your feet are still going to be stuck in Kool-Aid and have people screaming at you, you might as well stay in the car.

I also stopped off to see my cousin in New Orleans, but it seemed that whenever I showed up her and her husband got into a horrible fight. They finally got a divorce after three of my visits. She seemed happy and was doing well, so the guilt was starting to rise off of my shoulders, but last summer when I went down she and her daughter fought the whole time. I guess I just bring out the best in some people.

Every day on the road is a new adventure, especially if you're as bad as me at reading a map. My whole family was worried when I left because they know I can get lost going to the bathroom. But this wasn't just a freedom ride—it was a chance to prove to myself that I was capable of reading a map. I may not have proved that because a couple turnpikes kept coming up over and over. Georgia, Florida, Georgia, Florida, Georgia...I wish Little Red would have had one of those compasses in the mirror because it's hard to figure out north and south if you're like me and point up and down.

I think one of the best parts of my emancipation vacation was just driving forward full speed with the windows down and the radio blaring all of my favorite oldie tunes. Man, I love to sing along—of course sometimes it causes cars to pull over to the side. But hey, it's less traffic for me to contend with.

After a week on the road everything starts to look the same. That's when I started to wonder why I drove eleven hundred miles to go to a Wal-Mart and eat at Taco Bell. What's the point? That's also when the trouble started because I decided that I was out to experience something different: explore, discover, and traumatize myself bad enough to spend two hundred dollars for one night in a hotel where I felt safe. If you've ever been lost in the heart of a big city where it's not cars backfiring that you are hearing, it's okay to cry.

Here's a good bit of advice. Never pick up a hitchhiker, well, never let them ride inside your car. If they don't mind sitting on the back and holding onto the spoiler it's okay. I just feel sorry for people walking with a gas can on a desolate highway. I always think, *man, how many times has that been me?* Sometimes I still feel sorry for them sitting on the trunk if it's raining and a long way to the next gas station.

Roadside attractions really shouldn't be missed, as they are the epitome of America. It amazes me that someone will turn their entire yard into a rock garden village and people will pay ten bucks to walk through it and see all the crap they collected. A giant donut hole you can drive through to get a donut; now, that's fun. Don't forget to have someone take a picture of you and the monkey out front. But watch out for some places. It may look like a roadside attraction or yard sale but they may just be slobs with a really mean Doberman.

After two weeks on the road, you feel like you are getting into a routine. Drive, eat, stretch, drive, eat, stretch, drive, eat, stretch, and sleep.

After three weeks on the road, I pretty much figured out where not to go. There are signs, you know, you just have to be alert to them. Homeless people sleeping on the street are not a sign that the hotels are full. Antiquated kitchen chairs holding toothless old men along the roadside, sheds with house numbers on them, and lots of three-legged dogs is a pretty good sign you have entered a slum area and need to turn the map around. Never stop and ask for directions. Just keep driving and praying, especially if your handgun is packed in the trunk.

Sometimes toward the end of the money or trip, one is forced to sleep in their car. The best place to sleep is at a well-lighted 24-hour truck stop, or so I have been told. I know for a fact that the side of the road is not a good place, unless you are a light sleeper. It wakes you up fast when you feel your car moving upward. Thank God I didn't have to pay for the tow.

After a month on the road home starts to look pretty good, even if it's only a space at the local U-Store-It. One can only see so many gator farms, eat so many fritters, and sit in a cramped little Sunbird for endless fricking hours before you realize you weren't cut out to be free. Money was definitely an issue too. It was starting to remind me of my honeymoon so I hung a U-turn and headed homeward. I stopped at Graceland, but Elvis wasn't in. I tossed the monkey out somewhere in Arkansas. I was sick of his beady little eyes mocking my every word. I was counting the minutes to see my family and boyfriend. My boyfriend was busy working but I did catch up with him a few days later. This would have been a clue to any other woman, but naturally it didn't even faze me.

I have to say that my emancipation vacation was exactly what I needed to end those blasted dreams where I drive that little wind-up car inside the mouse maze never to reach the cheese. On the way home I started to make something of a plan, and then I realized I had forgotten to tell my boss that I was leaving. Either way, I was ready for a new start in every direction. I was slightly disappointed that I never found myself on the open road as I had hoped. However, I did find a nice pair of shoes. Usually you only find one. Why is that?

I think that getting away to find oneself is possibly one of those psychoses my therapist talked about. I think we're looking for someone other than who we are, and well, who we are is who we are. Unless you knock your noggin on the dashboard going 60 mph, chances are you are going to come back as the same person that left.

I guess I could have stayed home and figured out that I needed a job change and that my boyfriend was a workaholic. I'd probably always have to remind him I was alive. I'd pretty much accepted the fact that my kids were done with me before I drove 3,540 miles. I even learned that on the open road freedom can still feel mighty confining. You really can't go wherever you want, especially in a gator farm.

If I could do it all over again I would, but I would take a van not a Sunbird. I'd avoid Jackson, Florida all together, and dine only at restaurants that have real names not a verb in neon. I'd also not risk my life trying to take pictures while driving—the road looks pretty much the same after two or three thousand miles. The side shots all blur out and the truck drivers are not very understanding when you make them swerve, especially if they are carrying four thousand chickens.

Oh, and I would definitely get me a CB because when we used my sister's on a girlfriend trip it was really fun. After waving to a few good buddies in big rigs, you will have all sorts of road family trying to talk to you. You can toss the monkey right out of the chute.

Every now and then I still get the urge to just jump in my car and drive. But at three fricking dollars a gallon I usually pat Little Red on the hood, curse the big oil companies, and go make a cocktail and some brownies instead.

Chapter 21

Soul Mates or Something Close

I guess I need to back up here for a minute (not uncommon for me). Somewhere between the boys' release from the educational system and my ninth move due to the renters' rights crusade, I met a good man. Mind you, I didn't say perfect. Women who say, "oh my man is just perfect," are liars. If your man doesn't ever get on your nerves, I want the name of the doctor that writes your prescriptions.

As you know from Chapter Eight I've dated a lot of different men. Some I tolerated longer than others depending on what kind of gifts they gave. A few, I thought I really loved. *Thought* is the key word there. I now think that it was more just chemistry. I think people should say I'm *in chemistry* with someone. That way when the chemistry has fizzled out, and it will, you don't have to question your ability to love. Most people flunk chemistry anyway. People take the word "love" very seriously, and after you have loved twenty or thirty guys they start to look at you like *you* have the problem.

In about the three-hundredth year of childrearing I finally gave up on dating. I got a few cats and stopped seeing my therapist; he was never going to ask me out anyway. As soon as I surrendered to going crazy alone, I met Pookie. Love always has a way of whacking you in the head when you least expect it. It was love at first sight for me. How do I know it was love? Because we have passed the usual expiration date for my relationships. I know that sounds odd, but my relationships have an expiration date just like a jar of mayonnaise. After six years you best throw it out or risk bodily harm.

Pookie is the only boyfriend in my life worth naming in this book. Well, Pookie's parents didn't actually name him Pookie, that is my little term of endearment for him. Normally my terms of endearment for men are four-letter words; sometimes a whole string of them joined together.

Unfortunately Pookie didn't seem too interested in me at first. Probably because his ex-wife had him nailed to a cross while she stripped him of everything including his skin. I didn't know he was going through a divorce, so I just assumed he wasn't interested and I'd have to force myself on him like everyone else.

I was cocktailing at a fun little bar named Chippers to help make ends almost meet. I'da rather been tending bar because like I said, as a waitress, I stink. Put me on the other side of the bar and I can't walk and chew gum at the same time, much less serve others. But, they were a nice bunch of co-workers and customers so I made the best of it. I don't know how beneficial it was for my boss or me because some nights I'd take home a hundred and fifty dollars in tips. Other nights after I'd checked out I'd take home a dollar fifty. Those were both busy nights, but I guess it evened out. Damn the math!

Pookie only came in about twice a month and never stayed till he passed out. That was a good sign. I got all the other information I needed on him via my normal methods, though I was a little surprised that felony didn't show up.

I tried to flirt with him but my flirting skills are right up there with my waitressing skills. After a few months passed with little response and a few quick exits, I knew I'd have to trick him in to liking me. (It worked on my kids.) While I was scheming, another cocktail waitress informed me that she was going to make a move on him since he still hadn't asked me out. Pookie was a BIG tipper! After some guy pulled us apart she gave me another week, and I kicked my conniving into high gear.

Thanks to a few of his buddies I found out he was an avid hunter. This initiated a plan. I had just purchased a handgun for protection from a peeping tom that looked a lot like one of my old psycho boyfriends. If he hunted, he had guns, and hopefully he wouldn't refuse my proposal to teach me how to use mine.

Let me stop and say that I like guns, guns don't kill people, people kill people. And, if some weirdo is going to peep in my window and try to pick my locks, this people will kill that people if he gets in. Most people know the rules and yell, "don't shoot" when coming to visit me. As a matter of fact I yell the same thing when entering my sister's house—must be something in the genes.

* Here is the best argument I've ever heard in defense of guns. *If guns kill people then pencils make spelling mistakes.* Think about it: they've banned guns in England and everyone is hacking each other up with butcher knives and planting bombs. The bad guy will get the job done by any means. Might as well have a fighting chance.

Anyway, one fateful Friday night, unsuspecting Pookie

came in for a cold brewski. I raced to his side to make my move. I batted my overly mascaraed eyelashes and begged him to please teach me how to use my new firearm. His eyes twinkled, his mouth watered, his trigger finger twitched. He sipped his beer but remained silent. I leaned in for as much cleavage as I could muster up.

Sunday afternoon he loaded up his boat with an assortment of some of the finest weapons and ammo I'd ever seen. I brought a cooler full of wine, cheese, and my $89 Davis with a clip that jams every time you look at it. We made our way up the river, docked at a sandbar, and commenced to blow up the hillside. While we sipped some fine Missouri wines, Pookie instructed me on numerous safety issues. Well, except for shooting while intoxicated.

My mother was appalled that I would go out into the wilderness with alcohol and guns with a man I barely knew. I figured we were both armed and besides, if I made it back I could trust him with anything. I can. As a matter of fact over the years, I have learned to trust him much more than my own judgment. Which really isn't saying much for him, I guess.

They say it is very important that a man and a woman be friends first. I say if drinking wine from a bottle, discharging firearms, and slamming your exes all day doesn't make you friends, nothing will.

Pookie is a great guy. He's a hunting and fishing fanatic so he's not out at the bars (to the best of my knowledge). And, he's a fantastic fixer of anything. This is his most prized commodity, because repairmen are a single woman's worst nightmare. First off they speak in a foreign language: waternaters and altermiters, flangies, linear feet, and grommets. What the heck is a grommet anyway? I think men use the word "grommet" like we use the word "period" when they want you to leave the area they bring up the grommets. Either way if you don't understand what repairmen are saying you can bet it's going to cost you a lot. They actually calculate the rate by the confused look on your face and the amount of bobble head nodding.

Pookie also has two boys. That makes four. Now if that isn't a recipe for disaster nothing is. Fortunately for us, all of the boys seemed to get along rather well. By well, I mean little or no bloodshed on a regular basis. Usually if there was bloodshed it was drawn by their own sibling, which kept Pookie and me from exchanging words. The only problem was that my birdies were using their wings and his birdies were still at that funny fuzzy-coat stage requiring worms on a regular basis.

If there is one thing I never wanted to be it was a stepmother; I had a hard enough time being a mother. Women who take on kids from another marriage at a young age are either a saint or a sadist. I knew how Pete played Dick and me so there was no way I was going through that in a foursome.

I don't think Pookie was quite ready for me, usually people aren't. Pookie is the hardest worker I've ever known and he makes great money. Lucky for him I had lots of good ideas on how to spend it. He said he wanted to travel and I was ready to go anywhere. I like Jack and he likes the Captain. I also think he is very cute. I assume he thinks I'm okay. I'm going to ask him about that someday when he gets home from work.

For seven years we never mentioned the "M" word, partly due to the traumas of our first marriages and partly due to the possible trauma of having four boys under one roof. Mostly we had fun. After only a few weeks of dating he asked if I would like to go to Hawaii. I was packing while he was still asking. He would rent limos for a day at the winery, and he would take me to dine at places that didn't put your food in a paper sack. He sent me many a dozen roses and gave me a beautiful diamond ring, stating that it meant nothing. He would later regret that statement, as I would require another one for the "M" word. Pookie was as close to a knight in shining armor as any woman could get.

I guess they are right when they say opposites attract. I thought you had to have something in common, but apparently not. I am a very impulsive person and I over-react to everything, even poison ivy and green grapes. Pookie is a very calm person and rarely over-reacts to anything. I never stop talking and he never starts. He hates change, and I can't change things around fast enough. Poor guy learned real fast not to walk though a dark house if I was home all day. Pookie is a very stable man and mission-driven. It's a little too late to lie in the book now, so I will admit that I am unstable and my mission is still a mystery to me. Of course as we have aged we have more in common: we both eat more fiber and like to sit in the front yard and stare.

For a brief moment of instability I did move into his house but I think I moved out less than a week later and back into my own house. It seemed his youngest son had very possessive feelings toward the actual structure, as he repeatedly instructed me to get out of "his" house. I could have talked to Pookie about it, but one of us was always at work. So, I just up and left one day. By the end of the week he figured out I was gone. I'm not going to get into any of his kids—my kids stuff because it's apples and oranges. Fruits is fruit.

I'm not going to say we didn't have some trying times with the boys as that would be like saying prisons don't need bars. But, as long as I had my own apartment to go to when fists were flying or a cop was at the front door our relationship still had a chance.

We took the boys on a few vacations, against my warnings, which frankly marred me for life. Pookie didn't have the same travel rules my boys were used to. As a matter of fact Pookie didn't really have any rules at all. He didn't even have rules for the campfire. He went on the typical male theory that if no one is bleeding nothing is wrong. There was bleeding on every trip.

The Pook and I dated for six years. It's pretty hard not to get your lives tangled up over the course of six years. Before I knew what happened I was keeping his books and putting Ridex in his toilets. One can't keep up on their septic tank if they are at work all the time. Every now and then he'd fix my car or my plumbing, or recarpet my place. Together we were making it through the last couple hundred years of childrearing, never admitting that we might be looking in the same direction for the future.

Every woman, even those who have been burnt to a pile of crispy black ashes, will still gravitate toward marriage. It's always in a woman's mind just like cheating is for men. I think it's because we haven't married this particular man yet. There's always hope, right? A lot like pantyhose: maybe this pair will fit? Yet, they all bind and twist, run and snag, and the darn crotch is always six inches below yours. Between kids and husbands women naturally adapt; we figure if we aren't in the labor and delivery room, it's not that bad and it might get better.

To be honest, most of the time I don't know why Pookie is with me. My bad luck doesn't even seem to faze him, and I warned him. Everything we buy seems to break down and then it's a huge battle for justice. All of our billing is constantly messed up, the plumbing doesn't work, there have been two fires in the kitchen, and our fireplace doors have exploded into the living room twice. His investments go south as soon as he insists on putting my name on the document. The new cars won't run and the grass dies off no matter how much he works and spends on it. Yet, he just keeps working at it. He is a true optimist, and will whistle while he works right up until his arms and legs fall off and his spine snaps in half. I can't believe *he* hasn't moved away.

Pookie suffers better than any male I've ever known. He can sit in a tree for twelve hours, in torrential rain, starving, with seven hundred mosquitoes chewing on him and never say a word. That's the kind of man I need.

We finally married in 1999 when the last kid moved out (not that three of them haven't come back for refueling). I think we're pretty happy. I'm happy. I guess I should ask him about that, but yep, he's at work. That's okay. I'm not.

For six years we were friends and lovers. (That sounds like a song.) For six-and-one-half years (past expiration) we have been husband and wife and that sounds like my next book.

It's not that I haven't threatened Pookie with divorce when I'm in a "mood" as he says. He's pretty much figured out that if he shoves a Dove ice cream bar in my mouth I'm good with him for another six weeks. Dick used to just yell back and popped another can of beer for himself. That's not love. Dove Bars are love.

*Did you know that the man who invented Dove ice cream bars invented them just for his beloved wife? I'd like to meet his wife. Or maybe not?

Pookie is a good provider and I think I'm a good wife. We both do our jobs. He makes the money and I spend it. I went back into my old profession as a personal slave. It just felt right. Some people can't admit their purpose but I can, I was born to serve. My dad even told my sister and me on many occasions to, "Do the dishes because that is what you are for." I guess I should have believed him because I've not done much else and I am still doing the dishes.

I like to make Pookie a bowl of ice cream, and iced tea, and an ice pack in the evening. I like to search for the remote so he can change channels without rising. I like to jump up for the phone when it rings a foot from his reach. I enjoy picking up the hunting magazines, dishes, shoes, and duck calls after he heads to bed. It makes me feel like the kids are still home.

It's funny but when I watch other women wait on their man I think, *man, I'd make that jerk get his own roll of toilet paper,* but then I guess it's just because I'm not in love with *that* man. Though it is kind of fun to watch Pookie hobble to the linen closet with his pants around his ankles.

I am amazed when I look at older couples. They even start to look the same. I don't want to look like Pookie—that's why I shave my mustache off. I also don't want my nose and ears to keep growing until I die. Have you ever noticed how big old people's noses and ears are? Shouldn't they hear and smell better then instead of worse?

My parents have been together almost sixty years now. I'm sure they are soul mates. They are like a hand in a glove, I'm not sure which one is which, and I guess it alternates. Sometimes he keeps her warm, sometimes she keeps him warm, sometimes she rips him off and tosses him aside when it gets too hot. At which time he will go wait quietly in the drawer until she says it is time to be safely reattached. That's really cool because my father has learned the secret to a happy marriage and he proudly tells everyone: it's three little words. "She's always right."

Maybe, Pookie and I are soul mates? I just wonder why it takes you so long to find the right person. I'm really jealous of people who found their soul mate on the first hit.

That's something else I have to take up with God. I mean, if He has my whole life planned out, as the Bible says, did He plan for me to crap out ten times before meeting Pookie? A lot of people believe a good relationship is nothing more than fate. I like the fate theory much better than wondering if it has anything to do with *my* personality or God's sense of humor.

I guess I'm not really sure what soul mates are. When I think of souls I think of ghostly things and Heaven. Pookie doesn't want to go to Heaven. He said he doesn't want to go anywhere where there isn't any hunting or fishing. Whatever soul mates are I think we are it because I've never felt this way about anyone else for over twelve years. Counseling may prove otherwise.

Either way, I love him and he *says* he loves me. Ah, after all these years I still don't trust their species. Some things never change.

Chapter 22

Round Two

May 1, 1999 was the day I finally surrendered to the institution of marriage again. I figured the world was going to end in 2000 so at worst I would have to suffer for less than a year.

I don't know why I thought it was time for me to get married again. Maybe because the trauma of my first marriage was fading out of my memory banks just like account numbers, people's names, and my whereabouts, or maybe I was tired of going home alone to an empty apartment. My boys had pretty much quit coming to see me. They had lives.

When you live alone there's no one to argue with and it's hard to cook for one. How do you make lasagna for one? I hate frozen entrées. They never look like the picture. I once sent a scraggy slice of green pepper back to a manufacturer because it was supposed to be Pepper Steak dinner. The picture showed a delicious plate of steak, rice, and lots of green peppers. When I opened the box it had one slice of green pepper in it. So I wrapped it up in a snack size zippie and mailed it back with the front of the box. I got coupons for three free entrées, though I have to admit I gave them to my sister, the queen of canned ravioli. I didn't want to chance a stuffed pepper.

I don't function well all alone. I needed a warm body to put my cold feet on at night. Sure, I had the cats but they tend to like to sleep high, on your face, or they would make great feet warmers because they sure do keep your head toasty.

I don't know what made me think that Pookie and I would spend more time together if we were married. It seemed like it took forever for him to get off work, ready, and over to my house. I guess I figured we could spend all of that time we spent getting ready to go see each other together if we lived under the same roof. I didn't know he barely spent ten minutes getting ready to see me.

Why is that? Why do men get ready in ten minutes when it takes us the better part of a day? Six hours before it's time to go out I am picking out my outfit and doing my nails. Two hours before it's time, I'm picking out a different outfit and changing over my purse. One hour before I'm in the shower shaving, exfoliating, buffing, regenerating, and moisturizing. A half hour before I'm ripping hot curlers out of my hair while trying to pull up my pantyhose. Ten minutes after I was supposed to leave I'm checking the iron, coffee pot, and curlers for plugging status, again. Twenty minutes after I'm running to the car with my shoes in my hand and three jackets I will decide on later.

Men, on the other hand, watch TV until ten minutes before it's time to leave. Pookie actually has it down to a science. He watches the clock for fear of missing one minute of an *Uncle Buck's Cabin* rerun. When the little hand hits its mark he jumps in the shower and shaves while brushing his teeth. He's got a few scars. Then he gets out, semi-dries off, and digs a Q-Tip in to each ear. Six minutes before it's time to leave he puts on any shirt, black jeans, and one of his two pairs of shoes. He then accessorizes with his one goes-with-everything watch and is in the car two minutes early. That is not fair because he looks as good as I do without all of the work and stress.

Anyway, I decided it was time we got married. Someone in every relationship must make those judgment calls. Of course I had to break up with him before he agreed. I hate it when you have to keep calling someone to see if breaking up is what they really want. This procedure would usually tip off a normal person that the second party is happy where they are. But, I think we've already established I'm far from the norm, and I'm not usually one to give up a battle especially when there is a diamond involved.

After three very expensive limousine-driven dinners, and a slap upside the head, he finally popped the question. I was so happy. ☺

I was determined that this time I was going to be an integral part of my entire wedding, savoring every moment of the planning and event. I was hopeful that this time things would be perfect. Finally, I would have a wedding album without anyone's head cut out of the pictures and Brad Pitts glued on.

However, I found that weddings are a lot more fun when you're young and your mom does all of the work and your dad pays for it. But, lucky for me Pookie was paying and I managed to rope my sister and niece into helping with some of the work.

I felt kind of funny looking for wedding dresses next to

all of the young skinny little girls. They were all butterflies and hope, and it was hard not to school them on the darker side of marriage. But I managed to keep my mouth shut and muster up a little girlish giggle when I ripped the seams out of a two-grand designer McClintock.

I planned my entire wedding, reception, and honeymoon by myself. Pookie was working. My sister, niece, and I tried to attend as many wedding fairs as we could. I wish they would have had those back in the olden days. It's great to see what you're getting beforehand versus having someone deliver a surprise called in from the Yellow Pages. I also found out that there is now someone to do just about everything for you. Wedding planners are great. Boy, do they make big bucks and to be honest, if I was going to pay that sort of money I should have looked her up thirty years ago to plan my life. At least I could have blamed someone else.

There are all sorts of specialty services at wedding fairs too, even ones that make cute little guest favors for a giant fee. I bought a case of bubbles at Carnival Supply and threw it in a basket for under ten bucks. There were even experts to plan your meal. I think I can still pick out what I want to eat. They may be for people on their sixth or seventh marriage because they obviously are incapable of making good choices. "Yeah, we'll have smoked salmon... peanut butter...prime rib and popcorn...Yeah, that's the groom, why?"

The best part of a wedding fair is being the bride. Everyone wants to fuss over you, congratulate you, and empty out your bank account. It is hard not to be gluttonous around the elaborately decorated wedding cakes and free food samples. Of course if one splits their hooves at the fair one won't get into the overpriced gown being altered as we speak.

I cut a lot of corners on my second wedding because to be honest I'm used to pinching a penny so hard old Abe starts to wince. When you're a single mother for nineteen years there's a cheaper way of doing anything, even dental work. Ask the boys.

Of course Pookie gave me free rein of his checkbook to have whatever kind of a wedding I wanted. Family and friends thought me daft for not doing a Hoover on it, but I only tend to want to spend money freely when I can't or shouldn't. Go figure. I even made up my own pickle trays, but I got to eat a whole can of black olives while I did it so it wasn't really like work. Though it was a bit awkward dragging the platter to the church in my wedding dress.

Even though I swore I was going to be involved in every part of my second wedding it still seemed to slip right by me. One minute I was knee-deep in selecting Wal-Mart buck bushes and bows, the next minute the limo was there to pick me up for the ceremony.

Our wedding day went well, to the best of my knowledge—I had to have a few cocktails before the ceremony—against our pastor's advice at the rehearsal dinner. I guess he saw a little problem there. I knew in my heart that I loved Pookie, but it still made me think about that *hot cheese out of the oven* thing.

It turned out very pretty when it all came together. It was hard to picture all the boys in tuxedos without funny glasses and rubber noses on, but they all came through as perfect gentlemen. Well, until the reception.

I did freeze at the back of the church for a moment. I have to say I wanted to run. But with a few words of encouragement from my sister and niece, while they pried my hands off the door, I managed to regain my composure and quiver down the aisle. The moment I saw Pookie's smiling little face I wanted to suck boiling cheese off of a red-hot poker!

I was in love.

The reception went pretty well also, until I got there. I

actually stood up and announced to everyone that "I was there to party, glad they were all there, but I was there to party." I danced the night away and had a great time, right up until the minute I passed out.

Thank God we put those little disposable cameras on the tables for people to take pictures or we would have had none. I only paid for a church photographer, which seemed like a good idea at the time. I do remember snapping one of my parents but the flash was so damn bright I was unable to dance for a few songs. Their picture didn't turn out but someone's big fat nose did.

Here's a little tip. Don't use duct tape to attach your jelly boobs to your chest. They say models do that, but they forgot to tell you that it takes off all seven layers of your skin when removed. If you are going to a tropical paradise and love to sunbathe, stay out of the ocean. Salt water hurts really bad on exposed muscle.

My second honeymoon was much better than my first one was. This time I knew what I was doing and was extremely opinionated about it. Pookie paid for a top of the line all-inclusive resort and how the heck can you go wrong with that? We had a beautiful room with an elevated hot tub, champagne basket, ocean view, and five magnificent dining experiences whirling around us twenty-four hours a day. My hooves eventually split.

We did all sorts of fun tourist things too. I've never been able to do tours because they charge you money. Pookie and I snorkeled, drove little speedboats through the mangroves, and climbed to the top of a big pile of rocks the Inca-dinka Indians made. We shopped everywhere and I got to buy anything I wanted. That's when I knew this man would never get rid of me.

Ten days is not enough time for a really good vacation. I think we should work ten days and vacation 355. Of course we would all need huge pay raises.

I really liked Mexico. I don't know why all of their people are leaving to come and live here. Where do they vacation now, in Mexico?

My second honeymoon was the best trip of my life. Sure, a few little things went wrong, like a third-degree burn on my bones where the duct tape was. And, getting lost in Mexico when you don't speak Spanish is a little scary, but at least I had someone to run with me this time. And then there was that little "don't drink the water" issue. The Mexicans swear it's all the tequila we put in it but I'm not so sure because I drink whisky.

I mean if you're going to nit-pick over every little thing that happens, like being dropped off in town fifteen miles from the hotel with only your scuba gear, then you're never going to have the best trip. Walking in flippers can be very tricky though they are better than no shoes at all on extremely hot rocks.

When we got home Pookie even carried me over the threshold of our new home. Well, he tried, he does have a bad back and I did have a good time at all of the twenty-four hour buffets.

By now all of the boys were out on their own. I planned it that way. It was just the two of us walking into a pile of wedding presents and the nicest house I've ever lived in. I even like the flooring: no shag carpet. No carpet, new hardwood and ceramic: it pays to marry a flooring man.

Pookie went straight back to work, so I went back to work at a different branch of that major department store I mentioned before. However, it's very hard to get up and go to work each morning when you don't need the money to stay alive. When I calculated that I was only capable of making one dollar to his five hundred I decided it was more important for me to stay home and be a good wife and housekeeper. At this point in my life, liberation is more of a *not* having to prove something issue. I started to gather in a few stray cats, bought a few reams of paper, and settled in to be the domestic goddess/writer I'd always wanted to be.

He seemed so happy that I didn't work outside the home, probably because it cut the bitching in half or better. When he came home from work all I had to talk about was what the cats did and how many telemarkers called that day. This was pre opting-out days, so they kept me pretty busy. I would always have a nice dinner on the table and I would sit by his side and lovingly listen to him chew.

Of course I was scared to death, because this sort of thing just doesn't happen to me. I am constantly looking over my shoulder for auditors, hatchet murderers, and the Devil. I hate living with a feeling of impending doom. If we stop and think about things they can't really get any better. One, we are all aging. Two, we are all going to die; no one is getting out of this alive. That sure spells doom to me. I think it would have been nice if God could have given us some indication of how long we might be here, then at least we could have drank and done other things accordingly. I'd hoped to cross the finish line with all of my original parts but I'm already down by quite a few.

I have to say that I am happily married. They say that marriages are made in Heaven, but that's also where hurricanes, tornadoes, and hailstorms are made. I think marriages are made in the heart. If you both love each other and marry for that reason alone I think you will make it. But what the hell do I know?

Naturally Pookie and I took those marriage-training classes before we tied the knot, and to be honest they haven't improved much on the curriculum. Twenty years later the pastor was still talking about loving each other, loyalty, communication, and compassion. Fortunately I was

226

used to skid britches with the boys, and bill collectors were no longer a problem. The only thing I didn't realize was the fact that I married a mute. It's hard to communicate with a mute. If he won't talk and won't look away from the TV, even sign language is useless. Though it makes me feel better to send a few gestures anyway.

I guess I hadn't shut up long enough the six years we were dating to realize he didn't talk. No matter how long you date someone, the act of marriage will reveal amazing things about him or her.

I've often thought about opening a business called "Reality Check Marriage Course." All engaged couples would get a free set of boxing gloves upon graduation. There would be courses in *Fighting to Win, The Art of Back Pedaling, How to Hoard Money,* and *The Art of Physical Restraint Due to Capital Punishment.* The last class, of course, would only be for states that still have the death sentence. I think it would greatly reduce the number of divorces and murders in the country.

Of course there would have to be extra courses for men, like *What Not to Say to Your Wife* and *Why it's Just Easier to be Wrong.* Naturally there would be required courses on *The Art of Sending The Right Card at the Right Time,* and *If You're Running Late, How to Use a Phone.* I'd like to see it required like the blood test. I mean they worry about your blood mixing for a baby, when blood being spilled in battle is just as important. I think the most important course for women would have to be, *How to Live Alone, Married.* It's all a matter of adjustment, no different than after a natural disaster hits.

So, Pookie and I settled in to *live happily ever after...* I can't believe I even wrote that.

Chapter 23

Out West

One would think that with a brand-new vehicle, no kids, and plenty of money a driving vacation could be enjoyable. One would think.

Our first year as man and wife went rather well, I thought. Of course there were a few adjustments to make and a lot of compromising on his part, like cutting back on being at work seven days a week, and having an opinion.

We had just purchased a nice Chevy Tahoe so I decided we should take a road trip together out West. It would give us lots of time together with no chance of work calling him. All of our flying vacations went very well, except for a few minor glitches. Someone else might have been freaked out when left in the middle of an intersection at 1 A.M. by a psychotic bus driver. Pookie just climbed into the driver's seat and delivered the entire group of tourists to their respective hotels. He has a great sense of direction.

I had heard about the West a hundred times from my

sister's trips. I wanted to see everything she saw; unfortunately they were in five different states. I might have missed that part when my sister was telling the stories. Of course Pookie rarely tells me no, so he carefully mapped out my sites of interest. We had fourteen glorious days together, bonding, exploring, packed for any situation, ready to see the West.

There always seems to be important little things one should know before embarking on anything. I did not know that I could not let Pookie drive. If he has control of his timeframe it will be "a mission" and a mission must be completed in the least amount of time possible. There is no need to talk, eat, or pee while you are on a mission. It will only distract you from your mission. Pookie never fails at a mission. Everything is a mission.

We left at 4 A.M. and drove like my sister to a Famous-Barr White Sale.

Kansas reminds me of when the TV used to go off the air. Nothing. Our first stop was only long enough to use the restroom and grab some snacks. I refused to use the coffee can he brought for me. I thought he had brought it for fishing worms or something.

I was anxious to get to the West too so I didn't mind racing out there. I didn't really care that he hadn't said a word in over four hundred miles; at warp speed I wanted him to keep his mind on driving. I talked for both of us as usual—it just makes for a better conversation. In all honesty he did grunt a few times.

Onward we drove, flying past everything. I tried to read but I was told to watch the map. It never did anything. I turned on the radio and he turned it down to a whisper, as it was very distracting to the mission. I started to paint my toenails up to my ankles, but he reminded me it was a new vehicle. I fell asleep.

Finally we reached the amazing Corn Palace and glanced at it. I'm sure it has an interesting history but there was no time to read all the little signs they put up for people enjoying their vacation. I grabbed some brochures for the road. Besides I've seen corn before.

We had taken camping gear in case we couldn't find a room. But he thought we took it to actually use. Though, as a newlywed it seemed kind of romantic, sleeping in a cozy little tent on a bed of rocks in a land of vermin. Lucky for us we found a cabin for our first night out. We found it at 2 A.M. and checked out at 5 A.M.

We continued to drive. We drove and drove and drove... and then we drove some more. Finally we made it to Mount Rushmore. I managed to stay there a few hours by wandering off and hiding under Abe's nostril. When he realized there were too many heads he demanded we move on. The mission did not allow for this sort of senseless meandering.

I'm pretty sure I saw Crazy Horse, but the picture blurred out, we were going so damn fast. It was almost impossible to get things out of the glove box due to the G-force. The only upside to the speed was it straightened out my crows feet and laugh lines.

The Badlands didn't get their name by mistake. Miles and miles of rock, regular rocks, red rocks, black rocks, striped red-and-black rocks. Its flat rocks, jutting rocks, and very slippery rocks. There is nothing but fricking rocks! Breathtaking gorges of rock, dropping off five hundred feet down to more rocks below. I can just see and hear the pioneers when they were traveling west. "Now, Elizabeth, I know you're tired of riding, but these are some bad lands. At best we could grow a rock garden."

I have to say that the West is beautiful in its own special way, but even unending beauty gets old after your butt has grown to the seat. Yet we drove on...

We got lost in Custer State Park, well I swore we were lost but Pookie insisted it was just BIG. There are no restaurants in Custer State Park. I was ready to tie a bow on one of the buffalo because he was starting to look really familiar. If we passed him again he was going on a grill.

We had to camp in Custer because there are no hotels out West either. Well, none you can find and if you do happen on one it is full and rightfully so. No one wants to camp in bear country in a flimsy tent that can't even keep a prairie dog out. We cooked some canned crap over an open fire and collapsed inside of our homeless-people shelter. Sleep does not come easy in a big laundry bag when you have a boulder in your kidneys. Pookie went out like a light and snored up a storm. Normally I gouge him in the ribs to halt snoring, but I do believe that it kept the bears away; he sounded more vicious than anything roaming the wilderness.

Pook rose at 4 A.M. and collapsed the tent with me still in it. I clawed my way out and headed to the much-anticipated showers. However, a flock of prissy teenagers were hogging the one shower and tiny sink. Of course we didn't have time to wait so we drove onward as I wiped myself off with pop-ups.

By day three I still hadn't gotten to take a shower and I was out of pop-ups. I was only allowed to snap pictures from the car. He said it was too dangerous, I knew it was a time issue. I started a journal with tick marks going for the buffalo, elk, and bears. Oh my! I had to do something. I shouldn't have tossed my rubber monkey in Arkansas, but who would have thought I'da needed him after I was married.

When the traffic finally slowed us down to a crawl I demanded we take a walk and join a group of tourists standing out in a beautiful meadow. My knees were numb even though I straightened them occasionally by sticking my legs out the window.

After I ripped the keys from the steering column, he agreed to stretch his legs for five minutes. He set the timer on his watch. Together we strolled through the lovely meadow. A herd of majestic elk rested peacefully in the tall grass. I wanted at least a few clear pictures of these beautiful creatures. As we got closer the herd quickly arose, they and the entire group of tourists left. My guess was because we hadn't bathed in three days. We got back in the Tahoe and drove some more.

Finally we arrived at Yellowstone National Park. I was ecstatic to get out of the Tahoe, which I now hate with a passion. But, it was another sixty miles to Old Faithful. This park should be its own state. My sister had recommended a restaurant there so the dashboard was covered in drool of anticipation. I couldn't wait to eat something that didn't come out of a can that was on a real plate. We stayed there pretty long as Old Faithful only spews every so often. Thank God it wasn't spewing while we drove by.

I finally got to see the birdie boilers my sister spoke of, hot water boiling right out of the rocks. I have to say it was amazing to see, but at this point anything was better to look at than the dashboard or his hairy little ear. I had a terrible urge to grab a bar of soap and jump in one of the boilers.

Halfway through lunch Ed informed me that we must move on. That's right, his name is Ed; no more terms of endearment. Why, because it is eighty-seven miles to our campsite and we are *still* in the fricking park! It doesn't look that big on the map—well, nothing does. What is up with this quarter-inch equals two hundred miles crap? You know men set that measuring system up.

Once again we are forced to camp where everything you look at has a bear warning nailed to it. Even on the inside of the outhouse, nailed on the door facing you are ominous bear warnings. Needless to say it's easy to empty your colon. I'm normally not a coward but I've never come across a bear in the supermarket. There's a huge difference in being clipped by sculptured nails and shredded by bear claws. No way can I sleep in a tissue-paper tent terrorized by the thought of bears eating me. I sleep in the Tahoe amongst all the junk, which I now like again. I leave him in the tent as bait.

No showers, no campfire to cook on, it's too dry, and naturally more driving graced the rising of the sun. I filled my twelve-ounce empty water bottles from an odd pipe that sprung from the ground. A nice man from Canada helped me hang onto the little bottle as he raised the two-thousand-pound pressure handle. I thought he passed gas, but learned upon my first sip it was the water. Something about sulfur?

God was getting an earful by now.

Onward we go to Jenni Lake after a delicious breakfast of soda crackers and gummy bears. Jenni Lake was a beautiful place, but full. We rented a little boat with an eggbeater tied on the back with a "twisty" (all it required). Off we go across the big lake to fish. Why you cannot fish on the side you are on, I do not know. I wanted to sit on a wooden seat for four hours about as bad as I wanted to sleep in the Tahoe again. And I want to know why there is always time for fricking fishing.

As soon as we reached the other side a storm blew in over the mountains, which we were warned to watch out for. A storm coming over a huge mountain range is very scary. I panicked as always but Ed instantly kicked into survival mode. He is the person you want to be with in a natural disaster or when the world ends. It won't be comfortable, but you will stay alive.

We are trying to speed back to land, but we could have paddled faster with teaspoons then the water output stirred by the eggbeater attached to the wooden tub. Tarzan, I mean Ed, leaned into the water and wind with great passion while I bailed with my straw sunhat. I was calling upon God as usual but this time to save me from death. I had begged not to go out onto the lake with the storm warnings. I wanted to live long enough to kill my husband. No lake would take that joy from me. We made it back to the dry warmth of the wonderful Tahoe, alive.

Onward we went, driving... The West is too big, and a lot of it isn't very pretty. I think it should be broken down into areas... well, I guess that is... what states are? Anyway, I was going to have to have a few words with my sister when I got back.

As always we couldn't find anywhere to stay. Six hundred bazillion acres and no one thinks to build a damn hotel on any of them. We stopped and ask about a little place called GrosVenture that must have been misspelled and should have been printed Gross Adventure. The rangers laughed at me when I asked if it was full.

The campgrounds were desolate and weedy, with ice water in a two-hole outhouse. The faucets had spring tension on them like a leaf spring on a car. I had to grip it with all my might as I crammed my head into an eight-inch bowl to wash my hair. It was quite refreshing, especially on many body parts. I didn't care—I was taking a bath, of sorts. I didn't get to wash my feet because the floor was dirt, I believe. Tufts of prairie grass were growing in the corners by the burrows. I thought I saw a vermin pop his head out of the hole occasionally. Waiting for his turn I'd imagine.

I only packed a few canned goods and snacks. Ed

bought a case of Spam. One would think that there is a store on every corner, right? Wrong. The West doesn't have stores, hotels, gas stations, or showers. I hate canned meals; there's something about eating out of tin. But, who would have thought Spam and Cheez Whiz on a pretzel would taste so yummy. My sister always camps and said they eat lots of canned ravioli on their vacations. Her husband is as tight with money as a pickle jar lid when you're pregnant. God, what I would have given for a can of heated ravioli. A fifty-foot RV pulled up next to us, plugged in and through the cracks in the blinds I could see them eating hot food and watching TV in the air conditioning. Ed refused to help me let the air out of their tires.

I suffered through the night in the Tahoe draped over a cooler with a tackle box for a pillow, due to the very bold vermin that also like Spam. Ed slept like a baby on a rock with the vermin. The next morning we moved on bright and early, deeper into the Underworld. By this point I am in agony; my back pains me in a very expensive bed. My head was stuck to my shoulder for the better part of the day, I finally felt better around one o'clock when Ed pulled the fishing fly out of my back. I'm almost positive he saw it earlier in the day.

We drove, and drove, and drove... flat land and tumbleweed for endless hours. Wait, there is a cow. More flat land and tumbleweed. The West is a lot like Kansas. I now know the true meaning of the word barren. I never gave it much thought before but I now feel great sympathy for women in the Bible who were said to be "barren."

Finally we arrived in a little town called Jackson Hole. Jackson Hole is an oasis nestled in the middle of Hell's bowels. With the threat of divorce and no Dove Bars handy, Ed managed to bribe us into an overpriced hotel. I stayed in the shower until I was a prune.

We staggered around town the first evening like two rodeo cowboys that had been on a cattle drive for twenty months. Every now and then my knees would reverse flow and I would tumble backwards into an unsuspecting tourist or a bush. I've come to the conclusion that you either have to be able to feel your butt or your legs, both can't be numb at the same time while attempting to walk.

We stayed in Jackson Hole for two whole days because I refused to get into the Tahoe until my butt regained its shape. I stated this with a can of hair spray and a lighter. I begged Ed to sell the Tahoe and fly home, but since we had made only one payment he refused to do it. He reminded me that we were on a schedule, and that he was only trying to fulfill my dreams and wishes because he loved me. I got back in the Tahoe.

By now I will no longer touch the map because he loves to see me squint my eyes out only to give him the wrong direction, which he has no intention of following anyway. A few million miles of silence and tumbleweed passes...I keep busy planning his demise.

I finally agree to stay married, can't give away the master plan. I also know I cannot make it on my own out here in no man's land. Onward we head to Estes Park. I wish I would have known that Estes Park had bad memories for Ed, as his ex-wife's family apparently lived there. Information I could have used before I put it on my list of sites.

Along with all of my other medical issues I get sea sickness. I thought you had to be on water for it, but apparently not. Going into Estes Park is a snaking, winding, twisting, road, driven like you're in a bumper car. Of course Ed is making it worse now, probably because of some of the things I said to him earlier in the trip.

We finally get into Estes and I am green and ready to blow chunks; we stop off for breakfast. I get dry toast and he orders over easy eggs. He then douses them in hot sauce and catsup. My mascara is melting from the heat vapors rising from his plate across the table. My head is spinning and my stomach has risen somewhere between my lungs and my right nipple. Ed is pointing to his watch while gobbling down an embryo blood bath. Exit the restroom, again. I just love to hug a strange porcelain pedestal in a public restroom—it's one of those Kodak moments.

When I get out Ed is in the Tahoe with the engine running. I bolt for my freedom, yet he runs me down like a jackrabbit and stuffs me back into the Tahoe kicking and biting, to drive through the park to look at more fricking elks and deer. I'm sorry, but after a few million buffalo and hoofed creatures they lose their pizzazz. Now I know why the white man killed all the buffalo.

Silently we drive on until he stops at a cute little chalet, leaving me in the car like a damn dog. "Wait here," he commanded Fido. After about fifteen minutes he comes out smiling and carrying a small bag of the world's best donuts, for himself. He mentioned the wonderful owners. He paid no attention to the rabid creature he left behind, now busy cutting up his Powerworms with my pedicure scissor.

When he finally noticed bits of rubber worms stuck to the steering wheel and gauges he looked over rather puzzled. Happily munching on his donut, he asked, "is there a problem?"

Through gritted teeth I screeched, "Did it ever dawn on you that I might have wanted to throw up a donut, had you thought to ask? Did it ever dawn on you that I might like to get out of this fricking Tahoe and see how they make the best fricking donuts in the whole fricking world? Did you even notice that someone is on this fricking vacation with you?"

Quietly and carefully he tidied his moustache with a napkin, and then proceeded to calm the unhappy client. Ed is a very calm man. I think he learned patience from being in the customer service business. One must stay calm when dealing with irate people or spend the rest of one's life in prison behind bars. Problem is—I'm not one of his customers. I've told him this a thousand times.

"Well, I'm sorry. I thought you didn't feel well. Here, have a donut." Cautiously he handed me the bag. Which I pulverized until nothing remained but an extremely fine dust. He blinked a few times, binked a few sugar-dusted Powerworm bits off the steering wheel, and proceeded to drive on to the entrance of Estes Park in silence.

I hate people who can keep their composure through anything; how dare they stay calm and rational when it's time to spaz out. Nothing makes me more mad than someone who refuses to fight. I don't care if I spend the rest of my life in prison behind bars. Had I not seen him carry four hundred pound rolls of sheet vinyl on his shoulder, I would have attacked. Instead I stared out the window begging God to come and get me, whisk me up on angel wings away from this vile land they call the West. Rescue me from this alien creature that has taken over the body of the man I married and once loved. Please God, I prayed, knock the Tahoe off into a ditch so we can fly home. Bust off its wheels so there is no hope of repair. Rip off the back door so the last damn cans of Spam will explode like land mines made of pork and pork by-products. Oh, and please, break all the tips off his fishing rods. I can be downright evil when I am mad.

He drove on…I assume he still hadn't noticed someone was on the vacation with him.

At the front of the park a sign said it was a five hour drive due to traffic. I could feel an aneurysm forming in my frontal lobe. No way can I survive it. No way am I sitting (on my flat butt) in the Tahoe, winding through five hours of the same things I have seen for the last ten days. I'm ready to ride on the roof carrier just to be in a different position. I'm sure he was ready for me to ride there too.

"Stop!" I screamed at the top of my lungs. "I'm not going in there! I am not looking at any more fricking reindeer! I can't do it. I surrender. The West sucks, you were right, I was wrong." It was obvious I could never out-endure him at anything. I begged for mercy, I tried to put some of the Powerworms back together with spit. I banged my head on the dashboard until my contacts almost popped out of my eyes. "Have mercy, please!"

Carefully he stopped the vehicle. For a man of few words he had apparently been storing some up since May first of 1999. Calmly he informed me that he knew when we left it was impossible to see all of the sites I listed. No one could cover five states in fourteen days. Just because my sister suggested five hundred sites of interest didn't mean she saw them all in one trip. He then pointed at the map, or what was left of it, and emphasized how ridiculous it was to try to cover fifty billion acres in two weeks. He made a few references to some of my not-so-desirable traits and then he returned to his *cave*.

We both sat silent for what seemed like an eternity. He made good points. I decide to kill my sister instead as I needed him to drive me home. I then informed him that the, out west trip was over, it was time to take me home. Little did I know that is exactly what he wanted.

Glaze-eyed and on yet another mission we headed home. He drove fourteen hours non-stop through the night. As the miles rolled by, dreams of dinosaurs incinerating Ed and my sister, Tahoes rolling off of cliffs, and hot paved city streets void of elks and vermin comforted me.

Why is driving always such a mission to men? They get together after a trip and the first words out of their mouths are, "I made it in fourteen hours flat." The Dallas Cowboy cheerleaders could have been working out nude on the side of the road but the most important fact of the trip is always the road time. If men want to race through life I sure can hurry it up for them.

I finally awoke somewhere outside of Kansas City, rooted through the mangled camping junk, and commenced to gnaw on a hunk of Spam. I wasn't asking him to stop for anything. I even used the coffee can and then emptied it out his window. We both blinked and spit a few times but his eyes never left the road ahead.

We arrived home three days early and Ed went straight into work. Gospel truth! I unloaded the car and contemplated the destruction of him and the Tahoe. It took five days for my butt to regain its normal shape.

I now know two things about Ed. One, you always put him on a plane with a ticket that says you can't go anywhere until this date and time. Two, he needs to be sedated whatever the mode of transportation.

If I want to take a driving trip now I take it with my sister and niece. Yes, I let her live because I like to borrow her clothes. And never again will I go anywhere without my bottle of Jack Daniel's. I assumed I wouldn't need it with the absence of the boys. Wrong. And just so you know, there are no bars out West either. Or at least I didn't see any at warp speed.

Out West has now taken the top of my list for worst vacations ever. To this date when I hear people say the word *west,* I cringe and my butt falls asleep!

Chapter 24

Grandbabies

When I look at the boys' girlfriends, I'm sorry, but all I can see is a wonderful uterus ripe with grandbaby eggs. And yet, what very well may be another syndrome, I've lost track.

All I can think of is grandbabies and it doesn't help that my sister, Judi, got one before me. But then, she did birth a girl child and always got the good stuff before me. Excluding *the curse*. Boy children don't want to *make* babies—they just want to practice the procedure. Girl children dream about weddings, houses, and most of all, having babies. If you are lucky enough to spawn a girl child you're pretty secure on the grandbaby future, and the fact that you have *dibs*. Yes, *dibs* that the baby will be at your house most of the time.

My niece's mother-in-law bought a lovely crib for her new grandbaby. The crib stands at my sister's house. It's natural for a young mother to turn to *her* mother for guidance in child rearing. Even when a boy child produces a grandbaby, if something goes wrong they'll usually say, "I don't know, call *your* mother," especially if it's not half-time.

I have been blessed with a great-niece, and I have to say that a great-niece is just as wonderful as a grandbaby. As a favorite aunt you do get some *dibs*. For a brief moment my exuberance with my first great-niece scared my boys, as Repete told me often "don't burn yourself out on her. I'm going to have babies someday too!" However it was a short-lived terror because my great-niece just celebrated her fourth birthday and I am still grandbaby-less.

I have also been blessed with a *step*-grandbaby, however I do not have *dibs*. As a matter of fact when you get into *step*-things, I'm so far down on the *dibs* list her entire life of photos may not fill my key chain brag book. The poor child doesn't know what to call me and I don't know what to call myself. Step-grandma sounds so formal, but grandma could cause me severe bodily harm if my stepson's mother ever hears her call me that. Maybe I should pick out one of those generic grandparent names like Nana or Meme? Of course the next time I see her she will probably be old enough to understand the chain of command in grandparent land and just call me "hey you, got any fruit nubs?"

Extended families have really messed up a lot of things, and *dibs* is the worst. Seniority is a thing of the past in today's world. It used to be there were only two grandmas and they were old. Battles rarely ensued. Thanks to divorce first, second, and third wives are all potential grandmas. A forty-year-old is ready to rock and roll when the first grandbaby pops out. Who wants a half a grandbaby? It's just not worth it.

The only good part of having "grandbaby fever" is my

egg basket is gone and I can't satiate the urge by reproducing a baby myself. So, I am left only to dream, longing, in constant anticipation of someday seeing a little Pete or Repete running through the house. In the quiet moments I can hear the pitter-patter of little feet on my new hardwood floors. I can see the tiny little hand reaching out for my finger. I can hear myself singing lullabies, until someone yells from the living room, "shut that racket up!"

Sometimes I pretend like I'm already a grandma, or shall I say *practice*. Laylow doesn't mind wearing the dresses but the other cats are quite vocal about riding in the baby stroller. None of them like diaper changing. I guess the Desitin doesn't taste so good when grooming later? Lucky doesn't mind the pink bonnet at all, which worries me because he is a boy cat. Yes, even my pets are males. I thought I had a girl cat once but when I took her into get spayed she got neutered instead.

Does any of this seem a little odd? Oh, how quickly we forget—just sixteen short chapters ago I was ready to blow my brains out from stopped up toilets and crippling Legos. Now all of a sudden little kids are a wonderful gift from Heaven. Why is that? Well, I think we all know that grandbabies are different. You can give them back to the parents when they get to the Lego stage.

Grandparents can walk off the job at any given time and go to Florida for a while without even worrying if the babysitter is still alive. Grandparents get to buy their kid's kid Legos, lots of Legos, noisy musical instruments, and finger-paints, lots of finger-paints. Grandma can say, "sorry, we can't watch the baby tonight. Colic? Oh my, that is bad stuff. Pete had colic until he was seventeen. Call me in the morning and let me know how things went." I can see a whole new world of vengeance—I mean joy springing up before me.

Grandbabies

I'll admit that I miss my kids being around. I miss bath time and those cool colors we got to draw on the tile walls with. I miss naptime and especially snack time. I miss cuddling and rocking their tiny little bodies that couldn't talk back yet. I miss buying toys. Since they stopped coming around money is starting to pile up. We can't have that. Ed will think he doesn't need to work as much. Perhaps if the kids called me more often, this feeling of grandbaby urgency wouldn't be so overbearing? Hint.

I'm eager for a new phase in my life. I can't help it that baby clothes are so darn cute now. When my kids were little babies they had sleepers. Little boys had striped T's and elastic-waist corduroy pants. I don't know what little girls had. Now they've got adult fashions re-created to tiny size! Baby-size shrugs, designer jeans, beach shirts, skorts, halter-tops, jogging suits, it's unending. I can barely resist buying a pair of ugly shoes. How can I be expected to wait another day to spend forty bucks on a darling little twelve-inch outfit just like mine?

The room I waited many years to empty is boring, drab, and lifeless. At first the overpriced rose border that almost drove Ed to drinking was perfect. Now, it needs... bunnies and balloons in it. It needs to have a purpose. Like as a sleepover nursery. Sure, we have a houseguest now and then, but they won't let me rock them. I want someone that gets excited about eating off of the teddy bear dishes, someone who doesn't look at me like "what the hell" when I try to tie the cute *Grandma Loves Me* bib on. I want a grandbaby and this lack of a grandbaby thing is making me unstable. I mean...more than normal.

Everyone has a grandbaby except me. It's true, some people brag of having ten or twenty. Isn't that considered hoarding? Grandbabies are everywhere, some even look just like my kids when they were babies. Some grandbabies

244

I see are really scary looking and I still want one. I can't wait much longer. The other day I caught myself rocking a loaf of bread and humming a lullaby in *Shop'n Save* while waiting to check out.

So what if I picked up a stroller and car seat at a garage sale? Sooner or later I know I will need it. They're not going to waste—the cats love to sleep in 'em. And I know I shouldn't do this but I've tucked away a few cute little pink things for luck. Well, it's actually more of a little shrine set up so God will bless me with a girl grandbaby first. Well, to be honest it's a pretty big shrine now. I have pink barrettes and bows, booties, a bonnet, bunny bottles, blankets, and a box full of baby dolls all dressed in pink surrounded by pink candles I light on the first Monday of the month while chanting "girl babies, girl babies, girl babies..." I even picked up some cute little pink paper diapers, oblivious to the fact they will eventually be filled with mustard poop again.

I guess all I can do is wait. Badgering the boys has gotten me nowhere fast. Pete moved halfway across the country to be with his wife. Personally I think it had something to do with me introducing his fiancée as my soon-to-be uterus-in-law. Everyone is tired of me letting my stepson's girlfriend win at dominoes. She's figured out the key word for me to slip her a needed domino: *"grandbabies."* Repete is still idling and has been with a wonderful uterus, I mean girl, for almost four years now. However they are still not married... Though I took him out to look at rings, stating that I'm not getting any younger and my heart hasn't been feeling too good lately. I know it is right around the corner but I'm starting to worry now that God might come and get me like I requested before I get to hold my first grandbaby. Of course I'm sure God disregards most of my requests and He knows what is good for me as it's very apparent that I don't.

I didn't mean to scare Repete's someday-to-be-wife, but I felt compelled to inform her she may have to play catch-up and crank out a few sets of twins or triplets. Personally, I think one will be a challenge. Repete is about six-five and two hundred and sixty pounds. Keeks is about five-foot-one and ninety pounds soaking wet. Our family tends to crank out some galoot-size babies with great big heads. I fear she may be starting to connect the dots.

I won't allow anyone to tell childbirth stories around her. You know how people exaggerate. As soon as I had my baby I was overcome with joy. Heck, I barely remember my hips flying out of their sockets, because I was too busy holding my eyeballs in. Keeks has mentioned to me a few times that she is a bit nervous about having a baby. I just smile and tell her it's as easy as rolling off a log. Of course I don't finish that sentence: down a rocky gorge, through thousands of sticker bushes, and into a pool of molten-hot tar full of piranhas. I don't want to put any ideas into her head. We all like to remember childbirth in our own special way.

The best part of Keeks' having a grandbaby is that her mother and family live in California. Yep, that gives me *dibs*. I don't think they can run the baby across the country for a Friday night movie—making me the sole babysitter! I know I shouldn't think that way but I've been waiting a long time. Her mother also birthed four girl children, borderline hoarding if you ask me. Years ago when Keeks announced she was going to move to Missouri, I was doing the little "dibs dance" on the other end of the phone. I'm sure her family will travel out here to see the grandbaby, and I will try my very best to share. But for the most part, it's all mine. ☺ Unless Repete tries to ransom it to me.

I need to get a real job.

Chapter 25

A Typical Day in the Life of Me, 20 Years Later

Everyone hopes for retirement. It's the light at the end of the tunnel. I never thought that I would get to retire at such an early age. And, I guess I really shouldn't speak too soon as many things can throw one back into the world of *nose to the grindstone*. I sincerely hope that I never have to grind my nose again.

I find it hard to work for peanuts now that I don't have babies to feed and rent to pay. When I look back at the four hundred and fifty years of child rearing I remember scraping change together to buy groceries or gas. As I recall it took great effort to make it to the next paycheck many a week. Now I have to make an effort not to eat all of the groceries we have piled up in our pantry. Gas can still be a problem at these ridiculous prices. I had drive and incentive back in those days because it was work or perish. Now my only real concern of perishing comes from the failure of bodily organs due to overdoses of Parkay on a Sam's super muffin.

Sometimes I am in awe when I look back at old photo albums and see me in some of the many causes and crusades I managed to fit into my sixty-hour workweeks and endless child rearing. Now I'm lucky if I can fit a trip to the post office into my busy day of... I'm not sure.

I rise at 4 A.M. awakened by meows, purring, and paws. I stagger to the kitchen where I must *touch* Lucky's food bowl before he can eat the food sitting out on the no-fat-kitty-allowed table. Laylow, the twenty-two pound obese fur ball, must be fed his restricted quarter cup of diet food on the floor, and then be let outside to do whatever it is he does all day long. Lucky, the youngest cat will then return back to bed to sleep in my warm spot next to Daddy. I am not allowed to return to that spot. Peanut, one of the many animals dumped on us by our offspring and their college-bound friends, will follow me inches from my heels until I provide her a warm lap to lie on.

I make the coffee for my wonderful, hard-working man who I love dearly.

I like to go through a routine in the morning, especially my ten-minute sneezing fits and nose-blowing session. When I feel it is safe to go near hot liquid without blowing it into my face, I make a cup of green tea. Sometimes I make my wonderful, hard-working man a lunch. Sometimes I don't. I have many moods.

Ed springs out of bed, throws on some clothes, and runs out the door with his cup of coffee and anything I set out for him to take with him. He's taken some odd stuff to work because if it's on the edge of the counter he figures it's for him. A bag of old cell phones for the Humane Society, an envelope full of coupons for my grocery shopping, and some rotten food to be returned for a refund.

He didn't eat any of it, but he did question my love for him when he opened the bag at lunch time. I expect the rest of the guys did too.

I let Laylow back in and Lucky out. Peanut and I move to the sofa for our morning nap or possible read, if I need a dose of fiction from the newspaper. Peanut is an odd little cat. She has one broken ear that doesn't stand up and she's self-conscious about it. She hisses a lot at everything, some things no one can see but her. She sheds worse than a mountain lion in spring, and she loves a warm lap, friend or foe, she will mount any human that stalls too long and snuggle in for the duration of her life. She is very annoyed when the warm lap arises, because then she must follow you around meowing until you sit down again. She is a female, if you didn't notice that. I now have one of my own species in the house.

About nine o'clock I head in for my shower, and morning ritual of age resistance. I like to do a few exercises in the morning, like bending over to pick up Ed's socks and undies on the floor right next to the hamper. I also like to sit at my dressing table for a while as I apply thick layers of caulking. I have a great view of four acres of wooded land. I love nature. Squirrels are fun to watch, especially if one of them misses a branch. We also have a resident bird that doesn't know what glass is even after a couple hundred crashes. Sometimes I get to watch deer at the feeder or Laylow trying to bring down a twenty-five pound turkey. After my nature show I like to eat some breakfast. Peanut likes to lie on my lap while I eat it. Go figure.

I then let Laylow out and Lucky back in, and begin my many tasks of being a full-time housewife. Talk shows are turned on, laundry thrown in, and it's time for a break in the sunroom with another cup of tea with Peanut on my lap. If it's summer I have many more tasks because I love to plant things even if they don't usually grow. But in the winter most of my activities are restricted to indoors because Peanut and I desperately hate the cold. Time to let Lucky out and Laylow in again. I like to do this a lot.

Once a week I clean the entire house from top to bottom, unless I forget what I am doing somewhere along the line. It's very easy to get sidetracked when one isn't on a time schedule. Once again it is time to let Laylow out and time to toss Peanut out even though she protests this greatly. Anything can sidetrack me nowadays. Like a drawer full of interesting junk, a pile of mail long forgotten, a magazine, or an uncontrollable urge for homemade chocolate chip cookies. It's a good thing that didn't happen when I was younger or we would have all have starved to death and been buried in filth.

Around noon I like to make myself a little lunch and turn on the computer. This is where the trouble starts. Once I sit in front of the computer the clock speeds up. Before I know it, it's time to let Peanut, Lucky, and Laylow in. I know because they are all looking in the window at me, the window that I am staring out of in some sort of a coma. I have other tasks I could be doing but I have ample time now so I will put them off until the last bitter minute.

Around two it's time for more exercise as I walk one hundred and fifty feet to the mailbox to get the mail. Sometimes I get to talk to the mail lady, which is good for keeping my social skills sharp. If not, I just keep talking to the cats. One hundred and fifty feet is a lot longer than it sounds so Peanut and I fall asleep on the couch for our afternoon lulu.

Around four we like to start dinner for my hardworking husband who I love dearly. I really enjoy cooking and baking so every night is a delicious feast with a fancy dessert, unless I forget to get off the computer in time.

Then it's beans and weenies and cookies and milk. Ed is a great guy, as long as it's not a banana, he'll eat it.

Now I have to try to look busy. I don't want Ed to think I sit around all day long. I'm also tired of sitting around and feel an urge to move. Maybe I am nocturnal? While Ed stares at the TV in awe of anything on it, I putter around the house finishing the load of laundry I threw in at 9 A.M. and straighten up the kitchen after the dinner explosion. I truly believe that a good cook is a messy cook and I am a mighty fine cook from the looks of my kitchen. I love to bake but shouldn't be allowed around flour especially if there is rolling out involved. Grease is another dangerous item. I keep big boxes of baking soda near the stove. I love to try new recipes I cut out of magazines and the newspaper. Some of them work, some of them don't. Ed will eat them all as long as there isn't a banana in it.

Around eight we will either watch a movie or Ed will escape to the *shed.* It seems hard to believe but sometimes even with two hundred channels there isn't anything on TV to watch. Of course I am a lot more discriminating than Ed. Actually, Ed loves it when I decree there is nothing on worth watching because then he can vanish into the black hole, the *shed.* He will walk down the hill and not be seen for hours, days on the weekend, and months if he didn't have to work. Ed's shed is twenty-one-hundred square feet of junk with a basement. I'm guessing his Heaven will be a giant shed filled with greasy and rusty things. I guess that is why he doesn't want to go to Heaven, he's already there and has a refrigerator full of cold beer too.

It's hard to make friends when one stays home every day. But since they all tend to move away after they get to know me, I don't really bother trying to make them anymore. So, I will spend the rest of my evening yakking on the phone to my mom or sister while playing on the computer. And of course letting the cats in and out. Sometimes I feel a little lonely and wonder what it would be like to have buddies at work, friends to lunch with, and people without fur coats to talk to. But, I've remedied that problem, all I have to do is run down to the basement. Nothing makes you forget faster than running down to the basement, or up the steps for that matter.

Around ten I will travel to the shed in search of my hardworking husband whom I love dearly. He needs his rest so he can go to work tomorrow and I can stay home. After the kitties are fed and separated (Lucky is nocturnal too), I will begin my nightly ritual of age resistance. I will buff, exfoliate, moisturize, brush, and do a few windmills with my arms before retiring for the night. I might do some ironing. Kitties will be circumspectly placed throughout the bed and once this is done no one is allowed to move, except Laylow who now wants to go outside again.

My night will be much busier than my day. My bladder has shrunk to the size of a peach pit so I like to spend a lot of time in the bathroom. Lucky will usually take out a lamp or something of value while he shoots psychotically around the house in search of who knows what? Peanut will hiss like an old steam boiler at everyone for not staying put. Ed will snore through all of it. Most of my serious exercise program is done during the night, as I like to lie down, sit up, lie down, and sit up due to my bad back from twenty years of heavy cleaning.

The night is a happening place when you live in the country. Raccoons are busy little buggers, brazen and bold. I've chased many a forty-pound coon off of our upper deck with a broom or a BB gun. They love to uproot potted plants and drink the red Kool-Aid stuff out of the hummingbird feeders. They become quite the little acrobats to get to it too. As if the raccoons aren't enough fun everyone in the neighborhood turns his or her dogs and cats loose at night. This procedure results in party time in the wild. Raccoons fighting at night sounds just like babies screaming. It's shrill and terrifying the first time you hear it. Dogs and cats fighting sounds like dogs and cats fighting. Trashcans being turned over sounds like a messy morning. Ed snores through all of it.

Every now and then I will get a moment of enlightenment and race to the computer room to put down my thoughts. Why they can't come to me during the day I have no idea. The next day I usually can't find the documents I typed. Sometimes I will write my midnight musings down *close* to the paper on the desk or counter. My mother purchased a small hand-held tape recorder for me many years back, to record my moments of inspiration, but the next morning it sounded like someone with a mouth full of cotton and dental instruments.

Of course I have to guard us against the monsters at night too. Things that go bump in the night just may be those monsters come back from childhood or one of the lunatics you hear about on the evening news. Ed doesn't believe in monsters so I have to protect all of us. Well, excluding his ex-wife.

I will finally fall asleep around 4 A.M., right about the time Laylow needs to be let in or out—who could keep track? Sometimes I will let them all out and later they will be sitting on the desk by me. I know Peanut can open unlocked doors but she'd never let the nasty boy kitties back in with her. Life is a mystery and gets more mysterious with age.

As soon as I do fall asleep Ed will increase his snoring volume by about ten decibels. I bought him some snoring spray that really works well if he sprays it into his mouth like the instructions direct. However, a sleeping person sometimes tends to use it under the arm, on the cats, or in the eyes. Definitely not recommended. It doesn't help the snoring when not applied as directed. So, the short remainder of my night will be spent in the recliner, with Peanut on my lap and my fingers in my ears.

Tomorrow will be a bit more exciting because I have a doctor's appointment and some things to pick up for Ed at the *Tractor Supply Store*. It's almost as much fun as *Charlie's Farm and Home* or *Auto Zone*. Of course there is grocery-shopping day, and regular shopping days, which occur much more frequent than grocery-shopping days. There is my volunteer day at the pantry, and lunch with my mom day. But for the most part I'm bored to death and ready to type five hundred pages of *all work and no play makes Jack a dull boy...Red rum, red rum, red rum...*

Retirement is good.

Chapter 26

Inside Me

Nobody wants to be inside of me, not even me. I'd be scared but I've been here so long it feels like home. I've tried not to write about my dark side. We all have one. You know that side that wants to tell someone to "kiss my ass" when they cut you off. That side that wants to tell your neighbors, "I hope a tornado sucks all that crap up on the side of your house along with you and your yappy little dog." It's that side that wants to speak out and not worry about the feelings of the people who are definitely not worried about yours. That side that is standing on the cusp of Hell, saying, "fuck it, I'm tired of always being the nice guy!"

Well, I will spare you that side of me. Though I may put it to paper someday. The evils that lurk in my mind are countless. I am an evil person—ask anyone that has crossed my path, especially my children. May shame, retribution, and hot mozzarella cheese be heaped upon me, for I am just filled with selfish expectations of others. Especially of my children, who did not ask to be born. How dare I curse life upon them without their permission. Lucky for me my mind is a menagerie of moments and memories so I can't contemplate those expectations of others for very long. I have trouble contemplating whatever I am doing for very long, even what direction I am driving and why.

Where was I going with this? Oh yes. Everyone actually likes the dark side of people better, it's true. Dirty little secrets are juicy. Uncovering someone else's dark side makes you not feel so bad about yourself when you screw someone over. Everything is justifiable if you can make someone else look worse. Unfortunately my evil side turns on me more than anyone else, it's been out to get me from the very beginning. That is why I prefer the wacky side of myself better. The serious side of me is way too serious. Seriously.

When I read a book, I always want to know more about the author. I want to know what's in his or her head that makes them write what they write. I'm probably the only person that may read the introduction to a book a few times looking for clues. So, as an added treat I'm going to allow you inside of my head for awhile. It's kind of a deeper introduction to me, but not too deep because that is where the gargoyles lay in wait...

* * * * *

When I was a little kid I used to have dreams of big dinosaurs coming up the hill to incinerate our house. The sky was all runny, red and purple. The air was very hot, probably from the flames they were breathing. The trees were scorched off and most of my neighbors' houses were already melted into small asbestos puddles. I would stand at

256

the window and watch without saying a word. I could feel the house move with each step the monsters took. I never made a sound. I couldn't wake my parents—they had to go to work the next day. I had this dream for most of my childhood years. When I learned what the word extinct meant another whacked-out nightmare replaced it.

In the Seventies I dreamt about unending gas lines and finding bags of sugar. I had horrible nightmares of empty chocolate sections in the candy counter. That's when Corporate America first figured out how to ream the workingman by creating shortages. It was such a huge success they are still creating them in the twenty-first century. Nowadays I dream of pouring gas and sugar over CEOs. I'm eating a king-size Butterfinger and dancing scantily clothed around them like the kids in *Lord of the Flies.*

I hate recurring dreams, especially ones that haunt you for years. The worst one I remember was where I would enter a normal elevator and push the button for the ground floor. Immediately the button panel rises to the ceiling, displaying over one hundred floors. I am on the ninety-ninth floor. As soon as it begins to move I hear a cable snap and the elevator begins to fall. Floors fly by in the crack through the door as lights flash like an old-time flicker movie. My heart pounds in my ears as I move back and grasp onto the railings around the speeding mirrored box. It keeps going faster and faster, shaking harder and harder. I always wake up just before it hits, but I know that I will have to ride it again. It's just like going on a trail ride every summer with my sister.

One night I finally decided to ride the sucker out. I've never had a high tolerance for anything that is annoying me, even dreams. They say if you die in your dreams you will really die. I disagree. The dinosaurs melted my house and I'm still here. When the elevator begins to fall I move back and hang on tight to the handrails. Floors fly by, numbers decrease, it shakes and mirrors begin to crack. I hold on tight. Gusts of wind are blowing in my face. Finally the last number lights on the panel as a blast of fire and splinters of wood and glass fill the air. Dust clouds my sight. I cough. When it clears I am sitting on the floor in a wedding dress eating a chalupa and very much alive.

Of course I have the normal dreams too. I shop at the grocery store naked like everyone else. I find golden coins buried in the yard but can't dig it all up no matter how hard I try. I can fly, but only inside the Golden Triangle. I gorge myself at elaborate pastry buffets until I pop and then go ice-skating with the President. I dream every night, always have. If I could remember my baby dreams it was probably of empty boobs and gallons of strained spinach being pumped into my mouth.

I have dreams of Pete cussing me out and walking out the door, over and over. I wake up choking the living day lights out of my pillow. I have dreams of Repete giving me *the look* and then walking away...I have nightmares of being pregnant at fifty with twin boys—of course when I deliver them they have gargoyle heads.

I don't mind dreaming but it's a miracle I get any rest. I bought a book on dreams, but by the time I looked up each word and meaning I was more confused than by the dream itself. I even asked my shrink on a Blue Cross vacation the how and why of each dream. He increased my medication.

It's not bad enough that during the day my mind is either going a mile a minute or stalled at a dead stop. I have to spend the nights pondering the same mysteries of life only in cartoon style. I want to know why your legs are real heavy when you try to run in a dream. I want to know why one minute you're riding a beautiful white stallion and the next minute you're straddling a cardboard box. Can you imagine if our minds worked the same during the day as they do at night? It sure would be a lot more interesting in the grocery stores.

I can't stand people who say they never dream. How dare they sleep through the night, every night, without the threat of cannibals, electric hula-hoops, or maggot macaroni and cheese? I can't watch reality TV, as you may have surmised by the last image.

I once had a dream about not dreaming. I could see myself lying in my bed just sleeping like a baby. It was so nice and peaceful. Well, maybe that was one of those *out-of-body* episodes? Either way it was really nice.

Now that I don't have my kids around anymore my dream selection has greatly been reduced. I no longer have to save the boys from aliens or total nuclear annihilation. That's a big weight off my shoulders because running with lead legs carrying a sixteen and eighteen-year-old is exhausting. Though sometimes I still have to save the cats, which isn't easy, as they tend to run in every direction when the first blast goes off.

I hope my dreams don't get worse as I grow older. Do senile people have senile dreams? If so I suspect I'd be trying to evacuate my neighbors' pets from their house. Do people with Alzheimer's have the same dream every night? Do people with Alzheimer's have the same dream every night?

Sometimes I wish I didn't dream, but I expect the night would be rather long without it.

Ed doesn't dream, but he snores really loud. I'd rather dream. At least my mouth is closed. Most men say they don't dream, probably because they don't use their brains at night, just like during the day.

Most people won't admit their dreams because they fear

people will think they are crazy. However, if you ask other people if they ever dreamt of flying, finding money, or swimming in a pool of green Jell-O they will say yes. All right, maybe not about the Jell-O thing.

They say that dreaming is a way of sorting out things in our lives, or in ancient days, signs of things to come. I hope it's not signs of things to come because I really hate green Jell-O. In the olden days dreams were taken a lot more seriously. The Bible says God used them to enter people's thoughts. You never hear about that anymore, maybe because God doesn't like green Jell-O or some of the other ghastly things we have created.

The world has always been a pretty messed-up place, during the day, or in the shadows of the night. I guess people back in Bible times dreamt of lions chasing them around the Coliseum or strolling around the marketplace in the buff. Maybe they started out riding a gilded chariot and suddenly found themselves straddling a wheel-less ox-cart?

Aristotle says a lot about dreams and what their purpose is, but most of it doesn't make much sense because he tends to talk in circles if you ask me. Either way, a lot of the dead dudes seemed to believe that dreams were proof of a psychic world, messages from the soul, or an inner vision. They believed that dreams were inspired by divine powers and miraculous manifestations. Usually, they are brought on by pepperoni for me.

Dreams make me recall one of my mom's favorite sayings: *the Devil's mind is an idle workshop*. Or no, it's *an idle mind is the Devil's workshop*. Either way, when your mind is idling the Devil seems to dive in and stir up the natural flow of confusion. I don't think that's fair when you are sleeping; he's kind of hitting you when you are down. Guess that is why he is the Devil.

I'm not sure about the Devil; they say he comes in

many shapes and forms. I think his favorite is the politician. I've seen the Devil in my dreams and he always has Secret Service men around him, and of course they are all eating cotton candy and wearing red rubber noses.

I tend to daydream too. Daydreams seem to make more sense than sleepy dreams. I never daydream of people shopping naked, though I hear almost all men do. Usually my daydreams are more long blank spaces, just staring at something for a good period of time. Too bad I can't sleep that soundly. I usually tell people that I was calculating something. Of course if they know me they know that is a lie because it involves math.

I think I would have made a good philosopher. I like to ponder a lot, not *think* because that's not the same thing. Pondering is mulling life's mysteries over in your head with no real objective. There doesn't seem to be many philosophers in today's society. I think it would have been a cool job to be a philosopher back in the Biblical days. You get to stay in your house robe all day and just carry on about whatever you have been busy pondering on. Of course back then civilization was evolving so no one really knew much about anything. If you said the world was flat everyone bought it because no one had ventured much past the desert due to the lack of Igloo coolers.

I wonder how philosophers got to be philosophers. I wonder how anyone got a job back in those days. Did they drag in an eighty-pound slab of granite with their resume chiseled on it? Did it say *I can philosophize, chisel, and drive a chariot? I like to go to the coliseum and walk along the Nile. I am from the line of Noah. I have no references because the people before me couldn't write.*

Sometimes a pondering will up and capture my mind completely. Mostly they are short ponderous moments, too long and I forget what it was. I like to imagine what animals and small babies are thinking, especially when grown-ups are talking baby gibberish to them. Some of the looks on my great-niece's face were like, "do you realize I'm storing all of this for later use?" I think that could be why drunks talk stupid, baby talk resurfaces when the brain is pickled.

I wonder if a bird feels stupid for flying into a window. Do other birds laugh at him? Do fish get bored swimming in circles, and why don't they get pruney from being in the water all the time? Why does a hard-boiled egg explode after all the water boils away? What will I look like when I get to Heaven? If I die old will I be old there? Will there be babies there and who will tend to them? I hope I don't get diaper detail, because they say we will have a task in Heaven. I hope poop patrol isn't my task, but I wouldn't be at all surprised if it was. These are the mysteries of life I'd ponder if I were a philosopher. The trick to being a good philosopher is to philophize on things that can't be proven.

I'll be glad when I get to Heaven and have all the answers. There are a lot of people I want to say "I told you so" to. I wonder how the great philosophers of the past will feel there when the New Age people arrive and they start to exchange facts? "Man, I was way off on that one, Eucalyptasees. Who'da thought it was round!"

I love Paul Harvey; he's a modern-day philosopher. Our minds work exactly the same way, and that is unusual since he is male. I especially liked his thoughts on all the little bars of soap that are left after you wash them down. I used to feel bad about throwing them away too but they are so hard to hold onto. I think they should create an empty space in the middle; that way when you get to that last bit it just disappears. Voila! No more soap nubs to fret over.

When I was volunteering at the area food pantry someone donated all of their soap nubs to the poor. A huge

Zip-Lock bag of God-only-knows-where-they-were-used soap nubs. Wasn't that considerate? There's something people should think about when giving. If you don't want it, what makes you think someone else does?

The Bible says when you give gifts, give good gifts. Good grief, even way back in the Bible days they had to put warnings out for stupid people. Open a basket and there's a snake in it. "What the hell, Noah, didn't you bring any fruit or nuts?"

They say we only use about eight percent of our brains. That's not a very good ratio. It's kind of hard to use your brain, I mean it's not like you can lift weights with it while you're watching *Raymond*. I think I use my brain a lot less now that the kids have no need for me. I'm trying to keep it sharp for when I am a grandma, and may need it again.

When you're a young active mother your brain is very busy working for all of you. Moms have to think for their kids too because they aren't thinking most of the time. "Don't run out in front of that car. Don't stick your pencil in the fan. Don't tie the cat to the wagon; he can't pull that. Don't stuff green beans in the conch shell. Don't ask your brother to hold the hair dryer when he's standing in the tub." It goes on and on … there wasn't much time for pondering back then. Must be why all the philosophers were men—they weren't doing anything else unless there was a war going on and someone needed killing or plundering.

I used to think I'd like to get inside of Ed's head and see what makes him tick. How can anyone not like bananas? But after a few weeks of marriage counseling I decided bananas were minor and some places are better left unexplored.

If it were left up to me the world would be undeveloped, because I'm not a big explorer especially after *that* trip. Might be why the early explorers didn't take women on the expeditions. "There's nothing here, Ferdinand, let's go home." I know after a couple hundred miles of prairie grass and a wooden buckboard seat, I would have been bitching up a storm. Add some Indians and a snake and the country would have ended in the New England states. Makes me wonder how women did get out there. I expect men lied to them just like today. "I swear Baby, it's right around the next plateau!"

My mother says I am unique. I like the fact that there is only one of me. I bet you do too. It would be pretty scary if everyone out on the road driving seventy miles an hour had big blank spaces like I do. Though I have to say at times in rush hour traffic most of the people I pass appear to be in a blank space. Unless of course they are yakking on the fricking cell phone, then they are in my space and about eighteen inches over the white line.

Lately my mind had been misfiring. I sent an invitation to my cousin and his wife, but with his deceased wife's name on it. She has been gone for many years. I felt like a total fool and the only thing I could think to write in the apology card was "I'm sorry, I'm a total idiot, and my mind has gone bye-bye." That pretty much said it all. I've always been under the assumption that with age is supposed to come wisdom not worse stupidity. Maybe that is only in China?

I just wonder why my mind is misfiring so often, especially since I've cut way back on my drinking. I've had to make up really odd hypnosis tapes for myself now like, *Living in the Present, Why I go Down the Basement, The Importance of Unplugging Things,* and the one I use the most, *Pay Attention*—though I usually fall asleep on that one. I think they are helping; after all, you know it's all in the mind.

It's kind of scary to watch someone's mind leave. Not mentioning any names because my marriage depends on it, but when a loved one starts to lose it you just don't know what to do. I can guarantee it's not to write them a letter.

I was scared when I left my purse at home the other day. A handbag is an appendage to a woman. I worried about it for three days until I walked out to get the mail in my bra and blue jeans. I don't worry about little mental glitches so much now. I'm more worried about the big ones to come. After writing this book I've been looking over my shoulder for the men in the white coats. You think you are going along pretty well until you make a list and write it down. The more I proofread the scarier it gets. I now have one of those barn hex signs hanging over my office door and rabbits' feet tied to just about everything. They were already detached and dyed purple when I got them.

At the last minute I wasn't going to put this chapter in but then I thought, *why not*. People always say, "I want to get inside your head." Well, not my head in particular, but inside of other people's heads. They want to probe and discover what makes them tick especially if they don't agree with them. I think a lot of people want to know that they are not the only lunatics on the planet. I know I'm not alone.

I think that is why reality TV is so popular now. They let you get into other people's heads. And I have to say most of the people on these shows sure don't mind sharing their mental glitches with the whole damn world. I don't know if they are looking for their sixty seconds of fame or are really just that stupid. Maybe they haven't the ability to realize that they are telling the world when they spill their guts on television. Kind of like people who write books about their lives.

Well, now that you know what it's like inside of me, I guess I'll go make some double fudge cupcakes then take a little nap to see what new and exciting things are going on upstairs…I hope I don't run into any of the gargoyles.

Chapter 27

A Mother

This chapter is dedicated to mothers. I am a mother and that was by choice. However, I'm not exactly sure how much of that was my choice because I think God puts something inside of women that makes them want to be a mom more than anything else. It's an uncontrollable urge like the desire to consume mass amounts of chocolate and buy shoes.

My extent of medical knowledge could be put into a thimble with room for my big fat thumb, but I think the secret ingredient He puts into women are those darn hormones. Men get hormones but they get a different kind that makes them want to *make* babies, not actually *have* babies. I doubt that God used measuring cups when He was serving up helpings of hormones. It would be nice if He had, then no one would be fanning themselves in December screaming, "somebody open a damn window," or be putting babies in dumpsters like junk mail. Or in the case of males, trying to mate with anything that has a port of entry.

The dictionary says that maternal means *instincts of a mother*. Can you believe I had to look that up? I did. You have to have a prodigal son to constantly question your motherhood. I think I got my share of hormones when the boys were young but then when they had to take out my egg baskets and chutes problems arose. The doctor told me that my own body would still make some hormones—probably why I never actually strangled my kids. My few remaining maternal instincts kicked in when they started to turn blue.

I'm just kidding. I was a good mother, even if I'm the only one that feels that way. I think being a mother is a really hard job. Everyday life has a way of driving you crazy. It's hard enough trying to get yourself through this maze. But to be responsible for more little people who have self-centered, undeveloped brains the size of a raisin for the first twelve years of life it seems almost impossible at times.

I remember back before I got pregnant and how I was around little kids; I probably shouldn't have had any. I thought babies were cute, but only their heads smelled good. Little kids were cute from a distance and funny to watch because they say and do really goofy stuff. Toddlers are a hoot. Who else but little kids would stuff strange junk up their nose? Well, excluding druggies.

After kids get into school their cuteness really starts to narrow off. Once they learn how to count they think they know everything. They're loud, demanding, bouncy, and do really annoying stuff. They tell knock-knock jokes over and over that make no sense and sneeze right into your face. They have hissy fits with no regard to their whereabouts. I just don't understand that six-to-ten-year span; it's like that puppy chewing stage.

Medium-size kids, which I believe they call *tweens,* aren't too much fun either. I think this stage was better with boys because my friend has girls and they were rather moody and whined a lot. Her one daughter used to be able to drag a squeaky "moooomm..."out for two days. At least my boys just knocked each other out and the incident was forgotten. I hate to say it about my own species but females are whiny and can drag up old bones, thrash away at it until they turn to dust, then start digging for a new bone to gnaw on. It's like a sport.

Teenagers make me cringe, especially when they are painted up like death and have more holes pierced in them than a standing cheese grater. When I see a bratty punk in a store I just want to ask, "how can your mother love you? She must have a mountain of maternal hormones!" I feel so sorry for their poor mother trying to buy them a hundred-dollar pair of jeans—and all they can do is cop an attitude. I'm glad I wasn't like that when I was younger. Of course when we were younger we were taught to respect our parents and all of our elders; I believe there's even a commandment for it. The last time I quoted a commandment the kid looked at me and said, "That's not in the Constitution. I have freedom of speech." I don't think the Constitution protects cussing out your parents, but I'm sure the ACLU does.

After I got pregnant, which I was overpowered and compelled to do, I started to feel different about little kids. Not all kids. Definitely not my neighbor's kids, because they were possessed. I think Katy's two kids marred me for motherhood. I lived in terror of my sons turning out like hers. Her one son used to come over and spit loogies all over my dog. Buddy would unchain him, he would steal his collar and toys, and eventually he made my entire dog disappear. He told me he would, and mind you at age seven that is some pretty heavy magic. He also loved to set fires, in their yard, in my yard, in the park, and later on in life in buildings. I do have to give him credit for knowing his mission in life, he always said he wanted to be a fireman. Though he probably meant he wanted to be an arsonist.

I used to stare at my babies in their beds and pray for them a lot. Pray that I wouldn't mess them up. I used to ask God to give me maternal wisdom. I'm not so sure about God answering *all* of your prayers. I don't think there is anything in the Bible for baby maintenance. I guess God figured it would come natural. Maybe in the old days it did but since they invented formula, drugs, legal and illegal, cars, chopping, slicing and dicing tools, its gotten a lot more complicated to protect the little nippers. They say that a lot of the books of the Bible were left out, mostly books written by women. I bet the baby manual was axed by the same men who slipped in that word "obey."

I do remember having lots of fun with my kids, we played a lot. Probably because I was nothing more than a big kid when I had them. We made snowmen, flew kites, bicycled, hiked, built things, and went camping. Okay, the camping wasn't all that fun. I wish we could have played more and they would have fought with each other less. I have to say they fought more than my brother and I did. I wonder if my mom put the mother curse on me. It sure did work.

I've always hated the discipline part of being a mom. Kids don't realize that it really does hurt the parent more than the kid when they have to dole out corporal punishment. Sometimes after the boys had gotten into trouble I would send them to their rooms and set the timer on the stove. This was my cool-down and soften-up time. I would pace the kitchen wondering what to do. Should I spank or ground? Grounding was always more of a punishment for me. By the time the timer went off I wasn't frothing at the mouth anymore. Usually I would let them pick their punishment. They always picked the three swats on the butt, probably because my grounding was nothing shy of solitary confinement. With bread and water, of course. Nowadays, parents send their kids to an amusement park when they send them to their rooms. I removed all the fun stuff.

In one of the many versions of the Bible I found a passage, and I really had to hunt for it to be the way I wanted it. It said *not* to spare the rod and spoil the child. I don't think there is anything wrong with a butt whooping tempered with love. I don't hate my parents for swatting me. I learned right from wrong. I learned not to let your little brother ride his tricycle down a flight of concrete steps when you were told to watch him. But I was a girl child and I have to say that my brother took a lot longer to assimilate between bad behavior and corporal punishment. Pete, I don't believe, ever really figured it out.

Being a mother is endless. Even after my boys grew up, blew me off, and moved away, I'm still haunted by those maternal instincts. I wonder if they are all right, if they are taking their vitamins, eating vegetables, wearing their seatbelts, and if they have enough clean underwear. Mothering never stops, no matter how old you get or how old they get. When I see them I still want them to sit on my lap and rock them. Of course now they would be mortified and I would be a paper doll after they got up.

I feel even closer to my mother now that my sons have grown up and pretty much left me for dead; I know she didn't have to do all the things she did for me when I was little. It took me a long time to realize that she had a life of her own, and dreams, but she put all of that on hold for my sister, my brother, and me to be our mother. Lucky for me I never had any dreams, well, not counting the really weird ones where I go skydiving with a Snoopy umbrella. The only thing close to a futuristic dream was when I *thought* I wanted to be a schoolteacher, but somewhere along the line it clicked that I would be a temporary mother to thirty children like my little brother.

It always amazed my sister and me that our mother, really any mother, knows her child's cry. Whenever we got lost in a store from wandering off we would tell Bobby to yell for Mom. Once he let out a "Mom" yelp, a hundred women in the store would each tip an ear for a moment, then return to the sale table. Out of the crowd our mother would come running, dragging a fifty percent-off toaster behind her. Amazing, and only one word was uttered, the same word every one of them goes by. I'd know my boys' "Mom" in a crowded stadium with earmuffs on, but they rarely call me anymore.

Lucky for me I got a second chance at mothering, and I'm a really a good mommy to my cats. They all love me and can't seem to get enough of my affection as long as they are by their food bowl. I even took on an orphan that was only four weeks old. I fed him with a doll bottle and rocked and sang to him all the time, just like the boys. Well, I didn't use a doll bottle, I'da had to fill it eighty times for Pete.

I still rock Lucky in my arms like a baby, but he weights about twelve pounds now. He doesn't know that, he thinks he's still a baby. None of my cats have ever moved away and forgotten to call. I doubt, though I could be wrong, that any of my cats have ever even considered blaming me for their inability to succeed in life.

I know each of my cat's meows, too. I can tell which cat is walking down the hallway. I don't know why people say, "A cat's a better mother." I didn't give any of my babies away after they were weaned. I never carried them around by the scruff of their neck with my teeth. *With my teeth* is a key phrase there. Someday I would like to be a mama to a cute little wiener dog, but Ed says they are bait. I'm not going to try taking on any more human babies, I'll just keep sending money to the people who do.

I don't know why I got such a bad rap from my kids. I only beat them with a two-by-four with rusty nails in it on days that ended in y, or so they recall. *The Beating* on the way to the zoo was the only real spanking they ever received. And, a few slaps upside the head for being extremely rude and acting like goofballs in public places.

Nothing annoys me worse than a kid having a hissy fit in a store and the mother is just ignoring them. They are obviously the only person in the store capable of ignoring them; everyone else is gritting their teeth and chewing up dry Tylenol tablets. I want to scream, "They are not going to go away they came with you. Please, do something! I will gladly get you a pillow from housewares." Yet they just continue on while the kid blows out a vocal chord trying to get Mom to buy a bag of Pop Rocks. After ten minutes I want to buy the kid a snack from lawn and garden.

I guess there is nothing I can do to change the boys' opinion of me. I'm their mother. I will be their mother if they call or not. I think the boys could have done a lot worse. I've always told them I loved them and gave them lots of hugs and kisses. I never tried to sell them on the Internet—of course the Internet wasn't invented back then. I never put them in a dumpster unless we were looking for aluminum cans, and then it was more of a leg up. I never locked them in a closet unless we were playing hide and seek and I wanted to win.

I don't know why they don't have a sense of humor.

When we were being wild my mother used to yell, "Stop that or I will rip off your arm and beat you with the bloody stump!" It always got a big laugh out of us. I guess my boys just didn't inherit that wonderful trait from my side of the family. The sense of humor, not the arm ripping.

Perhaps I should have written down all of the great things I did for them and showed it to them when they got old enough to understand. Okay, maybe I'll have to wait another twenty years. I could have written down things like the time I unclogged a graham cracker from Pete's windpipe and the time I shoved Benadryl down Repete's throat and packed his foot in ice to save him from the deadly bee sting. I once carried them both across hot asphalt so they wouldn't burn their little feet. Why on earth none of us had shoes on I'll never know. I burned the dickens out of mine. Surely they would have been impressed if I had kept tick marks on how many diapers I changed, or how many times I allowed them to spit strained vegetable into my face. I wonder what they'd think if they knew I was hungry at McDonalds, but didn't eat because I didn't have enough money for all of us. They can't think they got this far all on their own, can they?

Being a mother is highly underrated. One crummy day out of the year we celebrate motherhood and that seems like a huge chore for my boys. And I don't know about anyone else, but we mothers usually end up doing some cooking and dishes on that day too. We have actually started a new tradition where all the moms get together and go out, with the girl children, for a nice lunch and spend a bunch of the men's money. We get the gifts we want, and the guys aren't whining that they had to waste a whole day at somebody's house when they could have been sitting in front of their own TV or in the *shed*. Instead of getting together on Father's Day now we let the men do whatever they want too, like go fishing, watch TV, or stay in the *shed*. We give 'em some camouflage gifts, make 'em a sandwich, and then the girls go out together and spend more of their money. It's a system that works well for us, you ought to try it.

Hopefully when my kids have children of their own they will understand what it means to be a mother. Well, a father, as they are both boys. Well, that isn't going to work because men don't have the same maternal instincts for parenting that women do. Well, I hope that sooner or later it opens their eyes to the fact I spent twenty-plus years of my life in the pursuit of their happiness. I did a lot for them and sometimes it seems like the only two things I gained in the four hundred and fifty years of child rearing is hemorrhoids and a lot of damn cats.

I think I've beaten this dead horse enough, *I ams what I ams*, their mother. To be totally honest, I don't think I was mean, most of the time they were just being sissies. My mother never allowed any of us to be a sissy. My brother was once piling up a bunch of little balsam wood boxes that my dad had brought home from a jobsite. He managed to get them very high right before they tumbled onto his head. Bobby screamed bloody murder for what seemed like forever. He didn't even have a mark, and we all knew it would take something much harder to penetrate his little blockhead. Finally, my mother, tired of trying to console him pinched him hard on his arm. "There!" she said. "Now you have something to cry for." At the time we thought that was very mean, but Bobby toughened up and has never been a sniveler like many people are today. None of us are snivelers. I'm glad she taught us that lesson. We learned to take the bad with the good and not to blame anyone but ourselves for piling the boxes too high.

I took my mother to lunch and shopping the other day

and I have to say she worries me. She's starting to bend over and she is slowing down. She used to out-shop everyone but now she tends to sit in an available chair and wait for me to look around. While writing out a check she takes great care and time, and then forgets to get out her ID. Other people in line seem annoyed. I want to punch them for not being patient with her. She doesn't drive much anymore, only on back roads close to home. She seems to get confused more often, though not as much as I do. She's seventy-six years old and that worries me.

My mother has been there for me for fifty-one years. I pray that she will be there for the rest of my years even if I must leave this world tomorrow to avoid her absence. I can't imagine life without her. We have our differences and we've had some rough times, probably due to my blockheaded nature. She spanked me and grounded me. She taught me to be a good person and to be grateful. She taught me about God, and right and wrong. She was strict about many things and pushed me so that I would be ready for the real world. She worked very hard for me. Most importantly she loved me. I love her too. I pray that I have never hurt her intentionally or unintentionally. I don't recall ever thinking anything but good of her.

Go call your mother.

Chapter 28

In Closing

I'm nearing the end of the story, as you can see by the remaining thickness of the book. It's not that I haven't more to say about my current relationship, it's more that I think it wise to keep my mouth shut. I'm learning and for someone that only opens her mouth to change feet, this is a pretty big accomplishment. I wish I would have learned that a tad bit earlier in life.

Sometimes I think I'm looking for something that doesn't exist. What makes people think that life should always be better than it is? Maybe because of all the crap we are bombarded with 24-7 on TV, in movies, and in magazines. Happiness is just a little gold ring, a new car, or a Happy Meal away.

Worse, we are filled with thoughts of an unrealistic utopia as children when we are the most impressionable. Of course we buy it because that knight-in-shining-armor deal never goes past the part where they get married in any of the Little Golden Books. Yeah, it says they lived happily ever after but we never really see that. Okay, *Shreck2* is the first time kids get to see after the honeymoon but she did marry a certified ogre so what did she expect?

I wonder what Cinderella looks like now. I wonder if she and Prince Charming are still together or if he ran off with an ugly sister, because he likes ugly women better. Some princes with big ears do that, you know. I wonder if the other two little pigs ever rebuilt with code materials. Sorry, got off track again.

I don't think stories should end with *and they lived happily ever after.* They have lots of other stupid laws forbidding stupid stuff. I think it's false advertising for marriage, plain and simple. How come the ACLU never lobbied against that—it works for any gender preference. I guess they don't care because God didn't say it?

Single or married, life is still a lot of hard work and effort. I know because I've had over a half of a century of it. I think marriage just makes it more vivid. I don't mind the hard work but it's nice to be acknowledged somewhere along the line for the effort. Or maybe be rewarded with a few tender, romantic moments.

Being a wife is almost as rewarding as being a mother to male children. And it doesn't get any better with time either. The only thing time does is make you question your existence even more. The other night Ed asked me if I wanted *some.* I think we all know what. When I said nah, he asked, "Are you sure because I wanted to drain off some toxic fluids." What am I now, a bio-hazard drum? I know I haven't got much of a waist anymore but geez. Not to be outdone by his romantic proposition I told him to drain it off in the shower tomorrow morning. The EPA will never know.

How come washing, cleaning, cooking, and *ironing* are

not as valued as making money? And what about grocery shopping—that is a chore! The last time I took Ed it cost us three times what I normally spend. He was grabbing the weirdest stuff; caviar at *Save A Lot*? Just because they sell it doesn't mean people buy it there. He never even looked at the list; he would have been mighty sad the next time he tried to dip his freedom fries in caviar. He also bought almond milk, who drinks a nut? I never took him again.

I think that taking care of a house and home is priceless and it takes a lot of skill and effort. Believe me, being a cleaning lady, I've seen many houses that are not taken care of. Over the years I have been forced to give myself a few awards for my effort, just so I'd keep going. You can buy them at any office store just fill in your name and the achievement. Like: *World's Greatest Cook* or *World's Greatest Ironer.*

If you are thinking right about now, what the heck happened to her two kids? I'll let you know as soon as I find out. I know they are around somewhere and will call any day. They just don't need anything right now or can't pay back the money they borrowed.

When I look back on my life I can't help but wonder if I was dropped on my head as a baby. I bet you were wondering the same thing a few chapters in. I'm fifty-something years into this dog-and-pony show and still don't have my act together. I've still got lots of unanswered questions, unresolved issues; well, many issues in general. I don't know where to go from here but I keep moving around, mostly for the amusement of others. Notice I didn't say forward and I'll never go straight.

I'm still talking to God but as you can surmise he hasn't come to get me yet. He's brought me very close and even in one of my darkest hours I tried to help him out.

I remember seeing the great bright light, and feeling

more peaceful than I had ever felt in my entire life. Then I woke up to a flashlight in my eye and a tic-tac-toe pattern on my chest. I was zapped with directed voltage; I'm surprised I didn't wake up with bolts in my neck. Unfortunately now I'm not really sure about the eternal light thing because a Maglite a quarter-inch from your pupil is damn bright.

About the only things that have really changed for me are my shape, my energy level, and my driving. I've moved over to the middle lane; those fast lane drivers are viciously stressed. Of course if I were going ninety-seven miles an hour a quarter-inch from the back bumper of a semi, I'd be stressed too.

I used to be five-foot-ten and somewhere along the line of life I lost an inch and a half, but I'm pretty sure it just pushed out to the sides. Some of my other stuff has relocated also. Unless I stand on my head it is physically impossible now to tan the underside of my butt.

I don't fight much anymore either because, well, to be honest, it's just too much like work. Though I can still give a vicious tongue lashing to a lengthy line leaper. Lucky for me they don't know my bark is a lot worse than my bite—too much dental work.

Now I didn't take any scientific poll to come up with this statistic but, trust me, most of the ones you read about didn't really either. It's like one month magazines say don't eat bacon, it will clog your arteries. The next month they say do eat bacon, it cures cancer. The beef industry published the first warning and the pork industry published the second. As I type, the poultry industry is working on their findings. I don't consider advertising ploys scientific.

So, the way I figure, I am in about the ninety-eight percent bracket of average people. I'm in the Jane and John Doe sector that are pretty much the jackasses pulling the cart for the other two percent. We ninety-eight percent are the consumers. We consume like locusts. I've consumed a lot in my life especially if you factor in chocolate. Looking back I now find this one of my noblest positions when compared to my other positions. I have helped my country move forward in a never-ending quest to be surpassed and someday owned by China. I have burned a million gallons of gasoline, used a million Energizers, and bought enough foreign-made junk to sink a small island. I am the cause not the solution. I've helped to over-populate the world and expand the ozone hole. That makes me one of the crowd. I've paid into Social Security for thirty years and like everyone else will eventually donate it to the pockets and pork projects of our out-of-control, lying, cheating government. I will continue to consume until I take my last breath for God and my country. Amen.

I am a true American and I don't believe you have to be born here to be one. If you can consume at a high clip, love this land with next to no regard for it most of the time, and believe the world revolves around you, you are a true American too. Might as well say it, it's the general consensus around the world anyway. They are just jealous.

Sometimes I get scared about seeing what is to come. I'm not sensing a real bright future for this old planet we call home. There are way too many natural disasters nowadays. Every summer is filled with worse droughts and floods, fires, tornadoes, and hurricanes; kind of makes one wonder if we are in the *end of days?* Might be why the CEOs are taking such bold chances. I don't want to see the end of the world, especially after reading Revelations. Lions with seven heads—lions are dangerous enough with one head. I hope God comes and gets me before that. I'd like to be sucked up in the Rapture, but I think that is only for really good people. I haven't been really good at anything except aging, losing friends, and pissing off my kids.

Most people my age are looking forward to retirement but I'm just not ready for real retirement yet. You know, when you are no longer employable—if I looked for a job I could be employed. Mentally I don't feel old enough for anything. In only a few short years I will be a certified senior citizen. I never thought I'd make it past thirty. Who am I kidding—I never thought I'd make it past ten, especially after I kissed that oak tree in the wagon.

Honestly, I don't want to get older, old people scare me. They have way too many pill bottles, doctor visits are the highlight of their day, and they love to talk about their bowel habits to strangers. They sit on top of the TV and then say, "what, I didn't see it." They nod off in the middle of a conversation and their clothes don't match. They either drive too slowly because they are scared or way too fast because they are over-medicated and oblivious. Though, it doesn't really matter because most of them can't see over the dashboard. Even worse, they pass gas in public and say "ahhh." That's not right at any age.

I'm just not seeing the golden years as real golden, so I'm going to keep looking somewhere else. Though, I sure don't want to go back to the child rearing years. When I hear about older couples in their sixties adopting babies, handicapped kids, and troubled homeless teenagers, I send 'em twenty bucks. At fifty I figure it's too late to make good on what I messed up on. Lately I'm scared to baby-sit for anyone. I figure I obviously messed up my kids, I sure don't want to mess up theirs and have more people avoiding me. What if I misplace their baby like I do my keys, purse, cup of tea, car...

I guess what it comes down to is, as always I don't know what to do or be. I've never really thought of myself as anything other than a mom (or grandmother) who doesn't look her age. Sure, I toyed with the idea of being the Queen of England, but I never bought a ticket to Europe to start my campaigning. I can't go back to school. I look at the TV Guide and forget what channel a movie is on as soon as I pick up the remote control. My brain has liquefied along with most of my joints.

If it weren't for Pookie I'd be living under a bridge. Not as a troll. I already spent the six hundred and thirty bucks I had saved for retirement. It seemed like a good idea at the time. I guess I could start saving again. But, since the Dollar Stores opened I just don't see me ever being able to do it.

I might be able to *set up a fund*. Every night on the news someone is setting one up for something. I heard of a woman who set up a fund on the Internet to pay off her bills that she racked up by living high on the hog. When she lost her job she asked people to have pity on her and apparently there are some mighty pitiful people out there because she raked in forty three thousand dollars. I guess I could set up a site to save the crazy old cat lady if Pookie ever wises up and moves away too.

Or maybe I just need to go back to work somewhere because being a personal slave to someone who works eighty hours a week and fishes the other eighty gives one's mind way too much time to wander asleep or awake. Problem is nothing interests me unless it's covered in chocolate. Ed always tells me to find something fun to do, but after I eat a bag of truffles I'm right back where I started with nothing to do.

He also tells me about once a month to take a trip. I think the exact words are "Go. Go somewhere. Go see someone. Go." I feel guilty going on trips without him. But I usually feel worse after I go with him on an unending outdoor marathon. We once fished on a lake from 5 A.M.

until 1 A.M. straight through a lighting storm that refused to strike me even though I was holding up the flagpole begging for rescue. Trips with a wilderness man are always kind of a dammed if you do, damned if you don't experience. Hopeful bonding usually only occurs when I'm straddling his back screaming frantically to escape some horrid aquatic creature.

Sometimes I think of something fun to do...sometimes I remember it, sometimes I don't. Perhaps I should write those thoughts down also.

Maybe I'll just keep moving around until God comes and gets me. Apparently He feels I can still do more damage and give out a lot more incentive. I was secretly hoping that by writing this I would have been enlightened and found a new direction, but no. I think my dad was right and ass-backwards just seems to work well for me. No use rocking the boat this late in the cruise. You know what? I'm just not going to think about it, that's always *worked well for me* too, though Dr. Phil might not agree.

I don't feel bad at all about my life, as I've never set out to purposely hurt anyone, not even my kids. I may have had the cart in front of the horse most of it, which didn't make it an easy journey, but it did make it an interesting one. I can also say that I have a clear conscience, though possibly due to memory loss. I've helped a lot of people and even successfully preformed CPR on a woman. I've made a lot of people smile in my lifetime even if they were laughing at me and not with me. I hope you are one of them.

Either way, that's my story and I'm sticking to it. Some of my friends and family wanted to read this, some of my friends and family didn't. Some weren't offered the option until I have some money to persuade them. Some I'm not sure can read. And, some of my friends won't be my friends after they read this book. Ed never stayed home long enough to read it. A dollar says he never does—there's no fish on the cover.

What have you learned, Dorothy? Absolutely nothing. But, I have finally finished something in my life, which is a good thing. So I am officially declaring it *Truffle Time*, then I'm gathering up all of this paper and heading off to the recycling center. ☺

God bless.

Dedication

This book is dedicated to my mother, to your mother, to all mothers, especially single mothers.

Special Thanks

To my mother who has read and saved every word I have ever written, even when they don't make sense. Thanks for egging me on. Thanks to my editor Christine Frank who is probably still in awe of my amazing ability to slaughter the English language. Also, thanks to my Co-Editor, Scott Schneider for taking over when Christine surrendered. Many thanks to my high school friend Diana Powers for her help, patience, and support. And, thanks for not moving away.

About the Author

Nancy A. Hausner: I was a unique child, the middle child, a child born on Wednesday. (Wednesday's child is full of woe.) Hence, I truly believe I am cursed. I've been busy scribbling words on paper ever since my pudgy little hand could wield a pencil. I'm not sure why. Most of my writing is locked away for fear of being locked up, again. Everything I've done I've done on impulse including reproducing, not once but twice. I'm not sure why. My education is as questionable as my sanity. I do not believe more college would have helped me be a better writer. Fourteen years of English ain't helped my grammar one bit. I am stubborn and prefer to stumble through life making mistakes. It works well for me.

9 781432 712778